WWII MILITARY RECORDS
A FAMILY HISTORIAN'S GUIDE

Other Books by MIE PUBLISHING

Find Anyone Fast

*How To Locate Anyone Who Is or Has Been in the Military:
Armed Forces Locator Guide*

*They Also Served:
Military Biographies of Uncommon Americans*

WWII MILITARY RECORDS
A FAMILY HISTORIAN'S GUIDE

By
Debra Johnson Knox

MIE PUBLISHING

MIE Publishing
PO Box 17118
Spartanburg, SC 29301
(800) 937-2133
www.militaryusa.com

Library of Congress Cataloging-in-Publication Data
Knox, Debra Johnson, 1964–
WWII military records: a family historian's guide / by Debra
Johnson Knox.

p. cm.
Includes Index
ISBN 1–877639–91–5

1. World War, 1939–1945—Registers. 2. World War, 1939–1945—
Registers of Dead—United States. 3. United States—Armed
Forces—Registers. 4. Veterans—United States—Societies, etc.—
Directories. 5. World War, 1939–1945—United States—Archival
resources. 6. United States—Genealogy—Archival resources.
I. Title: WW2 military records. II. Title: World War two military
records. III. Title: World War II military records. IV. Title: World
War 2 military records. V. Title.

D797.U6K56 2003
940.54'6773--dc21

2002045527

Dedication

This book is dedicated to my grandfather,

Major General Harry Hubbard Johnson
April 11, 1895 – August 8, 1986
World War I & World War II

Disclaimer

This book is designed to provide information and is sold with the understanding that the publisher and author are not engaged in rendering legal or professional services.

Every effort has been made to make this book as complete and accurate as possible. There may be mistakes, either typographical or in content. therefore, this book should be used as a general guide.

The author or MIE Publishing shall have neither liability nor responsibility to any person regarding loss or damage.

Acknowledgments

I wish to acknowledge the enormous contributions and support made by everyone associated with the project. This type of reference book couldn't be accomplished without a large support base behind it. Thank you, Dick Bielen—the guru of military records, Col. Frank Foster of Medals of America, Sabra Cox for endless hours of research, and to my family for their support.

Table of Contents

Introduction

I grew up as an Army brat. My father, Lt. Col. Richard S. Johnson (Ret), served 28 years in the Army and two tours in Vietnam. My grandfather was Major General Harry H. Johnson, a veteran of WWI and WWII.

I knew that my grandfather and others in my family had served during WWII, but when I was younger, it didn't seem to matter. I simply didn't care what they did or experienced during the war.

But later, after becoming involved in military records research, I decided to do some family military research of my own. Even as a professional military researcher, I had difficulty finding the resources that I needed. As others asked me to do military research for them, I decided to create a guide enabling other curious family members to start a WWII military research project.

While this book is a great resource for the records that are available concerning WWII, it would be an insurmountable task to include every resource or record housed in all of the archives or on the Internet.

It is my hope for you that this book unlocks the past and reveals a fascinating personal story from a unique era in history.

—Debra Johnson Knox

INDIVIDUAL MILITARY RECORDS

This chapter identifies and details the various types of military records available for a WWII veteran. The military personnel file, officer's registers and hospital admission cards are among the types of records maintained. These records pertain only to the individual military member and not the unit or organization.

Federal Military Records (201 File)

All of the federal government military records for WWII veterans of the Army, Navy, Marine Corps and Coast Guard are stored at the National Personnel Records Center (NPRC) in St. Louis, Missouri. The NPRC is part of the National Archives and Records Administration.

The privacy act *does* apply to military records and certain rules have to be followed when acquiring records. If the veteran is still living, only the veteran can obtain *complete* military records. If the veteran is deceased, then next of kin is entitled to the complete file. Next of kin as described by the NPRC are the unmarried widow or widower, son or daughter, father or mother, brother or sister of the veteran. Grandchildren, nieces or nephews are not generally included as next of kin.

If you are not the next of kin of a deceased veteran, it is suggested that you have the next of kin make the request for records. Complete records also can be obtained if you are the only living relative of a deceased veteran.

Following is some of the information contained in the military personnel file:

- Name
- Rank or grade
- Duty status
- Date of rank
- Geographic location of duty assignments
- Source of commission (if officer)
- Military and civilian education level
- Number
- Military job code (MOS)
- Awards, medals and decorations

- Date of birth*
- Official photograph (if available)
- Dependents' names, genders and ages*
- Military serial number
- Type of discharge*

*These items will be omitted if the request is made citing the Freedom of Information Act (see below). If the veteran is deceased and the requestor *is* next of kin *or* only living relative, then the information is included.

Military Medical Records

Free medical treatment was one of the benefits available to the men and women who served in the military during WWII. Before entering military service, each person was given a physical examination. Later, each person was given a series of immunizations to prevent certain diseases. Treatment for illnesses, wounds and injuries would be provided by military doctors, nurses or technicians. Normally, all of these actions would be recorded on paper and put into a person's medical treatment record. After the person left active duty that record along with the person's service record would have been sent to a record holding area. Today, there are only two federal agencies that may have those records: the National Personnel Records Center (NPRC) in St. Louis, Missouri or the Department of Veterans Affairs (VA).

Freedom of Information Act Request

The Freedom of Information Act entitles anyone to receive releasable information from a person's military record. Information that is not releasable is included above with an *. If you are *not* the next of kin *or* only living relative and still want basic information about someone who served during WWII, fill out the standard form 180 and cite the Freedom of Information Act request (FOIA). FOIA requests are not a priority to the NPRC and it can take up to six months to receive a response.

Fire at NPRC

In 1973, a fire at the National Personnel Records Center destroyed approximately 16-18 million official military personnel records. Eighty percent of the records were destroyed for Army personnel that were discharged from Nov. 1, 1912, to Jan. 1, 1960. Seventy-five percent of Air Force records for personnel who were discharged Sep. 25, 1947, to Jan. 1, 1964, beginning with last name Hubbard-Z, were destroyed.

The Army Air Corps was part of the Army during WWII and those records fall under the category of records that could have been destroyed by the fire.

Navy, Marine Corps and Coast Guard records were not destroyed in the fire. All of these records are still available.

Even if your relative's records may be in the burned category, go ahead and send in a request. Some reconstructed files were established when the veteran made a request. The NPRC used alternate record sources to verify military service. Therefore, some information may be in the file, although the complete record is no longer available. Don't let this discourage a request. See the information later in this chapter under *What if the Records were Burned?*

Request Military Personnel Records

To request the military records from the NPRC, you should fill out the standard form 180 (request pertaining to military records.) Fill out as much of the information as possible, including name, rank, branch of service, time period of service, serial number and date of birth. It is best to have a military serial number, if known (see military serial numbers below.) The only way the NPRC can tell the difference between veterans with the same name is by the serial number.

Standard Form 180 Sources

Internet: *www.nara.gov/regional/mprsf180.html*

Print out the form and fill it out by hand, or further down on the website, click on the "Standard Form 180 – fillable" form, type in the information on the screen and then print out the completed form. Don't forget to sign it before mailing. The NPRC is not taking electronic requests for records at this time.

By phone:

NPRC Customer Service number
(314) 801-0800
Leave your name and address. A SF 180 will be mailed.

Request in writing or by fax:

National Personnel Records Center
Military Personnel Records
9700 Page Avenue
St Louis, MO 63132-5100
(314) 801-9195 Fax

> If the veteran served in more than one branch of the military, make a separate request for each branch.

Private Records Researcher vs. NPRC

Requesting the records using the standard form 180 sent to the NPRC is a good way to obtain information from a person's military records. Be aware that you will most likely not receive every single piece of paper kept in the file. If the veteran served many years in the military, the file could be very large. In this case, it's recommended to hire a private researcher to handle the records request to ensure that every paper is included.

The NPRC has a list of researchers that can access the records with the proper authorization form from the veteran or next of kin, if the veteran is deceased. The same rules apply. Since they are private companies, they charge a fee for their services. But they will copy each document in the folder, no matter what it is.

> One family member obtained military records for a relative who served 30 years in the Army. Fortunately, the records were not touched by the fire and were more than 10 inches thick. The private researcher gave the family every paper and they received some important and meaningful documents.

U.S. Locator Service
PO Box 140194
St Louis, MO 63114-0194
(314) 423-0860 phone/fax
uslocator@earthlink.net

For a list of other available researchers, please contact the National Personnel Record Center in St. Louis, Missouri.

National Personnel Records Center
9700 Page Avenue
St Louis, MO 63132-5100
www.archives.gov/facilities/mo military_records.html

What if the Records were Burned?

Although the fire in 1973 destroyed millions of records, a large number survived and are kept at the National Personnel Records Center in St. Louis. Additionally, officials were able to find some alternate sources of information that could be helpful in providing proof of military service. Among these sources are 19 million final pay vouchers that provide some basic information such as dates of service, serial number, character of service and perhaps last major unit of assignment. These also are at the records center and often are used to generate a simple Certificate of Military Service.

Sometimes documents related to a veteran's military service can be found in other locations. For example, if a veteran ever went to the Department of Veterans Affairs for any medical treatment or made a claim before July 1973, the VA might still have the veteran's military medical records. These can provide some information about a person's service. Many states paid bonuses to veterans of WWII. State bonus files usually have copies of documents proving a person served in the military. See Appendix A (State Records).

Unfortunately, even if you find some alternate sources of information about a person's military service, it will never be as complete and detailed as the original service records would be.

National Guard Service

If the individual was in the National Guard before being called to federal service during WWII, the records for the National Guard service are maintained by the state's Adjutant General. See Appendix A (State Records) for addresses.

> On August 31, 1940, President Roosevelt called up the National Guard to active duty.

Military Serial Numbers

A military serial number was used by all branches of the service as the identifying number for military personnel. Today, the military uses the person's Social Security number as the identifying number. Having the military serial number will increase the chances that the records center will be able to find the correct military record. All WWII-era servicemen and women were issued a military serial number.

While most family members may know the date of birth and date of death of their relative, the military serial number may not be available. There are many different sources that can help locate this number. It's recommended to find the number if at all possible. If you've tried all sources and can't find a number, make the records request using name and date of birth.

Military Serial Number Sources

Officer Registers

Military Officer Registers provide a variety of useful information about Officers and Warrant Officers. These books were published each year by each branch of the military and include biographical data such as name, date of birth, serial number, rank, date of entry into the service, branch of service (such as Infantry) and military education.

These are great resources for date of birth and serial number for a WWII Officer or Warrant Officer, except that not all branches published books for each component. There are two components of military service: regular and reserve. The regular Officers were published in the books but the reserve Officers may not have been. More than 75 percent of the Officers serving during WWII were reserve component and not regular. It is advised to check the register to be sure.

Army Officer Register

Army Register

San Antonio Public Library
Texana/Genealogy
600 Soledad
San Antonio, TX 78205-1208
(Requests a donation for searches)

Jim Controvich
97 Mayfield Street
Springfield, MA 01108-3535
(413) 734-4856
*Research fee is $10. Contact him after 8 p.m. Eastern time.

THE ADJUTANT GENERAL'S OFFICE

Washington, January 1, 1943

OFFICIAL

ARMY REGISTER

▽

JANUARY 1, 1943

Published by order of the Secretary of War

in compliance with law

UNITED STATES

GOVERNMENT PRINTING OFFICE

WASHINGTON : 1943

ARMY REGISTER, 1943

Name, etc.	Record of service.
Aaron, Thomas R. (O12237). B—Va. 7 Dec. 95. A—M. A., Va. B. S., U. S. M. A., 18. Grad.: Inf. Sch., Co. Officers' Course, 30.	*lt. col. A. U. S. 15 Sept. 41; accepted 18 Sept. 41.*——Cadet M. A. 10 July 16; 2 lt. of Inf. 1 Nov. 18; 1 lt. 5 Dec. 19; (*) 2 lt. (Dec. 15, 22); 1 lt. 20 Apr. 23; capt. 30 Apr. 35; maj. 1 July 40; lt. col. 11 Dec. 42.
Abbey, Evers (O11810). B—Conn. 1 Feb. 95. A—N. Y. Grad. Air Serv. Photography Sch., 22, A. C. Tactical Sch., 35. Rated: Comd. Pil.; C. Obsr.; A. Obsr.	*Pvt. and corp. Cos. B and C, 502 Sup. Tn., and Fld. Sig. Bn., 251 Aero Sq., and 566 Proc. Aero Sq. 19 Sept. 17 to 15 Sept. 18; 2 lt. A. S., U. S. A. 14 Sept. 18; accepted 16 Sept. 18; vacated 10 Sept. 20; col. A. U. S. (AC) 1 Mar. 42.*——2 lt. A. S. 1 July 20; accepted 10 Sept. 20; 1 lt. 1 July 20; capt. 1 Oct. 34; maj. (temp.) 12 Oct. 37; accepted 14 Oct. 37; vacated maj. (temp.) 1 July 40; maj. 1 July 40; lt. col. (temp.) 15 July 41; vacated lt. col. (temp.) 11 Dec. 42; accepted 22 July 41; lt. col. 11 Dec. 42.
Abbey, Richard S. (O23022). B—N. Y. 3 Apr. 16. A—M. A., at lge. B. S., U. S. M. A., 40. Grad. A. C. Primary Flying Sch., 40. Rated: Pil.	*1 lt. A. U. S. 10 Oct. 41; accepted 16 Oct. 41; capt. A. U. S. (AC) 1 Mar. 42; capt. A. U. S. 13 June 42.*——Pvt. Hq. Btry., 2 C. Arty. July 35 to 29 June 36; cadet M. A. 1 July 36; 2 lt. of A. 1 June 40; trfd. to A. C. 21 Mar. 41.
Abbott, Oscar B. (O5748). B—Tex. 8 Oct. 90. A—Tex. G. S. C. 1 July 33 to 30 June 37; 5 Aug. 40. Grad.: Army War Coll. 33, C. and G. S. Sch. 31, Inf. Sch., Co. Officers' Course, 21, Advanced Course, 29. LL. B., Wash. Coll. of Law, 36.	*Sup. sgt. 2 Inf., Tex. N. G. 17 May 16 to 30 Mar. 17 and from 1 Apr. 17 to 15 July 17; col. A. U. S. 24 Dec. 41; accepted 24 Dec. 41.*——2 lt. of Cav. 14 June 17; accepted 16 July 17; 1 lt. 14 June 17; trfd. to Inf. 24 Aug. 17 (to rank from 14 June 17; capt. (temp.) 19 Dec. 17 to 30 June 20; capt. 1 July 20; maj. 1 Oct. 31; lt. col. 1 July 40.
Abbott, Ward T. (O17515). B—N. J. 19 June 08. A—M. A., N. J. B. S., U. S. M. A., 29. Grad. Engr. Sch., Regular Course, 38. C. E. 32, M. C. F. 33, Cornell Univ.	*Maj. A. U. S. 10 Oct. 41; accepted 17 Oct. 41; lt. col. A. U. S. 31 Jan. 42.*——Cadet M. A. 1 July 25; 2 lt. C. E. 13 June 29; A. C. 12 Sept. 29 to 16 Jan. 30; 1 lt. 1 Oct. 34; capt. 13 June 30.
Abdo, Edward S. (O25359) B—Tex. 6 July 18. A—Mich. B. S., Mich. State Coll. 41.	*2 lt. FA—Res. 14 June 41; accepted 14 June 41; active duty from 15 Aug. 41; 1 lt. A. U. S. 6 July 42.*——2 lt. of F. A. 5 Oct. 42; accepted 5 Oct. 42.
Abell, Julian D. (O18666). B—Ind. 15 Oct. 06. A—M. A., Ind. B. S., U. S. M. A., 32. Grad. Engr. Sch., Co. Officers' Course 37. A. B., Indiana Univ., 27. M. S. in E., Cornell Univ., 36.	*Capt. A. U. S. 9 Oct. 40; accepted 4 Oct. 40; maj. A. U. S. 26 June 42.*——Cadet M. A. 2 July 28; 2 lt. C. E. 10 June 32; A. C. 22 July 32 to 3 Mar. 33; 1 lt. 1 Aug. 35; capt. 10 June 42.
Aber, John E. (O23097). B—Tex. 24 Aug. 16. A—M. A., Calif. B. S., U. S. M. A., 40.	*1 lt. A. U. S. 10 Oct. 41; accepted 17 Oct. 41; capt. A. U. S. 30 June 42.*——Pvt. Btrys. A and B, 15 F. A. 1 July 35 to 19 June 36; cadet M. A. 1 July 36; 2 lt. C. A. C. 11 June 40.
Abercrombie, Jay A. (O20604). B—Ark. 9 Oct. 11. A—M. A., Colo. N. G. B. S., U. S. M. A., 37. B. S., Colo. Agri. Coll., 33. M. S. in C. E., Univ. of Calif., 40.	*Capt. A. U. S. 9 Sept. 40; accepted 2 Oct. 40; maj. A. U. S. 26 June 42; lt. col. A. U. S. 26 Dec. 42.*——Cadet M. A. 1 July 33; 2 lt. C. E. 12 June 37; 1 lt. 12 June 40.
Abert, George C. (O21337). B—N. Y. 21 July 12. A—M. A., N. Y. B. S. U. S. M. A., 38.	*1 lt. A. U. S. 9 Sept. 40; accepted 3 Oct. 40, capt. A. U. S. 10 Oct. 41; accepted 18 Oct. 41; maj. A. U. S. 24 June 42.*——Cadet M. A. 2 July 34; 2 lt. of Inf. 14 June 38; Q. M. C. 27 June 40; 1 lt. 14 June 41.
Abraham, Clyde R. (O2153). B—Pa. 17 July 83. A—M. A., Pa. B. S., U. S. M. A., 06. G. S. C. 1 July 28 to 30 June 32; 7 Aug. 34 to 20 Aug. 36; 1 May 39 to 12 June 39. Grad.: Army War Coll. 33, C. and G. S. Sch. 27, Inf. Sch., Advanced Course, 26.	*Maj. of Inf., N. A. 5 Aug. 17; accepted 23 Aug. 17; lt. col. of Inf., U. S. A. 23 Sept. 18; accepted 2 Oct. 18; hon. dis. 30 June 20; brig. gen. A. U. S. 1 Oct. 40; accepted col. 40; terminated brig. gen. A. U. S. 7 May 42.*——Cadet M. A. 16 June 02; 2 lt. of Inf. 12 June 06; 1 lt. 23 May 11; capt. 1 July 16; maj. 1 July 20; I. G. D. 27 Aug. 29 to 26 Aug. 24; lt. col. 2 Feb. 30; col. 1 Aug. 35; I. G. D. 13 June 39 to 25 Oct. 40.
Abrams, Creighton W., jr. (O20296). B—Mass. 16 Sept. 14. A—M. A., Mass. B. S., U. S. M. A., 36.	*Capt. A. U. S. 9 Sept. 40; accepted 17 Oct. 40; maj. A. U. S. 1 Feb. 42; lt. col. A. U. S. 3 Sept. 42.*——Cadet M. A. 1 July 32; 2 lt. of Cav. 12 June 36; 1 lt. 12 June 39.
Absher, Darius C. (O4287). B—N. C. 18 Dec. 82. A—N. C. Grad.: Army Med. Sch. 25, Med. Fld. Serv. Sch. 25, Advanced Course, 34, Army Med. Sch., Advanced Graduate Course, 39. M. D., Univ. of Md., 09.	*1 lt. Med. Sec., O. R. C. 24 Apr. 17; accepted 25 June 17; active duty 21 Sept. 17; capt. Med. Sec., O. R. C. 31 May 18; accepted 17 June 18; maj. M. C., U. S. A. 20 Sept. 18; accepted 2 Oct. 18; hon. dis. 1 Mar. 20; col. A. U. S. 18 Nov. 42.*——Maj. M. C. 1 July 20; accepted 1 Dec. 20; lt. col. 8 Aug. 37.

* Discharged as first lieutenant and appointed second lieutenant Dec. 15, 22, acts June 30, 22 and Sept. 14, 22.

7

Coast Guard Officer Register
List of Regular and Reserve Commissioned and Warrant Officers on Active Duty in Order of Precedence

Coast Guard Academy Museum
U.S. Coast Guard Academy Library
35 Mohegan Avenue
New London, CT 06320-8511
(860) 444-8511
www.uscg.mil//hq/g-cp/museum/museumindex.html

> For WWII years, the register does not contain date of birth. It lists the serial number (signal number), name, status, rank and dates of rank.

UNITED STATES COAST GUARD

———

List of Regular and Reserve Commissioned and Warrant Officers on Active Duty in Order of Precedence

February 1, 1943

Officers' Register

No.	Name	Vice Admiral	Rear Admiral	Captain	Commander	Lieut. Commander	Lieutenant	Lieut. (jg)	Ensign
30000	Russell R. Waesche........(*)	10 Mar.'42	14 Jun.'36	....	1 Jul.'26	12 Jan.'23	2 Apr.'17	2 Sep.'07	27 Oct.'06
30001	Thomas M. Molloy........(Ret.)		1 Jul.'38	1 Jul.'29	10 Sep.'25	10 Oct.'20	9 Mar.'09	14 Oct.'02	17 Aug.'99
30002	William H. Shea........(Ret.)		1 Sep.'41	8 Oct.'29	22 Dec.'25	25 Apr.'21	28 Jul.'10	11 Oct.'04	50 Jun.'02
30003	Lloyd T. Chalker........(*)		10 Mar.'42	1 Jun.'35	1 Jul.'26	12 Jan.'23	26 Jun.'16	20 Mar.'07	27 Oct.'06
30004	Edward D. Jones........(*)		10 Mar.'42	1 Oct.'35	1 Jul.'26	12 Jan.'23	26 Jun.'16	23 Jun.'07	27 Oct.'06
30005	Stanley V. Parker........(*)		10 Mar.'42	1 May '37	1 Jul.'26	12 Jan.'23	1 Dec.'16	25 Aug.'07	27 Oct.'06
30006	Harvey F. Johnson........(*)		10 Mar.'42	18 Dec.'35	1 Jul.'26	12 Jan.'23	11 Jan.'20	29 Jun.'09	13 Feb.'08
30007	James Pine........(*)		30 Jun.'42	25 May '40	1 Dec.'27	12 Jan.'23	21 May '20	30 Dec.'08	22 Dec.'08
30008	Frank J. Gorman........(*)		30 Jun.'42	1 Dec.'41	15 Jun.'32	21 Apr.'24	12 Jan.'23	3 Oct.'17	7 Jun.'13
30009	Robert Donohue........(*)		30 Jun.'42	1 Dec.'41	1 Oct.'34	21 Apr.'24	12 Jan.'23	7 Jun.'18	7 Jun.'13
30010	Edward N. Smith........(*)		30 Jun.'42	1 Dec.'41	21 Apr.'24	12 Jan.'23	7 Jun.'18	7 Jun.'13	
30011	Lorenzo C. Farwell........(Ret.)		1 Jul.'42	23 Apr.'30	1 Jul.'26	12 Jan.'23	2 May '12	21 Feb.'06	10 Jun.'02
30012	William H. Hunter........			23 Apr.'30	21 Apr.'24	31 May '20	22 Apr.'08	23 Sep.'03	2 Aug.'01
30013	California C. McMillan....(E Ret.)			23 Apr.'30	1 Jul.'26	12 Jan.'23	23 Aug.'12	22 Aug.'06	8 Aug.'02
30014	Lucien J. Ker........(E Ret.)			23 Apr.'30	26 Sep.'28	12 Jan.'23	3 Jan.'16	12 Dec.'07	15 Jul.'03
30015	James A. Alger........			1 Jan.'32	1 Jul.'28	12 Jan.'23	12 Sep.'12	8 Jul.'06	7 Aug.'05
30016	Ralph W. Dempwolf........			1 Oct.'34	1 Jul.'26	12 Jan.'23	17 Dec.'14	1 Oct.'05	25 Oct.'05
30017	Roger C. Weightman........(Ret.)			1 Oct.'34	1 Jul.'26	12 Jan.'23	16 Jul.'15	4 Nov.'06	25 Oct.'05
30018	Leroy Reinburg........			1 May '35	1 Jul.'26	12 Jan.'23	1 Aug.'15	23 Nov.'06	25 Oct.'05
30019	James L. Ahern........			7 Oct.'35	1 Jul.'26	12 Jan.'23	9 Nov.'15	17 Mar.'07	25 Jun.'06
30020	Thomas A. Shanley........			1 Jul.'38	1 Jul.'26	12 Jan.'23	3 Oct.'17	15 Dec.'07	19 Feb.'07
30021	Philip F. Roach........			25 May '39	1 Jul.'26	12 Jan.'23	21 Aug.'18	1 Jan.'08	19 Feb.'07
30022	Males A. Benham........			1 Jul.'39	1 Jul.'26	12 Jan.'23	27 Sep.'18	22 Jan.'08	19 Feb.'07
30023	Raymond L. Jack........(Ret.)			1 Jul.'39	1 Jul.'26	12 Jan.'23	27 Sep.'18	9 Mar.'08	19 Feb.'07
30024	Whitney H. Prall........			1 Jun.'39	1 Jul.'37	12 Jan.'23	18 Mar.'19	1 Jul.'08	29 Apr.'07
30025	George W. Cairnes........(E)			1 Mar.'38	1 Jul.'29	12 Jan.'23	21 Aug.'19	26 Jan.'09	28 May '07
30026	Fred A. Nichols........			1 Jul.'39	26 Oct.'25	12 Jan.'23	16 Mar.'19	9 Mar.'08	28 Jan.'08
30027	Chester H. Jones........			5 Aug.'39	1 Jun.'27	12 Jan.'23	2 Oct.'19	16 Apr.'08	17 Jan.'08
30028	Martin A. Doyle........(E Ret.)			1 Aug.'38	1 Jul.'29	12 Jan.'23	26 Dec.'20	1 Nov.'10	31 Aug.'08
30029	Norman B. Hall........(E)			23 Sep.'38	1 Jul.'29	12 Jan.'23	26 Apr.'21	5 Jan.'11	31 Aug.'08
30030	Phillip B. Eaton........(E)			1 Jul.'39	1 Jul.'29	12 Jan.'23	14 May '21	9 Aug.'11	11 Nov.'08
30031	William F. Towle........			29 Aug.'39	27 Sep.'27	12 Jan.'23	1 Jan.'20	2 Jan.'09	22 Dec.'08
30032	Charles A. Park........(X)			1 Dec.'39					
30033	Ralph R. Tinkham........			1 Dec.'39	----------	----------	----------	----------	----------
30034	Michael J. Ryan........			1 Jan.'40	27 Nov.'27	12 Jan.'23	11 May '20	2 Jan.'09	22 Dec.'08
30035	John H. Cornell........			1 Jul.'40	1 Jul.'29	12 Jan.'21	4 Jul.'20	9 Dec.'09	24 May '09
30036	Gordon T. Finlay........			4 Sep.'40	1 Jul.'29	12 Jan.'23	2 Feb.'21	28 Jul.'10	24 May '09
30037	Louis L. Bennett........			1 Oct.'40	1 Jul.'29	12 Jan.'23	23 Apr.'21	5 Oct.'10	26 May '09
30038	Charles J. Oden'Hal........(E Ret.)			1 Oct.'40	13 Jul.'29	21 Apr.'24	12 Jan.'23	10 Jun.'14	11 May '09
30039	Charles E. Sugden........(E)			1 Dec.'40	7 Jun.'30	12 Jan.'23		28 Aug.'12	11 Mar.'09
30040	Henry C. Roach........(E)			1 Dec.'40	18 Jul.'29	21 Apr.'24	12 Jan.'23	12 Jun.'14	26 Jun.'10
30041	William J. Kenster........			1 Dec.'40	1 Jul.'29	12 Jan.'23	14 Nov.'21	19 Dec.'10	14 Jan.'10
30042	Eugene A. Coffin........			1 May '41	1 Jul.'29	12 Jan.'23	30 Dec.'21	19 Jun.'11	14 Jan.'10
30043	Herbert H. Perham........(E)			1 Dec.'40	23 Apr.'30	21 Apr.'24	12 Jan.'23	7 Aug.'14	14 Jan.'10
30044	John S. Baylis........			25 May '41	1 Jul.'29	12 Jan.'23	19 Jan.'22	6 Jul.'11	25 May '10
30045	Charles G. Roemer........			25 May '41	1 Jul.'29	12 Jan.'23	10 Jul.'22	21 Aug.'11	6 Aug.'10
30046	Wilfred H. Derby........			26 Jul.'41	1 Jul.'29	12 Jan.'23	1 Sep.'22	13 Sep.'11	16 Jan.'11
30047	Clarence H. Dench........			1 Sep.'41	1 Jul.'29	12 Jan.'23	12 Jan.'23	27 Aug.'12	16 Jan.'11
30048	William K. Scammell........			1 Dec.'41	1 Jul.'29	21 Apr.'24	12 Jan.'23	12 Sep.'12	16 Jan.'11
30049	Russell L. Lucas........			1 Dec.'41	1 Jul.'29	21 Apr.'24	12 Jan.'23	19 Sep.'14	16 Jan.'11
30050	Stephen S. Yeandle........(*)			1 Dec.'41	13 Jul.'29	21 Apr.'24	12 Jan.'23	17 Dec.'14	18 Jan.'11
30051	Frederick C. Zeusler........(*)			1 Dec.'41	8 Oct.'29	21 Apr.'24	12 Jan.'23	16 Jun.'15	18 Jan.'11
30052	Joseph E. Stika........(*)			1 Dec.'41	1 Sep.'30	21 Apr.'24	12 Jan.'23	18 Jan.'16	18 Jan.'11
30053	Benjamin C. Thorn........(*)(E)			1 Jun.'41	23 Apr.'30	21 Apr.'24	12 Jan.'23	1 Aug.'15	18 Jan.'11
30054	Milton R. Daniels........(E)			1 Jun.'41	23 Apr.'30	21 Apr.'24	12 Jan.'23	11 Oct.'15	18 Jan.'11
30055	Ellis Reed-Hill........(E)			1 Dec.'41	1 Mar.'31	21 Apr.'24	12 Jan.'23	31 Mar.'16	18 Jan.'11
30056	Floyd Sexton........			1 Dec.'41	1 Mar.'31	21 Apr.'24	12 Jan.'23	1 Dec.'16	31 May '12
30057	Gustavus Stewart........			1 Dec.'41	15 Apr.'31	21 Apr.'24	12 Jan.'23	31 May '17	31 May '12
30058	Joseph F. Farley........(*)			1 Dec.'41	27 Jun.'31	21 Apr.'24	12 Jan.'23	31 May '17	31 May '12
30059	Gustavus R. O'Connor........(*)(E)			1 Dec.'41	15 Jun.'32	21 Apr.'24	12 Jan.'23	31 Aug.'16	3 Mar.'13
30060	Gordon M. MacLane........(*)			1 Dec.'41	1 Sep.'32	21 Apr.'24	12 Jan.'23	7 Jun.'18	7 Jun.'13
30061	Earl G. Rose........(*)			1 Dec.'41	1 Oct.'34	21 Apr.'24	12 Jan.'23	7 Jun.'18	7 Jun.'13
30062	Loyd V. Kielhorn........(*)			1 Dec.'41	1 Oct.'34	21 Apr.'24	12 Jan.'23	7 Jun.'18	7 Jun.'13
30063	Carl C. von Paulsen........(*)			1 Dec.'41	1 Jun.'35	21 Apr.'24	12 Jan.'23	7 Jun.'18	7 Jun.'13
30064	John E. Whitbeck........(*)			1 Dec.'41	7 Oct.'35	21 Apr.'24	12 Jan.'23	7 Jun.'18	7 Jun.'13
30065	Henry Coyle........(*)			1 Dec.'41	1 Jan.'36	21 Apr.'24	12 Jan.'23	7 Jun.'18	7 Jun.'13
30066	Henry G. Hemingway, Jr.....(*)			1 Apr.'42	28 Oct.'29	21 Apr.'24	12 Jan.'23	9 Nov.'15	16 Jan.'11
30067	Charles T. Henley........(*)(E)			1 Dec.'41	1 Apr.'36	21 Apr.'24	12 Jan.'23	3 Oct.'18	28 Aug.'15
30068	Edward F. Palmer........(*)(E)			1 Dec.'41	21 May '36		12 Jan.'23	26 Mar.'19	28 Aug.'15
30069	John H. Heiner........			3 Dec.'41	21 May '36	2 Feb.'25	12 Jan.'23	1 Dec.'19	7 Oct.'16
30070	Walter H. Troll........(*)(E)			1 Dec.'41	15 Jun.'32		12 Jan.'23	27 Sep.'18	3 Mar.'13
30071	Edward M. Webster........(*)(Ret.)			1 Jun.'42	21 Jun.'30		30 Oct.'23	31 May '17	31 May '12
30072	Lyndon Spencer........(*)			1 Dec.'42	1 Dec.'36	10 Jul.'25	12 Jan.'23	27 Sep.'18	4 Aug.'18
30073	Joseph Greenspun........(*)			1 Dec.'42	1 May '37	10 Sep.'25	12 Jan.'23	17 Nov.'13	31 Jul.'18
30074	Chester E. Dimick........(*)(P)			1 Dec.'42	17 Jun.'37				
30075	Louis W. Perkins........			1 Dec.'42	1 Mar.'38	4 Dec.'25	12 Jan.'23	20 May '19	1 Aug.'18
30076	Raymond T. McElligott........(*)			1 Dec.'42	1 Jul.'38	22 Dec.'25	12 Jan.'23	27 Jul.'18	16 Aug.'18
30077	Louis B. Olson........			1 Dec.'42	25 May '39	1 Oct.'26	12 Jan.'23	18 Dec.'19	1 Oct.'18
30078	Roger C. Heiner........			1 Dec.'42	25 May '39	1 Oct.'26	12 Jan.'23	12 Feb.'20	1 Oct.'18
30079	Charles W. Dean........(*)			1 Dec.'42	1 Jul.'39	22 Nov.'27	12 Jan.'23	18 May '20	22 Nov.'19
30080	Walfred G. Bloom........(*)			1 Dec.'42	1 Jul.'39	22 Nov.'27	12 Jan.'23	2 Jun.'20	22 Nov.'19

List of Regular and Reserve Commissioned and Warrant Officers on Active Duty in Order of Precedence, February 1, 1943.

Marine Corps & Navy Officer Register
Register of Commissioned and Warrant Officers of the United States Navy and Marine Corps

Naval Historical Center
Washington Navy Yard
805 Kidder Breese SE
Washington, DC 20374-5060
www.history.navy.mil

REGISTER

of

Commissioned and Warrant Officers of the United States Navy and Marine Corps

✦

JULY 1, 1942

UNITED STATES
GOVERNMENT PRINTING OFFICE
WASHINGTON : 1942

MARINE CORPS   753

MAJORS—Continued

No. in grade	Accepted commission	From—	Control date of commissioned service (see (N), Adm. notes)	Born Date	Born State	Total sea service Yr.	Mo.	Total foreign service Yr.	Mo.	Prior service not counted for pay purpose Yr.	Mo.	Expiration of last tour of sea or foreign service	Date of present duty
	28 Jan. 27	U. S. M. C.	28 Jan. 27	9 Apr. 05	N.Y	2	2	3	4	*3	7	May 33	28 June 40
	*2 June 27	U. S. N. A.	2 June 27	9 Aug. 05	Ariz	1	0	2	8	*3	11	Jan. 33	15 June 40
	...*do	U. S. N. A.	...do	30 Mar. 04	N.Y	1	11	4	2	*3	10	Mar. 42	22 Apr. 42
	*8 June 23	U. S. N. A.	8 June 23	22 Nov. 01	Pa	2	1	2	2	*4	0	Nov. 34	1 June 39
65	*2 June 27	U. S. N. A.	2 June 27	19 Mar. 06	Kans	3	7	2	2	*3	11	June 38	— July 42
	...*do	U. S. N. A.	...do	8 Apr. 05	Pa	6	3	0	11	*3	11	Nov. 34	1 July 40
	...*do	U. S. N. A.	...do	5 Sept. 05	N.Y	4	4	1	7	*3	11	June 34	— July 42
	...*do	U. S. N. A.	...do	19 July 03	W.Va	2	1	2	6	*3	11	Aug. 34	5 July 41
	...*do	U. S. N. A.	...do	7 Mar. 05	Iowa	0	8	7	0	*3	11	June 37	20 Apr. 40
70	...*do	U. S. N. A.	...do	20 May 06	Mont	1	11	5	8	*3	8	June 39	15 Feb. 41
	...*do	U. S. N. A.	...do	14 Feb. 05	Mo	2	0	6	8	*4	11	June 38	15 June 40
	...*do	U. S. N. A.	...do	29 Mar. 05	Ariz	1	9	4	8	*3	9	June 35	10 July 40
	...*do	U. S. N. A.	...do	28 Dec. 04	Okla	3	1	4	6	*3	11	Aug. 41	— July 42
	...*do	U. S. N. A.	...do	27 June 04	Nebr	0	11	4	5	*3	9	July 30	17 Sept. 41
75	...*do	U. S. N. A.	...do	14 July 05	Ky	2	0	5	10	*3	9	Apr. 42	1 May 42
	...*do	U. S. N. A.	...do	20 Apr. 03	Vt	2	0	3	11	**6	11	Aug. 41	3 Jan. 42
	...*do	U. S. N. A.	...do	22 Aug. 05	W.Va	3	4	3	11	*3	10	Feb. 42	— June 42
	...*do	U. S. N. A.	...do	9 Jan. 05	Ohio	1	11	1	8	*4	11	June 33	30 July 41
	...*do	U. S. N. A.	...do	9 Feb. 03	N.Y	4	0	2	9	*4	11	Dec. 41	5 Jan. 42
80	...*do	U. S. N. A.	...do	24 Sept. 04	Ala	2	1	4	4	*3	11	June 40	3 Mar. 42
	...*do	U. S. N. A.	...do	27 Dec. 04	Ala	3	9	0	6	*3	9	--------	4 June 41
	...*do	U. S. N. A.	...do	17 Oct. 06	Ark	4	11	4	6	*3	11	Mar. 41	10 June 41
	...*do	U. S. N. A.	...do	28 May 04	P.R	4	3	3	3	*3	11	Mar. 42	1 Apr. 42
	28 July 27	Md	14 July 27	19 Feb. 05	Md	3	2	2	5	f1	1	Mar. 36	5 Apr. 42
85	11 Aug. 27	Mass	11 Aug. 27	14 Sept. 03	Mass	4	5	2	0	0	0	June 40	— July 42
	9 Aug. 27	Nebr	9 Aug. 27	29 Nov. 04	Nebr	3	7	3	0	0	0	Sept. 41	17 Oct. 41
	...do	Nebr	...do	21 Feb. 04	Nebr	2	2	2	1	0	0	Jan. 33	10 Apr. 41
	1 Aug. 27	Va	1 Aug. 27	20 Nov. 03	Va	2	7	4	3	0	0	Sept. 39	16 Nov. 39
	10 Aug. 27	Md	10 Aug. 27	9 July 05	Md	2	5	4	1	0	0	Apr. 38	22 June 42
90	4 Feb. 28	U. S. M. C.	4 Feb. 28	27 Mar. 01	Mo	3	4	2	1	*2	4	Aug. 39	2 Aug. 39
	...do	U. S. M. C.	...do	22 Aug. 05	N.J	1	1	4	4	*4	10	July 41	— July 42
	...do	U. S. M. C.	...do	31 Aug. 03	Ohio	3	7	0	0	*2	5	June 33	1 May 42
	3 Mar. 28	U. S. M. C.	3 Mar. 28	9 Sept. 06	Fla	2	3	2	5	*2	9	Mar. 37	26 Dec. 39
	4 Feb. 28	U. S. M. C.	4 Feb. 28	4 Aug. 01	Ala	3	3	3	5	*2	3	Mar. 42	22 June 42
95	...do	U. S. M. C.	...do	3 Nov. 04	Ohio	2	4	2	1	*2	9	Feb. 37	29 Apr. 42
	...do	U. S. M. C.	...do	1 Dec. 04	Mass	2	1	1	10	b*4	6	June 39	18 Feb. 42
	*7 June 28	U. S. N. A.	7 June 28	23 Mar. 05	N.Y	0	4	1	4	a*5	8	Jan. 33	1 May 42
	...*do	U. S. N. A.	...do	25 Nov. 05	Mich	3	2	1	7	*3	11	...do	15 Aug. 39
	...*do	U. S. N. A.	...do	22 Oct. 04	Mich	1	2	2	0	*4	0	July 41	15 Sept. 41
100	...*do	U. S. N. A.	...do	27 Apr. 05	D.C	1	8	3	2	*4	0	Dec. 34	23 July 41
	...*do	U. S. N. A.	...do	30 Sept. 05	Pa	1	6	5	1	*4	0	Aug. 37	20 July 40
	...*do	U. S. N. A.	...do	1 Aug. 04	Conn	2	3	1	1	*4	0	Dec. 32	7 June 39
	...*do	U. S. N. A.	...do	17 July 04	Ohio	2	4	1	2	a*5	0	Nov. 34	— July 42
105	...*do	U. S. N. A.	...do	7 Oct. 04	Mich	2	0	3	10	a*4	10	Apr. 37	25 June 41
	...*do	U. S. N. A.	...do	9 June 04	Ill	1	11	4	2	*4	11	July 32	28 Mar. 41
	8 Sept. 26	Calif	8 Sept. 26	11 Sept. 03	Calif	1	9	6	7	0	0	June 36	29 Apr. 40
	*5 June 24	U. S. N. A.	5 June 24	1 May 00	Ohio	3	1	3	10	*4	0	Aug. 41	— July 42
	*3 June 26	U. S. N. A.	3 June 26	18 July 02	Minn	1	5	7	9	a*5	9	Oct. 35	25 Aug. 39
	18 July 25	Vt	18 July 25	24 July 03	Vt	4	8	2	4	0	0	Feb. 36	1 July 38
110	4 Feb. 28	U. S. M. C.	4 Feb. 28	7 Feb. 05	N.Y	3	7	1	0	*4	1	Mar. 42	1 Apr. 42
	7 June 28	U. S. N. A.	7 June 28	3 Aug. 04	Tex	1	10	3	11	*4	0	Aug. 39	3 Aug. 41
	...*do	U. S. N. A.	...do	4 Aug. 03	Iowa	3	2	0	7	a*6	11	Nov. 34	10 June 40
	12 Feb. 29	U. S. M. C.	12 Feb. 29	28 Feb. 04	Miss	3	10	1	10	*2	5	June 41	29 Dec. 42
	...do	U. S. M. C.	...do	26 Nov. 04	Ga	2	2	2	1	*2	7	May 41	30 Apr. 42
115	...do	U. S. M. C.	...do	4 Sept. 04	Pa	1	2	3	9	*2	6	Dec. 41	9 Mar. 42
	...do	U. S. M. C.	...do	15 May 03	Mich	2	0	1	11	*6	3	Jan. 38	16 Oct. 39
	...do	U. S. M. C.	...do	26 Mar. 04	Miss	2	8	0	9	a*5	0	Nov. 41	11 Mar. 42
	8 June 29	U. S. M. C.	8 June 29	3 Jan. 05	Ill	2	5	6	1	*3	6	Aug. 40	2 May 41
	12 Feb. 29	U. S. M. C.	12 Feb. 29	18 Sept. 03	Minn	2	3	3	4	*3	5	Aug. 39	29 Dec. 41
120	*6 June 29	U. S. N. A.	6 June 29	23 Feb. 08	Pa	1	9	2	11	*3	11	July 40	14 Aug. 40

*Date of rank of appointment as second lieutenant.

Register of Commissioned and Warrant Officers of the United States Navy and Marine Corps, July 1, 1942.

The registers also can be found in most government depository libraries. Check with your state or university libraries. They also can be requested using the interlibrary loan program.

Reserve & National Guard Officer Directories

Army Directory, Reserve and National Guard Officers on Active Duty

This book is much like that of the officer registers but for reserve and National Guard officers only. It lists the name, rank, serial number, organization and current base assignment. For the WWII–era, this book was printed in 1941, 1942 and 1943.

ARMY
DIRECTORY

Reserve and
National Guard Officers
On Active Duty

JULY 31, 1941

———

WAR DEPARTMENT
The Adjutant General's Office
Washington

United States Government Printing Office : Washington : 1941

RESERVE AND NATIONAL GUARD OFFICERS 1

Name, organization, and address	Name, organization, and address
AAB FRANKLIN G 0-240866 CAPT DC FORT HAYES OHIO	ABBOTT HAROLD S 0-395025 1 LT FA CAMP JOSEPH T ROBINSON ARK
AABEL BERNARD 0-402314 2 LT MAC CP FORREST TENN	ABBOTT HARRY P 0-129676 MAJ CH FORT KNOX KY
AAGESEN WALTER J 0-270275 MAJ MC LOVELL GEN HOSP FT DEVENS MASS	ABBOTT HENRY G 0-358458 1 LT CE CAMP SHELBY MISS
AAMODT JOHN F 0-363887 1 LT CAC FORT WINFIELD SCOTT CALIF	ABBOTT JAMES P 0-857156 CAPT CAV FORT RILEY KANS
AARNI JOHN C 0-363335 1 LT MC FORT HUACHUCA ARIZ	ABBOTT JOHN C 0-186525 MAJ FA ORG RES PRESIDIO OF SAN FRANCISCO CALIF
AAROE GLEN E 0-290234 1 LT FA CAMP SAN LUIS OBISPO CALIF	ABBOTT JOHN J 0-267629 CAPT MAC CAMP FORREST TENN
AARON EUGENE 0-419382 2 LT INF FT LEWIS WASH	ABBOTT JOHN L 0-353412 2 LT INF FORT CUSTER BATTLE CREEK MICH
AARON GEORGE 0-385976 1 LT MC CAMP LIVINGSTON LA	ABBOTT JOHN R 0-400984 1 LT DC CAMP FORREST TENN
AARON REID A 0-389878 2 LT AC SAVANNAH A B SAVANNAH GA	ABBOTT LEONARD J 0-377173 1 LT INF CAMP WOLTERS TEX
AARON WILLIAM DAYTON 0-419233 2 LT AC A C ADV FLYING SCH BARKSDALE FIELD LA	ABBOTT LYLE I 0-411757 2 LT INF CAMP JOSEPH T ROBINSON LITTLE ROCK ARK
AARONSON LEONARD 0-371388 1 LT INF FORT JACKSON S C	ABBOTT NATHAN M 0-378458 2 LT AC QUARRY HEIGHTS C Z
AASEN EDWIN K 0-351130 1 LT INF FT LEONARD WOOD MO	ABBOTT NORMAN F 0-394973 2 LT FA CAMP JOSEPH T ROBINSON ARK
AASER IVAR L 0-230667 1 LT DC FORT HUACHUCA ARIZ	ABBOTT OSLER A 0-384810 1 LT MC FORT KNOX KY
ABADIE LESTER C 0-354096 2 LT AC ALA INST OF AERO TUSCALOOSA ALA	ABBOTT RAYMOND B JR 0-351869 1 LT INF A C TECH SCH SCOTT FIELD BR SCOTT FIELD ILL
ABARBANEL MILTON G 0-415933 1 LT MC TALLAHASSEE FLA	ABBOTT ROBERT H 0-364950 2 LT ORD ABERDEEN PROVING GROUND MD
ABBAMONTE LOUIS W 0-294494 CAPT MC FT TOTTEN N Y	ABBOTT ROBERT O JR 0-411363 2 LT INF CAMP BLANDING FLA
ABBE WILLIAM C 0-403056 1 LT CH CAMP EDWARDS MASS	ABBOTT THOMAS H 0-307713 1 LT SC O C S O WASHINGTON D C
ABBEY JOHN C 0-395815 1 LT FA FORT LEONARD WOOD MO	ABBOTT TRUMAN C 0-289243 1 LT AC AC TRAIN DETCH CORSICANA TEXAS
ABBEY HARLAN I 0-281316 CAPT FA CAMP JOSEPH T ROBINSON ARK	ABBOTT WALTER R 0-406825 2 LT INF CAMP CLAIBORNE LA
ABBEY ROBERT J 0-377471 2 LT INF CAMP ROBERTS CALIF	ABBOTT WALTER R JR 0-340265 1 LT FA O UNDER SECY OF WAR WASHINGTON D C
ABBEY WALTER H 0-246670 MAJ CAC FORT STEVENS OREG	ABBOTT ZANE L 0-398491 2 LT AC A C BASIC FLYING SCH SAN ANGELO TEX
ABBITT CHARLES W 0-412629 2 LT INF FORT BENNING GA	ABBOTTS LLOYD F 0-423904 2 LT AC A C ADV FLYING SCH BARKSDALE FIELD LA
ABBITT WILLIAM H 0-364198 1 LT FA S C SCH FT MONMOUTH N J	ABDALAH ERNEST G 0-318113 1 LT AC MANCHESTER N H
ABBOTT ALBERT W 0-373312 2 LT CAV FT RILEY KANSAS	ABDO FRANCIS J 0-376568 1 LT MC FORT WINFIELD SCOTT CALIF
ABBOTT ALVIN S 0-338639 1 LT INF MANILA P I	ABEL ANTHONY C 0-365880 2 LT FA FT LEWIS WASH
ABBOTT ARTHUR J 0-361078 1 LT QMC ROBINSON RMT DEP FORT ROBINSON NEBR	ABEL NORMAN D 0-323358 1 LT CAC FORT CROCKETT TEX
ABBOTT FLOYD A 0-298781 CAPT MAC CAMP GRANT ILL	ABEL ORVAL J 0-322786 1 LT INF FORT BENNING GA
ABBOTT FRANCIS R 0-245478 CAPT CAC RNT DEP FT ROBINSON NEBR	ABEL RALPH S 0-373398 1 LT MAC FORT DIX N J
ABBOTT GARDNER JR 0-354859 1 LT FA BOLLING FIELD D C	ABEL RAYMOND E 0-342266 1 LT INF CAMP JOSEPH T ROBINSON LITTLE ROCK ARK
ABBOTT GEORGE C JR 0-398186 1 LT INF CAMP BLANDING FLA	ABEL RAYMOND L 0-100837 LT C CWS C W S PROC OFF AMERICAN BANK BLDG 6TH AND GRANT STS PITTSBURGH PA
ABBOTT GEORGE E 0-366856 1 LT MC HUNTER LIGGET MIL RES JOLAN CALIF	ABEL WILLARD E 0-320653 2 LT QMC FORT LEWIS WASH
ABBOTT GEORGE R 0-299413 1 LT INF PRES OF SAN FRANCISCO CALIF	ABELE LESTER J 0-267147 MAJ JAC CAMP SHELBY MISS
ABBOTT GEORGE W 0-415528 2 LT INF CAMP BLANDING STARKE FLA	

Army Directory, Reserve and National Guard Officers on Active Duty, July 31, 1941.

Jim Controvich
97 Mayfield Street
Springfield, MA 01108-3535
(413) 734-4856
*Research fee is $10. Contact him after 8 p.m. Eastern time.

This book may also be available from government depository libraries or using the interlibrary loan program.

County Clerk's Office

After a veteran was discharged, it was suggested that he file his discharge certificate at the county clerk's office, thereby protecting the document and allowing easy access if a copy was needed. Not all veterans filed their discharge certificates. If the county is known where the veteran lived during or after the war, check with the records department to see if a copy is available. They also may be stored at the state archives after so many years.

WWII Bonus Records

Many states paid a WWII bonus to veterans who served either stateside or overseas. Usually the payment was higher if the veteran served overseas. If the veteran served from a state that paid a bonus, the records may be searchable by name or name and date of birth. The serial number should be listed. See Appendix A (State Records).

Military Records Held by State Offices

State Archives, State Adjutant General's or State Veterans Affairs Offices may have WWII military records. Types of records vary by state. See Appendix A (State Records).

WWII Casualties

If your relative died during the war, he should be listed in the *World War II Honor List of Dead and Missing Army and Army Air Forces, Summary of War Casualties from World War II for Navy, Marine Corps, and Coast Guard Personnel*, WWII Roster of Dead or the American Battle Monuments Commission's database. These sources usually have the name, serial number, branch of service, rank, type of casualty and date of death. See Chapter Four (WWII Casualty Records).

Marine Corps

The Marine Corps has a complete list of all people who have served in the Marine Corps and they will give out a military serial number (but not a Social Security number). Contact them with the veteran's name, date of birth and time period of service.

U.S. Marine Corps – HQMC MMSB-17
2008 Elliot Road, Suite 203
Quantico, VA 22134-5030
(703) 784-3942, (703) 784-5792 Fax

> If the veteran entered the service during WWII and stayed in the military to retire, the person's serial number eventually changed to his or her Social Security number. Therefore, the standard form 180 should include the Social Security number as well as the military serial number.
>
> The Army and Air Force discontinued serial/service numbers on July 1, 1969; the Navy and Marine Corps on July 1, 1972, and the Coast Guard on October 1, 1974.

The NPRC or the individual military branches *will not* release a Social Security number. That is protected under the Privacy Act. If your relative is deceased and you need to obtain the Social Security number, there are several avenues available.

Social Security Number Sources

Social Security Death Index

The Social Security Death Index on the Internet can be searched by name and date of birth or name only (if the name is unique). It lists the Social Security number, first name, last name and possibly middle initial, date of birth, date of death and place the Social Security death payment was sent. The Social Security death index can be found on the Internet at *www.ancestry.com* or *http://ssdi.genealogy.rootsweb.com*.

Officer Registers

Officer Registers were published each year by each branch of the military. After the services switched from a serial number to a Social Security number, the Registers included the military member's Social Security number. The books were not released to libraries after 1980. If you relative stayed in the service after the number was changed, the register would be a source for the Social Security number.

Underage Veterans

The minimum age to enlist during WWII was 17 years old. Many lied about their age and would simply change the age on their birth certificate or provide some source of documentation to substantiate their false age. If your relative served underage, it's possible that this may cause some problems in obtaining the military record if the serial number is not available. Make a note on the standard form 180 that the year of birth may be different in the records. Give an idea of what years to search for.

Story

I worked on a case in which a 16-year-old boy lied about his age to enlist in the Army during WWII. After his death, his daughter tried to obtain his military records and gave his correct date of birth, not the one he used during enlistment. The request was sent back stating "No Record Found." After talking with other relatives, she learned about his underage service. She simply reapplied for the records giving a range of years. His records were located finally and sent to her.

Hospital Admission Cards

The office of the Surgeon General, Department of the Army (1942–1945 and 1950–1954) created information from the hospital admission cards. For the WWII period (1942–1945), it only covers active duty Army and Army Air Corps. It contains the serial number of the veteran and *does not* list the veteran's name. Important information can be utilized from the report, including rank, time period in service and place of admission. This would be extremely useful if the veteran's records were burned in the fire. The National Personnel Records Center uses these records as an alternative source to verify military service.

National Personnel Records Center
9700 Page Avenue
St Louis, MO 63132-5100

```
                INFORMATION FROM THE HOSPITAL ADMISSION CARDS CREATED     02/07/2001
                BY THE OFFICE OF THE SURGEON GENERAL, DEPARTMENT OF        LACin
                      THE ARMY (1942-1945 and 1950-1954)

        THIS INFORMATION WAS FOUND IN THE FILE FOR THE YEAR 1944 .

           SERVICE NUMBER:   348897██

              CATEGORY:      CODE:        EXPLANATION:
        RANK:                2          Enlisted Man
        ARM OF SERVICE:      98         Transportation Corps
        AGE:                 37         37
        RACE:                1          White, includes Mexican
        YEARS OF SVC:        01         0 Year(s),1 Month(s)
        MO/YR OF ADMISSION:  014        January 1944
        STATION OF ADMISSION: D248      Camp Gordon Johnston, Florida
        FINAL TRMT FACILITY: 6          Station hospital
        INVALID/DIED IN PRSN: 0         Not a special classification
        TYPE OF CASE:        1          Disease
        TYPE OF ADMISSION:   1          New
        TYPE OF DIAGNOSIS:   1          Sole diagnosis, no history of prior disease, injur
                                          y or battle casualty
        LINE OF DUTY:        1          In line of duty

        FIRST DIAGNOSIS:     6213       Nasopharyngitis, acute
          LOCATION:          -          Not Found
          OPERATION:         -          Not Found

        SECOND DIAGNOSIS:    -          Not found
          LOCATION:          -          Not Found
          OPERATION:         -          Not Found

        THIRD DIAGNOSIS:     -          Not found

        CAUSATIVE AGENT:     -          Not found
        FINAL RESULT:        -          Not found
        DISPOSITION:         6          Duty
        FIELD OF CAUSE OF
          DEATH OR DISCHARGE: 0         Not death nor discharge (incl cases remaining in h
                                          osp at end of 1944
        DISPOSITION DATE:    014        JANUARY 1944

        NON-EFFECTIVE DAYS
          Total Days:        009        009 .      *000 = case incl
          Hospital Days:     009        009.       for statistical
          Cur Yr/GenHosp OS: 009        009   ·    purposes only

        UNSPECIFIED FIELD:   -          Not found
        UNSPECIFIED FIELD:   -          Not found
        SAMPLE SIZE:         2          20%

        Source:  This information was obtained from the Hospital Admission Card data
        files (1942-1945; 1950-1954), created by the Office of the Surgeon General
        Department of the Army.  During 1988, this secondary source material was made
        available to the National Personnel Records Center by the National Research
        Council, a current custodian of the data file.  This file was originally
        compiled for statistical purposes.  Therefore, name identification does not
        exist and sampling techniques were used with the result that not all hospital
        admissions are included.  Veterans on the file are identified by service number
        and other data related to hospital admission.
```

Hospital Admission Card Data Files (1942–1945; 1950–1954)

Department of Veterans Affairs Files

As a result of having served in the military, most veterans are eligible for certain benefits from the Department of Veterans Affairs (VA). These benefits can include medical treatment, home loans, life insurance and educational payments. Whenever a veteran files a claim for a benefit with the VA, a claim folder is established and usually kept at a regional office in the state where the veteran lives. These claim folders can sometimes contain military service and medical documents, family information and even copies of marriage and birth certificates.

To determine if a claim folder exists, call (800) 827-1000. You will be connected to the nearest VA regional office. It's best to have the veteran's identifying information available, such as full name, date of birth, Social Security number or military serial number. The VA maintains a database of claims and claim folder locations. If a folder exists, ask how you can obtain a copy of the folder. Depending on the location of the folder, it could take several months for you receive the copies. If the veteran is deceased and you are next of kin, you may need proof of death if the database does not show date of death.

WWII Prisoner of War Files

The Prisoner of War (POW) Information Bureau under the Office of the Provost Marshal General put together punch cards with information pertaining to military and civilian POWs and internees. This data was converted to electronic media and is available on the National Archives website. Information includes serial number, name, grade, grade code, service code, arm of service, arm of service code, date reported, race, state of residence, type of organization, parent unit number, parent unit type, area, latest report date, source of report, status, detaining power, place of detention (camp code), repatriation status, and whether the POW was on a Japanese ship that sank, or if he died during transport to the Philippine Islands.

- American POWs returned alive from the European Theater A-V (85,541 records)
- American POWs returned alive from the European Theater Vititoe – Zywot (6,952 records)
- American POWs returned alive from the Pacific Theater (19,202 records)
- American Civilian POWs [Released and Dead] Interned by Japanese (13,750 records)
- Deceased American Military POWs Japanese (7,041 records)
- Deceased American Military POWs Japanese Died in Ship Sinkings 1944 (3,299 records)
- Deceased American [Military] POWs [Germany] (2,523 records)
- Neutral Internees [U.S. Military Personnel Interned in a Neutral Country] (2,164 records)
- Escapees/KIA [Japan] (21 records)
- Never POW [Japan] (92 records)
- Missing-in-Action Returned to Military Control (1,554 records)
- Civilians A-Z [Worldwide] Non U.S. Citizens (488 records)
- Civilians – Unofficial A-Z [Japan] (747 records)

Center for Electronic Records
National Archives at College Park
8601 Adelphi Road
College Park, MD 20740-6001
*www.archives.gov/research_room/research_topics/
wwii_pow_punchcards.html*

Navy POW Records Microfiche F-454 (two fiche) is a list of Officers and enlisted POWs as of 25 September 1945. Arranged alphabetically, the list includes service number, rank or rate, date of capture and the prisoner of war camp designation. Another microfiche F-455 (two fiche) is an alphabetical list of the officer and enlisted POWs in the Pacific and Asiatic areas as of 28 July 1945. It provides the same information as fiche F-454.

Naval Historical Center
Operational Archives Division
805 Kidder Breese SE
Washington, DC 20374-5060
www.history.navy.mil

Military Academies & Colleges

During WWII, graduates from the three military
academies were required to serve in the military for a
specified period of time. If your relative either attended or
graduated from one of these schools, you should contact the
institution to acquire as much information as possible. The
academies have student records. The alumni associations
also may have a *Register of Graduates* that might provide
military service information.

U.S. Military Academy
West Point, NY 10996
(845) 938-4011
www.usma.edu

U.S. Coast Guard Academy
Annapolis, MD 21402
(860) 444-8501
www.cga.edu

U.S. Naval Academy
121 Blake Rd
Annapolis, MD 21402-5000
(410) 293-1000
www.usna.edu

While the military academies mandated military service,
other military colleges such as Texas A&M and The Citadel had
cadet programs but did not require military service, although
many of their graduates did enter the military. During WWII,
many may have enlisted for service or were required to serve
under the draft. If your relative attended one of these schools,
photographs and other information of value for a family

history may be available. Contact the school directly for its policy about releasing photographs or school records.

The Citadel
171 Moultrie Street
Charleston, SC 29409
www.citadel.edu

Norwich University
158 Harmon Drive
Northfield, VT 05663-1035
(802) 485-2001
www.norwich.edu

Texas A&M University
College Station, TX 77843-1227
(979) 845-2811
www.tamu.edu

Virginia Military Institute
Lexington, VA 24450
(540) 464-7311
www.vmi.edu

Virginia Tech
Blacksburg, VA 24061-0213
(540) 321-6413
www.vt.edu
More than 7,000 students served during WWII.

Military Occupation Specialty (MOS/Ratings) Codes

Each military member was assigned an MOS (other branches used different terms), which is a job code. An MOS could range from truck driver to surgeon. Once you have the person's military records, information available from the states and other military service information, search out the definition of the MOS. Each branch has an average of more than 100 MOS descriptions. Due to the volume, the information can't be printed in this book.

MOS Sources

Army and Army Air Corps
U.S. Army Military History Institute
22 Ashburn Drive
Carlisle, PA 17013-5008
(717) 245-3711 Fax
http://carlisle-www.army.mil/usamhi

Coast Guard
Coast Guard Historian's Office
U.S. Coast Guard Headquarters
2100 Second St, SW
Washington, DC 20593-4309
www.uscg/mil/hq/g-cp/history/collect/html

Marine Corps
Marine Corps Historical Center
1254 Charles Morris St. SE
Washington, DC 20374-5040
(202) 433-0780, (202) 433-4691 Fax

Navy
Naval Historical Center
Washington Navy Yard
805 Kidder Breese SE
Washington, DC 20374-5060
www.history.navy.mil

Replacement Medals

Replacement medals are issued to the veteran or next of kin, if the veteran is deceased. Fill out the standard form 180 and mail to the address listed below for the appropriate branch of service. Medals may also be purchased from companies such as Medals of America and placed in a frame comemerating the veteran's military service. See Chapter Five (WWII Medals).

Air Force & Army Air Corps
National Personnel Records Center
Air Force Reference Branch (NRPMF)
9700 Page Avenue
St Louis, MO 63132-5100

Army
National Personnel Records Center
Medals Section (NRPMA-M)
9700 Page Avenue
St Louis, MO 63132-5100

Coast Guard, Marine Corps, Navy
Bureau of Naval Personnel
Liaison Office Room 5409
9700 Page Avenue
St Louis, MO 63132-5100

Photographs

Most family members would love to have a photograph of their relative in their military uniform. Unfortunately, it is the most requested item but the most difficult to locate. The military records for WWII–era most likely will not contain a photograph. Although thousands of photographs were taken of the war, it's extremely difficult to locate one with specific military members identified. Local newspapers and county historical and genealogical societies will be the best method to find a photograph of a veteran. But this, too, is a hit-and-miss situation. Unless a photograph can be located among the family mementos, it may be next to impossible to find a one from government sources.

National Archives and Records Administration
Still Picture Reference
Special Media Archives Services Division
National Archives at College Park
8601 Adelphi Road
College Park, MD 20740-6001
*www.archives.gov/research_room/obtain_copies/
still_pictures.html#select*

ORGANIZATIONAL
MILITARY RECORDS

Military organizations literally kept track of everything and of everybody. To accomplish this, they kept meticulous records. Historically, these documents can tell us important and valuable information about the place a unit was serving, the daily operations of a unit, who were the members of a unit at a particular time, how many personnel reported for duty or who were wounded, killed or missing members. Once you've obtained the individual military records of your relative and know the unit or ship assignments, you can now begin to research the history of the organization.

There are several types of official documents that military units create, usually on a daily basis, to keep track of personnel and duty assignments. These include morning reports, unit rosters, deck logs, muster rolls, and unit diaries. These historical documents can provide priceless information such as serial number, rank, middle initial, and whereabouts of a unit at a certain time period.

You must specifically identify the type of document desired, clearly identify the unit or ship, and give the month and year needed. Units should be identified by the company, battery or troop, and battalion or regiment (i.e., 46th Quartermaster Company; Company B, 127th Infantry or USS Enterprise.)

The majority of these official organizational records are archived at various records centers or military historical agencies. Be aware that most request times for records will take a minimum of three months or longer to receive. Some documents may take years. It's recommended to check for other possible sources of information before requesting records that will take months to receive. Other military museums, archives, or historical centers may have previously obtained the documents needed and will be a much quicker resource for documents. A good example of this is the Iowa Gold Star Museum that contains the morning reports and rosters for the 34th Infantry Division that were donated to the museum. Another example might be a ship that has been preserved as a museum that might have records there, which could take months to locate elsewhere. Check Appendix A (State Records) or Appendix

C (Military Museums) for other sources of unit or ship museums.

It also should be mentioned that the archives and other facilities that maintain organizational military records do charge a fee for research. Usually, they will provide a bill before doing the work. They will *not* do detailed historical research, but do provide a list of private researchers that can be hired to handle these types of requests, also for a fee.

Question: The base my grandfather served on during WWII is still in operation. Can't I just go to the installation and get the information about my grandfather and his unit?

Answer: Military installations did not maintain records on individuals, but may have some historical information about movements and units that were assigned to the base. If the base is still in existence, then contact the base historian or base librarian and ask what information is available for a certain organization. If the base is closed, then it's recommended to acquire the history or other organizational records.

Army Records

Unit Roster

A unit roster contains a list of personnel who served in a military unit at a certain point in time. These rosters have the rank, last name, first name, and serial number. In some cases, hometown and MOS may be listed.

Unit rosters were destroyed for the years 1944, 1945, and 1946. It's recommended to request morning reports instead of unit rosters for those years.

Morning Reports

Morning reports were produced on a daily basis by Army units to show any important changes in the availability or state of personnel. This would include initial assignment of a person to the unit, sick days, hospitalization, absence without leave, ordinary leave, killed, wounded or missing in action, change in rank or occupation code specialty, and reassignment out of the unit. You may find a list of personnel attached to some of these reports. If the rosters were destroyed, a morning report is the only other source that may provide lists of personnel in a unit. These reports can be used to prove hospitalization, unit location on a certain date, or to identify other members of a unit.

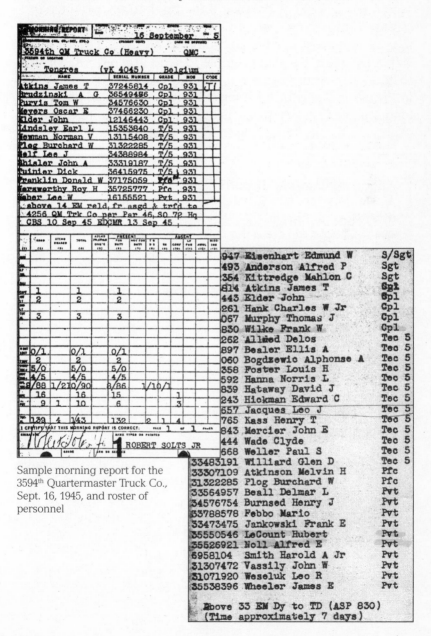

Sample morning report for the 3594th Quartermaster Truck Co., Sept. 16, 1945, and roster of personnel

Army unit rosters and morning reports for WWII years are available from the National Personnel Records Center (NPRC). The NPRC requires a search fee to access these records: an hourly rate of $13.25 and a copy fee (six pages for $3.50 with each additional page at $.10). The minimum search fee is $8.30. A deposit of the minimum search fee is required to begin a search, with any additional costs billed to you. A request can be submitted using the standard form 180 or by letter. It's also possible to send in a request for unit rosters or morning reports citing the Freedom of Information Act. But be aware that though this will take longer since FOIA requests are not a priority, no fees will be charged. Checks should be made payable to the "National Archives Trust Fund."

National Personnel Records Center
ATTN: ORU
9700 Page Avenue
St Louis, MO 63132-5100

Army reserve units:
US Army Reserve Personnel Command
ATTN: ARPC-IMP-F
9700 Page Avenue
St Louis, MO 63123-5200

National Guard units activated during WWII:
Check the appropriate state's Adjutant General, state's National Guard museum, or the state archives. See Appendix A (State Records).

After-action reports, S-3 journals, G-3 journals, histories, and commendations are other types of records maintained. After-action reports are known also as operations reports and were monthly reports describing unit activities. Journals were detailed accounts of a unit's activities and contain an hourly account, which was reported daily. Unit histories offer brief overviews and general duties of a unit.

3594TH QM TRUCK COMPANY
APO 350; U. S. ARMY

HISTORICAL RECORD   8 November 1943

Company B, Supply Battalion, 8th Armored Division, N
Cp Polk, Louisiana, Relieved from attachment to 8th A.D. and
attached to Second Hq & Hq Detachment, Special Troops, Third
Army, Fort Sam Houston, Texas, per GO #124, Hq, 3d Army, Ft.
Sam Houston, Texas dated 3 November 43 as of 2 Nov 43.

Company B, Supply Battalion, 8th A.D., redesignated to
3494th QM Truck Company per Letter, Second Headquarters,
Special Troops, Third Army, Camp Claiborne, La. dated 16 Nov 43.

3494th QM Truck Company redesignated to the 3594th QM
Truck Company per Ltr, Second Headquarters, Special Troops,
Third Army, Cp Claiborne, La. dated 16 Nov 43.

Place of Organization------Camp Polk, Louisiana.

Personnel acquired from
original unit, Co B, Sup Bn
8th A.D., during regesignation of Company

PRINCIPAL OFFICERS:

Co Commander----Capt. John F. Peavey
Asgd to Co------Capt. Stanley A. Holeva
1st Plat Ldr----1st Lt. Robert Solts, Jr.
2d Plat Ldr-----2d Lt. Richard J. Boyer
3d Plat Ldr-----2d Lt. Kenneth w. Kapallusch
Maint Officer--2d Lt. Clarence Maxey
PX Officer------2d Lt. Cleo Misel
DS to 1st Prov
QM Car Co-------2d Lt. Waldo R. Blanke

6 June 1944

This was the day. It happened early in the morning before
realizing the actual truth. Everybody was excitedly giving their
vent to their own feelings. "Give 'em hell", as eyes turned to
the skies as fighter plaes and bombers passed overhead. There
was an inward tingle of excitement as all felt the import of
the support of the bxxxx planes for the men at the front.

On this day three separate missions were issued by the company
dispatcher, Cpl Rudolph Koller. For the company it wasn't an
unusually difficult day nor was it for the dispatcher, who manytimes
stax must stay up all night to get vehicles dispatched for vehicles.
The fact remained that all knew what they were driveing for. These
missions were exclusively for the purpose of hauling personnel
from the D Camp mustering reas to the landing crafts. A total
of fx 1400 troops were carried from Camps D-7, D-10 and D-11.

Sample Unit History for the 3594th Quartermaster Truck Co., Nov. 8, 1943, and June 6, 1944.

Modern Military Records Unit
National Archives at College Park
8601 Adelphi Road
College Park, MD 20740-6001
www.archives.gov/facilities/md/archives_2.html

The National Archives at College Park allows researchers
to come in and do their own research at no charge. The fee
for research is limited to five files at a time for a fee of $0.50
per page.

The U.S. Army Military History Institute maintains
unofficial Army historical collections that include books,
oral histories, photographs, manuscripts (diaries, letters,
memoirs), military publications, manuals, and maps.

U.S. Army Military History Institute
22 Ashburn Drive
Carlisle, PA 17013-5008
http://carlisle-www.army.mil/usamhi

Internet Sources for Army Histories
www.wfrgames.com
Has Infantry and Armored Division Histories

www.army.mil/cmh-pg/lineage/cc/cc.htm
www.grunts.net/army/airborne.html
Army Unit Histories

www.mtpublishing.com/historym.html
Published Unit Histories for all branches

www.lettersfromthewar.com
Rosters for the 36th Infantry Division

www2.powercom.net/~rokats/normandy.html
Normandy Roll of Honor. Listings of divisions and units
that obtained battle credit for participation in D-Day

Army Air Corps Records

The Army Air Force began maintaining unit histories in 1942.

Air Force History Support Office
AFHSO/HOR
Reference and Analysis Division
B-3 Brookley Ave., Box 94
Bolling AFB, DC 20032-5000
(202) 404-2264
www.airforcehistory.hq.af.mil

Air Force Historical Research Agency
600 Chennault Circle, Bldg. 1405
Maxwell AFB, AL 36112-6424
(334) 953-2395
http://afhra.maxwell.af.mil

Air Force Historical Information

Historical background on numbered Air Force units, Air Force commands, linage and honors, as well as acronyms and abbreviations.

http://afhra.maxwell.af.mil/wwwroot/rso/rso_index.html
Missing Air Crew Reports of the US Army Air Corps 1942–45.

This contains information pertaining to missing air crewmembers or failure of a plane to return. The names of missing aircrew are listed by crew position, rank, serial number, and status of crew members (prisoner of war or missing in action.) Other information includes the tail number of the aircraft, nickname or squadron identification letter, and the type, model, and serial number of the engine or machine gun. The name of the military base, unit information, (squadron, group, or air force) to which an aircraft was assigned are also listed. Microfilm collection.

Air Force Historical Research Agency
600 Chennault Circle, Bldg. 1405
Maxwell AFB, AL 36112-6424
(334) 953-2395
http://afhra.maxwell.af.mil

Missing Air Crew Reports of the US Army Air Corps 1942–45. (Microfilm ID M1380/Record Group RG018)

Mission and Combat Reports of the Fifth Fighter Command, 1942–45. (Microfilm ID M1065/ Record Group RG 018)

To order a copy of the microfilm collection contact:

National Archives Trust Fund
Cashier (NAT)
8601 Adelphi Road, Room 5100
College Park, MD 20740-6001

Aircraft Research

The Air Force Historical Agency has detailed records for specific aircraft by tail number, including manufacturer, place of production, date of delivery, units of assignments, duty stations, and final disposition. WWII–era planes only contain the theater of operation and not the unit of assignment.

Air Force Historical Research Agency
600 Chennault Circle, Bldg 1405
Maxwell AFB, AL 36112-6424
(334) 953-2395
http://afhra.maxwell.af.mil

Coast Guard Records

Musters rolls from 1940 to present for vessels, districts, lifeboat stations, miscellaneous units, and recruiting stations show dates of enlistment, duty stations, changes in ratings, transfers, absences, surrenders, deliveries separations, and leave. Available by ship or by station. Request record by giving name of ship or station, and month and year.

War Diaries for Coast Guard units/vessels 1942–1945
Narrative Histories of Coast Guard Districts
Log books for Coast Guard ships

Request by name of ship, month, and year.

National Archives and Records Administration
700 Pennsylvania Ave, NW
Washington, DC 20408
(866) 325-7208
www.archives.gov

Unit histories for WWII district Coast Guard units; logs of
Coast Guard vessels and installations for Alaska Coast
Guard District. *RG 26*

National Archives – Alaska Region
654 Third Avenue
Anchorage, AK 99501-2145
(907) 817-2441

Marine Corps Records

Muster rolls/unit diaries for WWII years are available
from the National Archives at College Park. The term
muster roll changed to unit diary sometime after WWII.
These documents show duty stations, dates of enlistments,
dates received on board, changes in ratings, transfers,
absences, surrenders, separations, deliveries, and leave.
Microfilm.

Modern Military Records Unit
National Archives at College Park
8601 Adelphi Road
College Park, MD 20740-6001
www.archives.gov/facilities/md/archives_2.html

Internet source for Marine Corps Histories
http://hqinet001.hqmc.usmc.mil/HD/Historical/
Frequently_Requested.htm
Battle Honors of the Six Marine Divisions in World War II

www.usmc.mil/history.nsf
Lists statistics of numbers of Marines that served and died during the war. Includes dates of battles and campaigns involving Marines.

Navy Records

Muster Rolls & Deck Logs

A ship's muster roll lists the rank, last name, first name, middle initial, and serial number of all enlisted persons aboard a ship. The deck logs usually will list only Officers. Muster rolls and deck logs should be requested by month and year. By using both listings, a complete list of crew can be obtained. Other documents of interest include war diaries, action reports, and submarine war patrol reports.

Modern Military Records Unit
National Archives at College Park
8601 Adelphi Road
College Park, MD 20740-6001
www.archives.gov/facilities/md/archives_2.html

> When putting together a list of those who served aboard ship, don't overlook those that may have died during the War. See Chapter Four (WWII Casualty Records) for casualties by ship or unit.

Ship's Histories

www.hazegray.org/danfs
The book *Dictionary of Naval Fighting Ships* was published from 1959 to 1991 and contains histories of more than 7,000 ships. Online version are available on this website.

Ship's histories for purchase are available from Seaweed's Ships Histories. They are quality histories suitable for framing.

Seaweed's Ships Histories
PO Box 154
Sistersville, WV 26175-0154
(800) 732-9333
www.uss-seaweed.com

United States Ship

U.S.S. NORTH CAROLINA (BB-55)

(BB-55: dp. 35,000; l. 728'9"; b. 108'4"; dr. 26'8"; s. 27 k.; cpl. 1,800; a. 9 16", 20 5", 16 1.1", 12 .50-cal.mg.; cl. North Carolina)

The third North Carolina (BB-55) was laid down on 27 October 1937 by the New York Naval Shipyard; launched on 13 June 1940; sponsored by Miss Isabel Hoey, daughter of the Governor of North Carolina; and commissioned at New York on 9 April 1941, Captain Olaf M. Hustvedt in command. North Carolina entered the Pacific on 10 June 1942. North Carolina and the Navy began the long island-hopping campaign for victory over the Japanese by landing marines on Guadalcanal and Tulagi on 7 August 1942. On 24 August the Battle of the Eastern Solomons erupted. The Americans struck first, sinking the carrier Ryujo. In an 8-minute action, North Carolina shot down between 7 and 14 enemy aircraft. One man was killed by a strafer, but the ship was undamaged. On 6 September, she maneuvered successfully, dodging a torpedo which passed 300 yards off the port beam. Nine days later, sailing with Hornet (CV-8), North Carolina took a torpedo portside, 20 feet below her waterline, and five of her men were killed. After repairs at Pearl Harbor, North Carolina screened Enterprise and Saratoga. Supporting the Gilberts campaign and preparing the assault on the Marshalls, North Carolina's highly accurate big guns bombarded Nauru on 8 December. During the assault and capture of the Marshall Islands, North Carolina illustrated the classic battleship functions of World War II. The battlewagon then protected carriers in the massive air strike on Truk, the Japanese fleet base in the Carolines, where 39 large ships were left sunk, and 211 planes were destroyed. With Majuro as her base, North Carolina joined in the attacks on Palau and Woleai 31 March to 1 April, shooting down another enemy plane. At Truk, North Carolina's planes were catapulted to rescue an American aviator downed off the reef. The next day, North Carolina destroyed coast defense guns, antiaircraft batteries, and airfields at Ponape. The battleship then sailed to repair her rudder at Pearl Harbor.

Returning to Majuro, North Carolina sortied with the Enterprise group 6 June for the Marianas. At dusk on invasion day, 15 June, the battleship downed one of the only two Japanese aircraft able to penetrate the combat air patrol. On 18 June, North Carolina cleared the islands with the carriers to confront the Japanese 1st Mobile Fleet. On that day and the next, American air and submarine attacks, with the fierce antiaircraft fire of such ships as North Carolina virtually ended any future threat from Japanese naval aviation; three carriers were sunk, and two tankers severely damaged. After supporting air operations in the Marianas for another two weeks, North Carolina sailed for overhaul at Puget Sound Navy Yard. She rejoined the carriers off Ulithi on 7 November as a furious typhoon struck the group. With Ulithi now her base, North Carolina screened wide-ranging carrier strikes on Formosa, the coast of Indo-China and China, and the Ryukyus in January. Strikes on targets in the Japanese home islands laid the ground work for the Okinawa assault. On 6 April, she downed three kamikazes, but took a 5-inch hit from a friendly ship. Three men were killed and 44 wounded. North Carolina splashed an enemy plane, and she shot down two more on 17 April. After overhaul at Pearl Harbor, North Carolina rejoined the carriers for a month of air strikes and naval bombardment on the Japanese home islands. North Carolina sent both sailors and members of her Marine Detachment ashore for preliminary occupation duty in Japan. North Carolina anchored in Tokyo Bay on 5 September to reembark her men. Carrying passengers from Okinawa, North Carolina sailed for home, reaching the Panama Canal on 8 October. She anchored at Boston on 17 October. After inactivation, North Carolina decommissioned at New York on 27 June 1947. Struck from the Navy list on 1 June 1960, she was transferred to the people of North Carolina on 6 September 1961. On 29 April 1962 she was dedicated at Wilmington, North Carolina, as a memorial to North Carolinians of all services killed in World War II. Splendidly maintained and most appropriately displayed - including a spectacular "sound and light" presentation - "Showboat" still serves to strengthen and inspire our nation. North Carolina received 15 battle stars for World War II service.

USS North Carolina, Seaweed's Ships Histories

www.navsource.org
Naval Source is a non–profit organization dedicated to the preservation of information pertaining to the Navy. It provides lists brief histories with thousands of photographs available online.

www.history.navy.mil/branches/org11-2.htm
The Naval Historical Center's listings of Navy photographs and images include brief histories and gives details on how to order photographic reproductions.

Naval Aviation

Microfilm copies of naval aircraft accident reports, 1920–1953

Unpublished histories of aviation–type ships and aviation squadrons serving on ships, 1942–1952

Naval Historical Center
Naval Aviation History Branch
Bldg. 200, First Floor
Washington Navy Yard, DC 20374-0571
www.history.navy.mil/branches/nhcorg4.htm

U.S. Navy Cruise Books

Cruise books were not official publications but were put together by the crew. They contain mostly photographs taken while aboard of the crew and ports of call. Some cruise books may contain rosters of personnel. For a list of WWII cruise books, check the book *Cruise Books of the United States Navy in World War II: A Bibliography* by Dean L. Mawdsley. The online version is available at *www.history.navy.mil/biblio/biblio2/biblio2.htm*. This details the name of the cruise books available.

Naval Historical Center
The Navy Department Library
805 Kidder Breese SE
Washington, DC 20374-5060
www.history.navy.mil/library/index.htm

New York Public Library
5th Avenue & 42nd Street
New York, NY 10018
www.nypl.org
Maintains large collection of cruise books for Navy ships

Ship & Submarine Museums

Many ships have been preserved as museums, such as the USS North Carolina and the USS Yorktown. If a particular ship is now a museum, a wealth of information is available from the museum or museum historian. Museum gift shops have photographs and ship's histories for sale. Check the following website for a listings of naval vessels that are now preserved as museums. *www.maritime.org/ hnsa-class.htm#BB*. See Appendix C (Military Museums).

Damaged Ships
www.history.navy.mil/faqs/faq82-1.htm
Provides brief information and listings of Navy and Coast Guard ships that were sunk, damaged, or beyond repair during WWII.

Navy College Programs
V–12 unit records, Dartmouth College, Hanover, NH, 1942–46. RG 24. The records include information about the unit's organization, operation, faculty, curriculum, student body, correspondence, logbooks, muster rolls, orders, and reports.

National Archives Northeast Region (Boston)
Frederick C Murphy Federal Center
380 Trapelo Road
Waltham, MA 02452-6399
(866) 406-2379

Indoctrination School, Fort Schuyler, New York, 1941–46. Records include information pertaining to school and students. Muster cards list name, date and place of enlistment, qualifications, enlisted men as well as officers.

National Archives Northeast Region (New York City)
201 Varick Street
New York, NY 10014-4811
(212) 337-1300

Military Historical Offices

For general historical questions or the whereabouts of certain historical documents, please contact the following. These agencies will most likely provide some assistance but will not do detailed research projects. The Army's official records are held by the National Archives.

Army
U.S. Army Military History Institute
22 Ashburn Drive
Carlisle, PA 17013-5008

Army Air Corps/Air Force
Air Force History Support Office
AFHSO/HOR
Reference and Analysis Division
B-3 Brookley Ave., Box 94
Bolling AFB, DC 20032-5000
E-mail: afhso.research@pentagon.af.mil
(202) 404-2264

Coast Guard
Coast Guard Historian's Office
U.S. Coast Guard Headquarters
2100 Second St., S.W.
Washington, DC 20593-0001
(202) 267-1394
www.uscg.mil/hq/g-cp/history/collect.html

Marine Corps
Marine Corps Historical Center
1254 Charles Morris St. SE
Washington Navy Yard, DC 20374-5040
(202) 433-3483
http://hqinet001.hqmc.usmc.mil/HD

Navy
Naval Historical Center
Washington Navy Yard
805 Kidder Breese, S.E.
Washington, DC 20374-5060
www.history.navy.mil

Published Histories

Airborne Unit History Books

North Bay Listings
PO Box 7131
Cotati, CA 94931
(707) 794-8665
www.norbay.com

Army, Air Force, Marine Corps, Navy Histories.

Turner Publishing
(800) 788-3350
www.turneronline.com

Private Researchers

Most government sources may not be able to do research for the public. If that is the case, ask them for a list of private researchers that can, for a fee, perform research. This may be listed on their website. Here are a few private researchers that handle a variety of military records searches.

Lyon Research
627 Echols St, SE
Vienna, VA 22180
(301) 442-5330
www.lyonresearch.com

Army and Air Force Unit Histories

Jim Controvich
97 Mayfield Street
Springfield, MA 01108-3535
E-mail: unithistory@worldnet.att.net
(413) 734-4856 (after 8:00 p.m. Eastern Time)

Army, Army Air Corps, Marine Corps, Navy Unit Records

Pike Military Research
(202) 345-3591, (202) 338-4249 Fax
www.militaryunits.com

WWII DRAFT RECORDS

There were six regular draft registrations that took place during WWII. This chapter provides details concerning the WWII draft registrations, how to obtain your relative's records, and the type of information contained in these records.

The draft registration card contains a wealth of personal information. More than 10,000,000 military personnel entered the service through the Selective Service System during WWII.

A WWII Draft registration card asked for the following information:

- Name (first, middle and last)
- Place of residence (town, township, village or city, county and state)
- Mailing address (if different then place of residence)
- Telephone (exchange and number)
- Age in years and date of birth
- Place of birth (town or county and state or country)
- Occupation
- Name and address of person who will always know your address
- Employer's name and address
- Place of employment or business
- Signature
- Race (White, Negro, Oriental, Indian or Filipino)
- Height
- Eye color
- Hair color
- Complexion
- Other obvious physical characteristics that will aid in identification
- Registrar for local board (board number, city or county and state)
- Date of registration
- Stamp of local board (has date of registration and address of local board)

The Selective Service System kept two types of records: a Selective Service registration card and a classification record.

The registration card was created when the person first registered for the draft, and contains the information listed above. The classification record lists the person's name, selective service number, classification code and various data concerning draft registration.

Serial Number and Order Number

"For the age groups liable for military service-the first second, third, and fifth registrations-the local boards, after the registration, at a time set by National Headquarters, shuffled the cards of the registrants indiscriminately, and then gave to each a serial number. Then to be sure that there was no manipulation of the process, a National lottery based on the serial numbers was held to determine by chance the order in which the registrants would be considered for classification and induction. The number that was given to each card is called the order number. In the later registrations, the fifth and the sixth, the order numbers within the local board areas are determined by the birthday of the registrant; and for registrants born on the same day, the alphabetical order of their names determines which is called first."

Selective Service in Wartime: Second Report of the Director of Selective Service 1941–1942. Government Printing Office, 1943.

WWII Draft Registrations

By order of the President, there were six regular draft registrations from the years 1940-1946, and one special draft registration of male citizens living abroad.

1st Draft Registration

October 16, 1940: Men born on or after October 17, 1904, and on or before October 16, 1919

Serial number prefix: none

Order number: began with one

SERIAL NUMBER | 1. NAME (Print) | ORDER NUMBER

1464 | ARTHUR HOLMAN KENNEDY | 1670

(First) (Middle) (Last)

2. ADDRESS (Print)

933 E. ST. CATHERINE, LOUISVILLE JEFFERSON KY JR

(Number and street or R. F. D. number) (Town) (County) (State)

3. TELEPHONE | 4. AGE IN YEARS | 5. PLACE OF BIRTH | 6. COUNTRY OF CITIZENSHIP

— | 22 | LOUISVILLE

(Town or county)

DATE OF BIRTH | KENTUCKY | U.S.A.

— | 4 | 1 | 18 | (State or country)

(Exchange) (Number) | (Mo.) (Day) (Yr.)

7. NAME OF PERSON WHO WILL ALWAYS KNOW YOUR ADDRESS | 8. RELATIONSHIP OF THAT PERSON

MRS MARIE THOMPSON KENNEDY WIFE

(Mr., Mrs., Miss) (First) (Middle) (Last)

9. ADDRESS OF THAT PERSON

933 E. St Catherine Louisville Ky.

(Number and street or R. F. D. number) (Town) (County) (State)

10. EMPLOYER'S NAME

Coca Cola Co.

11. PLACE OF EMPLOYMENT OR BUSINESS

1513 Bank St Louisville Ky.

(Number and street or R. F. D. number) (Town) (County) (State)

I AFFIRM THAT I HAVE VERIFIED ABOVE ANSWERS AND THAT THEY ARE TRUE.

REGISTRATION CARD
D. S. S. FORM 1 (over) 16—17105

Arthur Holman Kennedy

(Registrant's signature)

REGISTRAR'S REPORT

DESCRIPTION OF REGISTRANT

RACE		HEIGHT (Approx.)	WEIGHT (Approx.)	COMPLEXION	
White	✓	6' 0"	150		
		EYES	HAIR	Sallow	
Negro				Light	
		Blue	Blonde	Ruddy	
		Gray	Red	Dark	✓
Oriental		Hazel ✓	Brown ✓	Freckled	
		Brown ✓	Black	Light brown	
Indian		Black	Gray	Dark brown	
			Bald	Black	
Filipino					

Other obvious physical characteristics that will aid in identification. None

I certify that my answers are true; that the person registered has read or has had read to him his own answers; that I have witnessed his signature or mark and that all of his answers of which I have knowledge are true, except as follows:

(Signature of Registrar)

Registrar for 1 2 La Ky

(Precinct) (Ward) (City or county) (State)

Date of registration 10-16-40

LOCAL BOARD No. 71
311 NORTON BLDG.
LOUISVILLE, JEFFERSON COUNTY
KENTUCKY

(STAMP OF LOCAL BOARD)

(The stamp of the Local Board having jurisdiction of the registrant shall be placed in the above space.)

U. S. GOVERNMENT PRINTING OFFICE 16—17105

Sample of 1st Draft Registration Card (front and back)

2nd Draft Registration

July 1, 1941: Men born on or after October 17, 1919, and on or before July 12, 1920, and born on or after October 17, 1904, and on or before October 16, 1919, who had failed to register

Serial number prefix: "T" then numbered from one up

Order number: "S" then numbered one up

3rd Draft Registration

February 16, 1942: Men born on or after February 17, 1897, and on or before December 31, 1921

Serial number prefix: "T" then numbered from one up

Order number: began with 10,001

Sample of 3rd Draft Registration Card

4th Draft Registration

April 27, 1942: Men born on or before April 28, 1877, and on or before February 16, 1897

Serial number prefix: "U"

Order number: None (were not liable for military service) Approximately 14,000,000 men register for this draft.

Some of the Ohio registration cards are available from digital copies at the National Archives website (*www.archives.gov*). The series title is: *The Selective Service System Registration Cards for Ohio Men born April 28, 1877, through February 16, 1997.*

Sample of 4th Draft Registration Card

National Archives and Records Administration. The Selective Service System Registration Cards for Ohio Men born April 28, 1877, through February 16, 1897. (www.archives.gov)

The 4th draft registration was for men that were between the ages of 45 and 65 in 1942. The military needed men with construction skills for the Navy Seabees. These men were not liable for military service and no order number was given to these cards. These draft records are now open to the public and can be obtained from the Federal Records Centers. See Appendix F (Federal Records Centers). You must know the county and state where they registered to acquire a copy of the card.

5th Draft Registration

June 30, 1942: Men born on or after January 1, 1922, and on or before June 30, 1924

Serial number prefix: "N" then numbered one up by birthday and alphabetically

Order number: followed other numbers

Sample of 5th Draft Registration Card

Men ages 18 and 19 were not liable for military service at this time. As a result, the cards were sorted by date of birth and then assigned serial numbers. Cards came up as the person became eligible for service.

6th Draft Registration

December 11-31, 1942: Men born on or after July 1, 1924, and on or before December 31, 1924. Also for men as they reach their 18th birthday on or after January 1, 1943

Serial number prefix: "W" then numbered one up by birthday and alphabetically

Order number: followed numbers after 5th registration

Sample of 6th Draft Registration

Special Draft Registration

November 16-December 31, 1943: Men born after
December 31, 1898, and before January 1, 1926, and men
born on or after January 1, 1926, on their 18th birthday
Were liable for military service
In excess of 25,000 registered.

The first, second, third, fifth, sixth and subsequent
registration cards are protected under the privacy act.
Obtaining the WWII draft registration (other than the 4th
draft) card for your relative is much like requesting the
person's military records held by the National Personnel
Records Center. If the veteran is living, then the request has
to come from the veteran. If the veteran is deceased, next of
kin can acquire the record. Proof of death of the veteran
must be given. This can be a print out from the Social
Security Death Index (Chapter Six), a print out from state
death index (Chapter Six), a death certificate or an obituary.
Name, date of birth, city, county and state where he
registered for the draft should be given when requesting a
draft registration card.

Selective Service System
Records Division
Arlington, VA 22206-2425
(703) 605-4000, (703) 605-4071 Fax
www.sss.gov

Army Draftees

The 30,000,000 and 40,000,000 series of Army serial numbers all entered the military through the Selective Service System. On January 1, 1943, all enlistees had to go through the Selective Service to enter and were not allowed to enlist. Exceptions to the rule were men that were 17 years old and over 36. Therefore, any military member with a 30,000,000 or 40,000,000 series serial number should in theory have a draft registration card.

Example of Serial Numbers

35616924: Serial number for an **inductee** under the Selective Service Act of 1940

13031437: Serial number for an **enlistee** in the regular Army on or after July 1, 1940

You can not determine if a person was drafted based solely on the draftee serial number, since the military made it mandatory to volunteer using the Selective Service System beginning January 1, 1943.

Military Serial Number vs. Selective Service System Serial Number

On the upper left corner of the WWII draft card is a number entitled serial number. On the first draft registration card, there is no prefix but on the subsequent registrations a prefix is added to the serial number. Please do not confuse this number with the military serial number used to identify military members. A military serial number would have been issued after a person entered the service. The draft card does not include a military member's identification (serial) number.

Men already serving in one of the military branches or attending one of the military academies were not required to register.

Brief Chronology of the U.S. Selective Service (Draft) during WWII

1939, September 8. President Roosevelt declares a limited national emergency.

1940, August 31. President orders National Guard to active duty.

1940, September 16. Selective Training and Service Act of 1940 enacted.

1940, October 7. First local draft boards appointed.

1940, October 16. First draft registration. Men ages 21-35 must register with Selective Service.

1940, November 18. First inductees sent to Army induction centers.

1941, July 1. Second draft registration.

1942, February 16. Third draft registration.

1942, April 27. Fourth draft registration.

1942, June 30. Fifth draft registration.

1942, December 11-31. Sixth draft registration.

1943, January 1. Voluntary enlistments prohibited for men 18-37; all* must enter armed forces through Selective Service.

1943, November 16-December 31. Special Registration for male citizens living abroad.

1947, March 31. Selective Training and Service Act allowed to expire.

*All except 17-year-olds and those over 36. These men were allowed to enlist. The Navy had an upper age limit of 51 to enlist older men with construction skills for the Seabees.

Registration and Selective Service, 1945.

Some Internet sites have copies of WWII draft lists from their county newspapers. These listings give their name, draft number and place of residence. Check your county newspaper for something similar. Most WWII–era newspapers are available on microfilm. Here's a sample of one of the county draft listings from the Internet. *www.rootsweb.com/~miisabel/militaryWWII.htm*

WWII Selective Service Statistics

November, 1940–October, 1946: 10,110,104 men entered the service through the Selective Service System.

1940	18,633	1944	1,591,942
1941	923,842	1945	945,862
1942	3,033,361	1946	183,383
1943	3,323,970*		

*On January 1, 1943, anyone who entered the service was to enter through the Selective Service System, with the exception of 17-year-olds and those over 36, who were allowed to enlist.

Selective Service System. (www.sss.gov)

Chapter 4

WWII CASUALTY RECORDS

More than 400,000 Americans died during WWII. A computerized searchable database of WWII casualties does not exist, but there are several resources that are available for death listings, such as a microfilm collection of war casualties, books of casualties and military casualty records.

In this section, the term casualty describes those who were killed in action, wounded or held as a prisoner of war. The majority of data refers to those killed, but some resources also contain information on wounded or prisoners of war.

When researching a military member that died during the war, most family researchers would like to find the following information:

- Date of death
- Place of death
- Cause of death
- Place of burial
- Dates of service
- Military serial number
- Branch of service
- Rank
- Awards and medals
- Unit or ship assignment
- Obituary
- Casualty report

Each WWII casualty listing varies in the amount of information available. While one source will have a military serial number, it may not have the date of death or cause of death. Since it's important to acquire as much information as possible, it's suggested to research all sources to obtain all available information.

Sources for WWII Casualties

- Roster of WWII Dead
- WWII casualty books
- Death burial files
- Military academies or military school libraries
- Officer registers

- Marine Corps casualty records
- Navy casualty records
- American Battle Monuments Commission
- National Cemetery System
- State records
- Local newspapers
- Internet websites
- Military reunion associations

Roster of WWII Dead

Although this is the most accurate listing of WWII dead, it is only on microfiche and not widely available. This is the only complete list arranged alphabetically by last name. Information includes last name, first name and middle initial or complete middle name, military serial number, branch of service, rank, religion, race, permanent interment site, temporary cemetery and disposition code. This is the only casualty source that identifies if the veteran was Army Air Force. For those interned in an American cemetery overseas, the plot, row and grave number is given. The roster also includes information pertaining to Merchant Marines and civilians killed in the war. Obvious exclusions from this source are date of death and cause of death.

1201	C	6	9ZABELLA JOSEPH S JR	T SC	36603328	1		1220	2 1	
			ZABEN ROBERT C	PVT	35240248	1			2 1	
7500			ZABICKI HENRY J	SGT	37610826	1		6515	2 1	1
2322			ZABILSKI CHESTER W	S SG	32582231	1		1260	2 1	1
5222			ZABINSKI ALPHONSE A	S SG	32833859	1		4650	2 1	1
7701	L	6	76ZABINSKI LOUIS A	F1	9449206	2		8078	2 1	
			ZABITCH JOSEPH	PVT	19003246	1			1 1	
5200			ZABKA HENRY H	PFC	33465720	1		8078	2 1	
1300			ZABKA JOHN	PFC	31023417	1		4568	2 1	
			ZABKA JOSEPH W	SEA1	8990640	2			6	
6100			ZABKAR FRANK K	PVT	36775615	1		3582	2 1	
5202	I	6	17ZABLER KENNETH A	PVT	36723990	1		5260	2 1	
6100			ZABLOCK ERNEST A	SGT	36743081	1		3574	2 1	
5100			ZABLOCKI FRANK		8	24080	5		3574	2 1	
2300			ZABLOCKI JOHN L	2 LT	0	1017826	1	3568	2 1	
7522			ZABLOCKI WALTER A	T SG	36048468	1		9970	2 1	1
5300			ZABLOTNY THEODORE B	S SG	35516801	1		1240	2 1	
7600			ZABLOUDIL STEVEN L	S SG	37466358	1		3574	2 1	
6300			ZABLUDOWSKI JOHN P	PFC	36280830	1		3582	2 1	
5504	K	16	5ZABLUDOWSKI M J	PFC	32153699	1		3578	2 1	
2300			ZABOLOTSKY MILTON	SGT	12185728	1		5210	3 1	1

WWII Roster of Dead

If only a name of a service member is known, not the state he entered the service from, then use the microfiche first to obtain the permanent cemetery or military serial number. Then check the WWII casualty books and other sources for additional information.

Since the microfiche is not widely available, check your state archives for a copy. If the last name is not common, it may be useful to have all of the entries by last name.

WWII Casualty Books

In 1946, the War Department and the Navy Department printed in book form a list of WWII casualties by state. The War Department's book included Army and Army Air Corps personnel who died in the line of duty. The Department of the Navy, which included the Marine Corps and Coast Guard, included casualties, wounded and prisoners of war.

World War II Honor List of Dead and Missing Army and Army Air Forces is the War Department's casualty book. It's arranged by county, and then alphabetically by last name. It lists the last name, first name and middle initial, rank, military serial number and cause of death.

WORLD WAR II
HONOR LIST
OF DEAD AND MISSING

STATE OF
ARIZONA

WAR DEPT   **JUNE 1946**

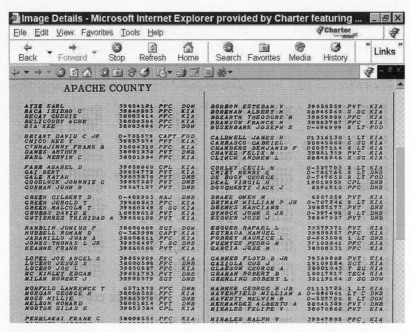

World War II Honor List of Dead and Missing Army and Army Air Forces Personnel from Arizona. 1946 Series from Record Group 407: Records of the Adjutant General's Office, 1917- [AGO], 1905-1981 (www.archives.gov/research_room/arc)

> Does not include date of death or cause of death and does not designate if the service member was a member of the Army Air Corps.

- Descriptions of Cause of Death
- KIA = Killed in Action
- DNB = Died Non Battle
- DOW = Died of Wounds
- DOI = Died of Injuries
- FOD = Finding of Death
- M = Missing Person

State Summary of War Casualties from World War II for Navy, Marine Corps, and Coast Guard Personnel. This book was published by the Navy Department in 1946. It lists casualties by state and then alphabetically by last name. Information includes last name, first name, middle name, rank, branch of service, relationship and address of next of kin. It also has sections on wounded, prisoners of war that died or were killed, and prisoners of war that were released.

Another published source for Navy casualties is the *United States Submarine Losses, World War II.* Naval History Division, 1963. This includes crew lists.

State Summary of
War Casualties
[FLORIDA]

U. S. NAVY
1946

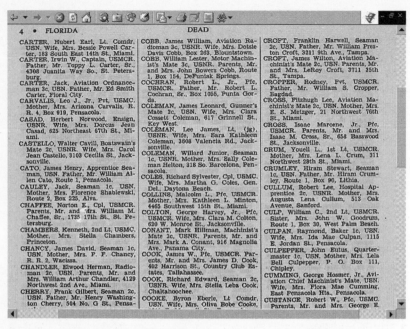

State Summary of War Casualties from World War II for Navy, Marine Corps, and Coast Guard Personnel from Florida, 1946. Item from Record Group 24: Records of the Bureau of Naval Personnel, 1798- 1970 (www.archives.gov/research_room/arc)

Does not include military serial number, date of death or cause of death.

www.accessgenealogy.com/worldwar

This website has already put together the copy of the War Department's casualty book by state and then county. This site provides easy access.

All of the WWII casualty books for the War Department and the Navy Department are available on the National Archives and Records Administration's website at *www.archives.gov*. It's a bit tricky to find; use the following instructions:

- Go to: www.archives.gov/research_room/arc/
- Click on the large search button.
- For Navy casualties, type {*War Casualties*} *and Navy*.
- For the Army and Army Air Corps casualties, type {*honor list*} *and Army*.
- Check the box that says "descriptions of archival materials linked to digital copies."
- Hit the go button.

The first page for each state book should now come up on the screen. If your state isn't listed, then hit the next page button until you find the correct state. Once the state has been located, it will display the individual pages. Remember that the Navy book is listed alphabetically by last name by killed and then wounded or prisoner of war. The War Department's book is listed by state, by county and then alphabetically by last name.

Check with the specific state's archives, library or historical agency for a copy of the book. Not all archives have these books or one but not both might be available. See Appendix A (State Records) for a listing by state.

Military Academies and Military Colleges

The military academies and military colleges may have additional information about WWII casualties who either graduated or attended their schools.

U.S. Military Academy
West Point, NY 10996
(845) 938-4011
www.usma.edu

U.S. Coast Guard Academy
Annapolis, MD 21402
(860) 444-8501
www.cga.edu

U.S. Naval Academy
121 Blake Road
Annapolis, MD 21402-5000
(410) 293-1000
www.usna.edu

The Citadel
171 Moultrie Street
Charleston, SC 29409
(843) 953-5116
http://citadel.edu/library

Norwich University
158 Harmon Drive
Northfield, VT 05663-1035
(802) 485-2001
www.norwich.edu

Virginia Military Institute
J.T.L. Preston Library
Lexington, VA 24450
(540) 464-7000
www.vmi.edu

Virginia Tech
Blacksburg, VA 24061-0213
(540) 321-6413
www.vt.edu

More than 7,000 served in WWII; 300 were killed.

The officer's register should list the college graduated.

ACTIVE LIST	381
Harrell, Ben (O19276). B—Oreg. 15 Mar. 11. A—M. A., Oreg. B. S., U. S. M. A., 33. G. S. C. 25 May 42. Grad. Inf. Sch., Regular Course, 40.	Capt. A. U. S. 9 Sept. 40; accepted 3 Oct. 40; maj. A. U. S. 1 Feb. 42; lt. col. A. U. S. 22 Oct. 42.——Cadet M. A. 1 July 29; 2 lt. of Inf. 13 June 33; A. C. 13 Sept. 33 to 15 Jan. 34; 1 lt. 13 June 36.
Harrell, Henry C. (O22307). B—Tex. 14 June 08. A—Tex. Grad. Med. Fld. Serv. Sch., Basic Course, 40. M. D., Univ. of Tex., 33.	Capt. A. U. S. 9 Sept. 40; accepted 3 Oct. 40; maj. A. U. S. 1 Feb. 42.——1 lt. M. C. 29 July 39; accepted 29 July 39; capt. 29 July 42.
Harrell, Howell (O11329). B—Okla. 16 Feb. 95. A—Okla. Grad.: Inf. Sch. Basic Course, 22, Q. M. Sch., 37.	Pvt. 1 cl. and corp. Tr. B, Cav., Okla. N. G. and 111 Am. Tn. 5 Aug. 17 to 1 July 18; 2 lt. Q. M. C., N. A. 1 July 18; accepted 2 July 18; hon. dis. 3 June 19; 1t. col. A. U. S. 15 Sept. 41; accepted 17 Sept. 41; col. A. U. S. 15 June 42.——2 lt. Q. M. C. 1 July 20; accepted 20 Sept. 20; 1 lt. 1 July 20; trfd. to Inf. 25 July 21; capt. 1 Nov. 33; Q. M. C. 1 July 34; trfd. to Q. M. C. 24 Jan. 38; maj. 18 June 40; lt. col. 21 Oct. 42.
Harrell, Joe (O18929). B—Tex. 16 Dec. 06. A—Tex. Grad.: Army Med. Sch., 33, Med. Fld. Serv. Sch., 33. A. B. and M. D., Baylor Univ., 30.	1 lt. Med-Res. 2 June 30; accepted 2 June 30; active duty 1 July 30 to 3 Aug. 32; maj. A. U. S. 24 Dec. 41; lt. col. A. U. S. 30 Oct. 42.——1 lt. M. C. 1 July 32; accepted 4 Aug. 32; capt. 1 July 33; resigned 24 Mar. 36; 1 lt. M. C. 21 Sept. 38; accepted 22 Sept. 38; capt. 21 Sept. 38.
Harrell, John W., Jr. (O24722). B—Ala. 6 Aug. 19. A—M. A., Ala. B. S., U. S. M. A., 42. Grad. A. C. Advanced Flying Sch., 42.	Cadet M. A. 1 July 38; 2 lt. of Inf. 29 May 42.

Army Register, 1943.

Officer Casualties

Each branch of the military published a yearly book that included biographical and background information for regular Army officers and Navy and Marine Corps officers. These books contain lists of officers that died on active duty. It lists the officer's name, serial number and date of death.

Army
Army Register

Navy and Marine Corps
Register of Commissioned and Warrant Officers of the United States Navy and Marine Corps

If the death is listed in the register, it can be a source for date of death, date of birth, rank, military education, dates of service and awards.

This source is not a complete list of officer casualties and may have someone who died on active duty who was not a war casualty.

CASUALTIES

ACTIVE LIST

Resigned

Major Maurice C. Bisson, Air Corps, June 4, 1942.
Major Charles' Francis Haughey, Medical Corps, May 26, 1942.
Captain Emil W. Geitner, Chaplain, March 23, 1942.
Captain Newell Charles James, Field Artillery, January 28, 1942.
Captain LeRoy H. Rook, Quartermaster Corps, May 12, 1942.

Died

Major General Herbert A. Dargue, December 12, 1941, *in the vicinity of Bishop, California.*
Major General Frank C. Mahin, July 24, 1942, *near Waynesboro, Tennessee.*
Brigadier General Harold H. George, April 30, 1942, *near Darwin, Australia.*
Brigadier General Albert K. B. Lyman, August 13, 1942, *at Honolulu, Territory of Hawaii.*
Brigadier General Alfred J. Lyon, December 1, 1942, *at Walter Reed General Hospital, Washington, D. C.*
Colonel Edward H. Bertram, Infantry, June 10, 1942, *at Denver, Colorado.*
Colonel Clifford P. Bradley, Air Corps, October 4, 1942, *at Botwood, Newfoundland.*
Colonel Charles W. Bundy, General Staff Corps, December 12, 1941, *in the vicinity of Bishop, California.*

Army Register, 1945.

DEATHS (268)

Deaths on active list (160)

Name	Date	Name	Date
Wilcox, John W., Jr., rear admiral	27 Mar. 1942	Janz, Clifford T., lieutenant	7 Dec. 1941
Bristol, Arthur L. Jr., vice admiral	20 Apr. 1942	Blessman, Edward M., lieutenant	4 Feb. 1942
Kidd, Isaac C., rear admiral	7 Dec. 1941	Sisko, William J., lieutenant	19 Aug. 1941
Van Valkenburgh, Franklin, captain	Do.	Ghetzler, Benjamin, lieutenant	31 Oct. 1941
Bennion, Mervyn S., captain	Do.	Bailey, Walter C., lieutenant	1 Mar. 1942
Picking, Sherwood, captain	1 Sept. 1941	Hurst, Edwin W., lieutenant	9 June 1942
Meadows, Pal L., captain	26 June 1942	Oates, Albert E., Jr., lieutenant	10 Dec. 1941
Dugger, Greene W., Jr., commander	26 Aug. 1941	Koivisto, Martin M., lieutenant	19 Feb. 1942
Patterson, John J., III., commander	13 Sept. 1941	Hutchinson, George L., lieutenant	21 Jan. 1942
Burrow, John G., commander	1 May 1942	Peters, Thomas V., lieutenant	27 Jan. 1942
Craig, James E., lieutenant commander	7 Dec. 1941	Fernald, Frank S., lieutenant	12 Apr. 1942
Healy, Howard R., lieutenant commander	8 May 1942	Ingersoll, Royal R., lieutenant	4 June 1942
French, John E., lieutenant commander	7 Dec. 1941	Newman, Arthur L., lieutenant	18 Feb. 1942
Evans, Thomas C., lieutenant commander	8 Apr. 1942	Johnston, Dewey G., lieutenant	31 Oct. 1941
Hopping, Hallsted L., lieutenant commander	1 Feb. 1942	Davis, George E., Jr., lieutenant	4 Feb. 1942
Tammany, William P., lieutenant commander	24 Mar. 1942	Anderson, Elmer D., lieutenant	18 Feb. 1942
Bedford, Stephen R., lieutenant commander	5 May 1942	Ricketts, Milton E., lieutenant	8 May 1942
Bielka, Rudolph P., lieutenant commander	7 Dec. 1941	Hood, Clark A., Jr., lieutenant	11 June 1942
Register, Paul J., lieutenant commander	Do.	Denney, Edward F., lieutenant	12 Apr. 1942
Baron, Richard S., lieutenant commander	15 Mar. 1942	Gustafson, Arthur L., lieutenant	19 Feb. 1942
Edwards, Heywood L., lieutenant commander	31 Oct. 1941	Patterson, Donald D., lieutenant	14 Jan. 1942
Reybold, John K., lieutenant commander	19 Mar. 1942	Henderson, Frank H., Jr., lieutenant	18 May 1942
Black, Hugh D., lieutenant commander	28 Feb. 1942	Simpson, Fred H., lieutenant (Jr. Gr.)	26 May 1942
Hickox, Ralph, lieutenant commander	18 Feb. 1942	Davis, Joel A., Jr., lieutenant (Jr. Gr.)	23 Dec. 1941
Morris, Loren A., lieutenant commander	12 Apr. 1942	Gadrow, Victor M., lieutenant (Jr. Gr.)	22 Dec. 1941
Winters, Robert C., lieutenant commander	6 May 1942	Ferguson, Jack C., lieutenant (Jr. Gr.)	6 Nov. 1941
Rounds, Clinton S., lieutenant commander	8 June 1942	Little, John G. III, lieutenant (Jr. Gr.)	7 Dec. 1941
Riggs, J. Clark, lieutenant commander	6 May 1942	Daub, John J., Jr., lieutenant (Jr. Gr.)	31 Oct. 1941
Lovelace, Donald A., lieutenant commander	2 June 1942	Hebel, Francis F., lieutenant (Jr. Gr.)	7 Dec. 1941
Bermingham, John M., lieutenant commander	19 Feb. 1942	Hughes, Richard B., lieutenant (Jr. Gr.)	8 Dec. 1941
Pennewill, William E., lieutenant commander	23 June 1942	Shricker, Harold D., lieutenant (Jr. Gr.)	23 Dec. 1941
Carpenter, Gilbert C., lieutenant commander	18 May 1942	Harveson, Herold A., lieutenant (Jr. Gr.)	7 Dec. 1941
Marshall, Thomas W., Jr., lieutenant Commander	28 Feb. 1942	Wilcox, Jesse A., lieutenant (Jr. Gr.)	24 Sept. 1941
Jordan, Julian B., lieutenant	7 Dec. 1941	Sooy, Charles D., lieutenant (Jr. Gr.)	27 Oct. 1941
Davis, Eugene E., lieutenant	23 May 1941	Case, Frank D., Jr., (Jr. Gr.)	23 Feb. 1942
McRoberts, James J., lieutenant	23 Dec. 1941	Reimann, Charles J., lieutenant (Jr. Gr.)	8 Mar. 1942
Clarkson, James S., lieutenant	9 Feb. 1942	Allen, Eric, lieutenant (Jr. Gr.)	7 Dec. 1941
Ashworth, Thomas, lieutenant	21 Oct. 1941	Danforth, James W., lieutenant (Jr. Gr.)	18 Feb. 1942
Elden, Ralph W., lieutenant	6 June 1942	Ginn, James B., lieutenant (Jr. Gr.)	8 Dec. 1941
		Zink, Oseald A., lieutenant (Jr. Gr.)	13 Dec. 1941

Register of Commissioned and Warrant Officers of the United States Navy and Marine Corps. July, 1942.

Coast Guard *List of Regular and Reserve Commissioned and Warrant Officers on Active Duty in Order of Precedence* does not have casualties for WWII.

Sources for Officer Registers

Army Officer Registers

Army Register

San Antonio Public Library
Texana/Genealogy
600 Soledad
San Antonio, TX 78205-1208
(A donation for searches is requested.)

Navy & Marine Corps Officer Registers

Register of Commissioned and Warrant Officers of the United States Navy and Marine Corps

Department of the Navy
Naval Historical Center
805 Kidder Breese SE
Washington, DC 20374-5060
www.history.navy.mil

Coast Guard Officer Registers

List of Regular and Reserve Commissioned and Warrant Officers on Active Duty in Order of Precedence

Coast Guard Academy Museum
U.S. Coast Guard Academy Library
35 Mohegan Avenue
New London, CT 06320-8511
(860) 444-8511
www.uscg.mil/hq/g-cp/museum/museumindex.html

The registers also can be found in most government depository libraries. Check with your local state or university library. They also can be requested using the interlibrary loan program.

Death Burial Files

U.S. Army Total Personnel Command
ATTN: TAPC-PAO (FOIA)
200 Stovall Street
Alexandria, VA 22332-0404
(703) 325-4054

They have WWII death burial files for all branches of the military. After 50 years, privacy issues no longer apply to these records. Make your request citing the Freedom of Information Act. See Appendix H (Forms and Worksheets)

Name, branch and military serial number are needed to identify the correct record. The death burial files contains a copy of the letter sent to the next of kin notifying them of the death, date of death and a copy of the certificate of death along with information pertaining to the cause of death, etc.

Army WWII Casualty Records

The Modern Military Records unit of the National Archives has casualty lists of WWII U.S. Army divisions and their permanently attached units. They are arranged by unit, then alphabetically by name of casualty. The list also includes the serial number, rank or grade, branch of service and type of casualty. Date of death appears on about 65 percent of the file. (Record Group 407, Records of the Adjutant General's Office).

National Archives and Records Administration
Modern Military Records
8601 Adelphi Road
College Park, MD 20740-6001

Coast Guard WWII Casualty Records

Per the U.S. Coast Guard's web page, 241,093 coast-guardsmen participated in WWII. Total casualties were 1,917. The Coast Guard Historian's office has an additional resource for Coast Guard casualties: a handwritten ledger that contains the name, rank, serial number, place of death and date of death.

Coast Guard Historian's Office
U.S. Coast Guard Headquarters
2100 Second Street, SW
Washington, DC 20593-0001
(202) 267-1394
www.uscg.mil/hq/g-cp/history/collection/html

Marine Corps Casualty Records

The Marine Corps Casualty office maintains a list of WWII Marine Corps casualties on microfiche. Request the casualty report by citing the Freedom of Information Act and providing the name only or name and serial number of the Marine.

Headquarters U.S. Marine Corps
ATTN: MRC/Casualty Records
3280 Russell Road
Quantico, VA 22134
(800) 847-1597

Marine Corps Casualty Cards

The Marine Corps Historical Center has casualty cards on microfilm for WWII. A casualty can include those who were killed, wounded or prisoner of war. These records have more detailed information pertaining to the MarineCorps casualty. Privacy issues do apply to this set of records. The location of next of kin will not be released. Information on the card includes the complete name, rank, branch and component of service, service number, date of casualty, type and place casualty occurred, date entered service, date of birth, place of induction, home of record, next of kin and burial information.

Marine Corps Historical Center
1254 Charles Morris St, SE
Washington Navy Yard, DC 20374-5040
(202) 433-0780, (202) 433-4691 Fax

If more information is needed about next of kin of a Marine Corps, Coast Guard or Navy casualty, check the Navy Department's casualty book available on the Internet. The next of kin information is not restricted in those records. See section titled WWII Casualty Books.

Navy WWII Casualty Records

The Bureau of Naval Personnel Casualty IBM printout is another source for a navy casualty list. The Bureau of Naval Personnel made this list available in 1947. It's listed chronologically by the campaign, then has a listing of the ships and units, and contains the casualties alphabetically by last name. It includes name, rank, serial number, casualty type (either wounded or killed), and date of casualty.

This resource provides much more information than the WWII Navy casualty book, such as the campaign and the ship or unit, as well as the date of casualty and type of casualty.

The entire file is available on microfilm or microfiche from the Naval Historical Center. If they are unable to do a search, the center has a list of commercial researchers available for hire. See the website for listings.

Naval Historical Center
Washington Navy Yard
805 Kidder Breese Street, SE
Washington Navy Yard, DC 20374-5060
www.history.navy.mil

United States Submarine Losses, World War II is a book published by the Navy Department and contains crew lists. Contact your local university or government depository library or request from your local library using the interlibrary loan program.

Purple Heart Cards

Index cards were maintained for those that received or were considered for the Purple Heart medal. The card list the veteran's name, rank or rating, and serial number. Date of casualty, ship or assignment, name and address of next of kin, date of the award also is included. Not all received the medal. Give name and rank when requesting a card.

The Operational Archives Branch of the Navy Historical Center has several other lists of personnel casualties on microfiche. Microfiche F458 contains a list of personnel killed or wounded on merchant ships and Army transports arranged chronologically and then alphabetically under the unit. The name, service number, rank or rate, casualty code, and date of casualty are included.

Microfiche F454 lists officers and enlisted prisoners of war as of 25 September 1945. The list is alphabetical by name, and includes service number, rank or rate, date of capture and the prisoner of war camp designation.

Operational Archives Branch
Naval Historical Center
805 Kidder Breese Street SE
Washington Navy Yard, DC 20374-5060
www.history.navy.mil

Department of Veterans Affairs

The Department of Veterans Affairs may have additional information pertaining to a WWII casualty. Date of death may be in its records, which is not available from most WWII casualty sources. Contact the Veterans Affairs Regional Office at (800) 827-1000. See Appendix A (State Records).

American Battle Monuments Commission

The American Battle Monuments Commission is a government agency that maintains all of the overseas cemeteries and war monuments in the United States. According to records, 93,242 WWII veterans are buried in the cemeteries and there are 78,976 names of those missing, lost or buried at sea. The WWII Memorial is under this agency.

Ardennes American Cemetery and Memorial
Ardennes, Belgium
5,328 interred; 462 missing
Most died in the Battle of the Bulge.

Brittany American Cemetery and Memorial
Brittany, France
4,410 interred; 498 missing
Casualties were from Normandy and Brittany campaigns
in 1944.

Cabanatuan American Memorial
Cabanatuan, Phillipines
Lists those that died in the internment camp during
WWII.

Cambridge American Cemetery and Memorial
Cambridge, England
3,812 interred, 5,126 missing
Most died in the battle of the Atlantic or in bombings in
the Northwest Europe.

East Coast Memorial
Battery Park, New York
4,601 missing due to loss of life in the Atlantic waters
during WWII. Inscribed are the names, rank, organization and state.

Epinal American Cemetery and Memorial
Epinal, France
5,255 interred; 424 missing

Florence American Cemetery and Memorial
Florence, Italy
4,402 interred; 1,409 missing
Casualties were from fighting after the liberation of Rome
in June 1944 from the 5th Army and also from Apennines.

Guadalcanal American Memorial
Guadalcanal, Soloman Islands
Died during the Guadalcanal Campaign August 7, 1942–
February 9, 1943.

Henri-Chapelle American Cemetery and Memorial
Henri-Chapelle, Belgium
7,989 interred; 450 missing
Most died due to entry into the Germany during WWII.

Honolulu Memorial
Honolulu, Hawaii
18,096 missing, lost or buried at sea in the Pacific.

Lorraine American Cemetery and Memorial
Lorraine, France
10,489 interred; 444 missing

Luxembourg American Cemetery and Memorial
Luxembourg, Luxembourg
5,076 interred; 371 missing
Battle of the Bulge and Ardennes.

Manila American Cemetery and Memorial
Manila, Philippines
17,206 interred; 36,282 missing
Pacific theater, China, India and Burma. *Largest of
WWII burials

Netherlands American Cemetery and Memorial
Netherlands
8,302 interred; 1,723 missing

Normandy American Cemetery and Memorial
Normandy, France
9,387 interred; 1,557 missing
Casualties were from D-Day invasions and later
European battles.

North Africa American Cemetery and Memorial
Carthage, Tunisia
2,841 interred; 3,724 missing.

Rhone American Cemetery and Memorial
Rhone, France
861 interred; 294 missing.

Suresnes American Cemetery
Suresnes, France
24 unknown WWII dead

Sicily-Rome American Cemetery and Memorial
Nettuno, Italy
7,861 interred; 3,095 missing.

West Coast Memorial
San Francisco, California
Inscribed with the names, rank, organization and state of
412 missing due to loss of life in the Pacific waters.

The American Battle Monuments Commission's online
database has only a small number of those who died during
the war, but for those listed, it has an abundance of
information. Information includes the full name, military
serial number, rank, branch of service, veteran's home of
record, date of death, name of overseas cemetery and
location of grave, or where the name is listed if the veteran
was missing or buried at sea. Lists the awards given and,
most importantly, the unit, if known.

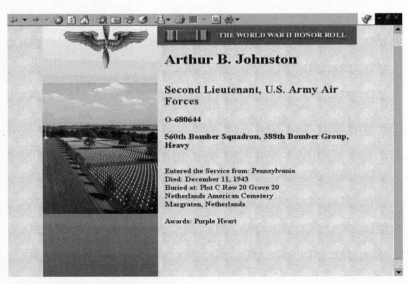

Sample of a WWII casualty buried in an overseas cemetery.
American Battle Monuments Commission. www.abmc.gov

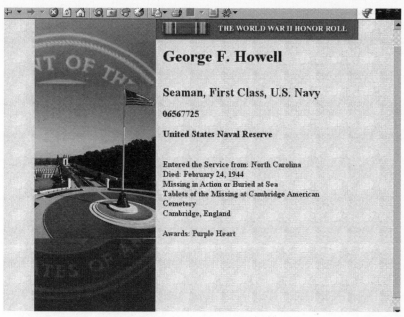

Sample of a WWII casualty missing in action or buried at sea.
American Battle Monuments Commission. www.abmc.gov

American Battle Monuments Commission
Courthouse Plaza II, Suite 500
2300 Clarendon Boulevard
Arlington, VA 22201
(703) 696-6897
www.abmc.gov

A photo or lithograph of the decedent's headstone or marker is available upon request. Please see the website or write for additional information.

Story

A female cousin of a WWII casualty called my office for guidance on researching her cousin's military service. She had been unable to find anything about her cousin's military background up to this point. At my suggestion, she used the information from the WWII microfiche, WWII casualty books and the information obtained from the American Battle Monuments Commission, and was able to learn in just a few minutes about her cousin who died during the war. She had misspelled the name. By checking some quick sources, she learned the correct spelling, branch of service, serial number, date of death and cause of death.

She told us that she last saw him when he was leaving for the Pacific theater. He was killed just a few days later.

Veterans Affairs National Cemeteries

The Department of Veteran Affairs National Cemetery Administration consists of 120 national cemeteries across the country. A database of burials is on the Internet at *www.findagrave.com* and *www.interment.net*. Information includes the veteran's name, date of birth, date of death, rank, branch of service, cemetery name, city, county and state, and location of grave. Please be aware that the verification process has not been completed on all the files. If there is any question as to the grave listing, contact that particular cemetery or the Veterans Affairs office directly at (800) 827-1000.

www.findagrave.com

Click on search 4.1 million graves. This includes the database of the Department of Veterans Affairs National Cemeteries. Search by name and state or by name only. Lists name, date of birth, date of death, name and location of cemetery. In some records, rank, time period of service and unit may be listed.

www.interment.net

This online database can be searched by name or by cemetery. They include the same information as *findagrave.*

The cemetery may have additional information than what is listed on the website. For example, the headstones usually tell the time period of service of the veteran, such as WWI and WWII, or the cemetery records may have names of dependents buried in the same cemetery. Photographs or sketchings are available from the cemetery. For listing of the cemeteries, check Appendix D (Department of Veterans Affairs National Cemeteries).

Department of the Army Cemeteries

The Department of the Army operates two cemeteries: Arlington National Cemetery and the U.S. Soldiers' & Airmen's Home National Cemetery. For information pertaining to those buried in these cemeteries, contact the following:

Arlington National Cemetery
Interment Services Branch
Arlington, VA 22211
(703) 695-3250/3255
www.arlingtoncemetery.org

U.S. Soldiers' & Airmen's Home National Cemetery
21 Harewood Road, N.W.
Washington, DC 20011
(202) 829-1829

A searchable database of those buried in the Department of the Army cemeteries is not available online. A partial list is available at *www.interment.net*. Please check with the cemeteries directly.

State Veterans Cemeteries

State Veterans Cemeteries are not part of the Veterans Affairs cemeteries. They are under the jurisdiction of the state and have certain criteria for burial. A list of state veterans cemeteries is available on the Internet at *www.cem.va.gov/lsvc.htm*. A searchable database of burials isn't available. Please make your request to each cemetery or state office.

State Records

Military records maintained by the individual states all vary. Some states such as Connecticut have many resources for WWII military service, while others may have little information pertaining to the individual military member. Please don't overlook what information may be obtained from the State Veterans Affairs Office, State Adjutant General, State Archives or State Genealogical or Historical Associations.

Many thousands of records burned in the 1973 fire at the National Personnel Records Center in St. Louis, Missouri. If your relative's records were among those burned, state records may be an important alternate source of military service. Some states received and maintained discharge certificates as far back as WWII. Although privacy laws apply, the next of kin of a deceased veteran can apply for those records. See Appendix A (State Records).

Local Newspapers

County or city newspapers are treasure chests of information pertaining to WWII. Most local newspapers carried information concerning their citizens involved in the war. This may include notices of promotions, orders for overseas duty, listings of service members from the area, reports of injury or death and obituaries.

JOHN E. HARDY
KILLED IN ACTION

John Ellis Hardy, pharmacist's mate third class attached to the U. S. Marines, has been killed in action in the Southwest Pacific theatre of war, according to information received by his parents, Mr. and Mrs. W. E. Hardy, Route 5, Box 505.

Young Hary was a graduate of Winslow High School. He enlisted in the navy November, 1942, and was attached to the marines four months before going overseas.
. In addition to his parents he leaves four brothers, George and Caleb of Tucson and Charley and Oliver of Winslow, and seven sisters, Mrs. Herbert Messinger, Mrs. Alonzo Oliver Stephens. Mrs. Howard Martineau, Mrs. Martha St. Aubin, Miss Laura Hardy and Miss Barbara Hardy of Tucson and Mrs. Walter Teague Johnson of Seattle, Wash.

His brother, George, has enlisted in the marines and will leave January 20 for boot camp training.

The Arizona Daily Star, Tucson, Arizona January 16, 1944, page 4.

State Summary of War Casualties from World War II for Navy, Marine Corps, and Coast Guard Personnel from Arizona, 1946. Item from Record Group 24: Records of the Bureau of Naval Personnel, 1798- 1970. www.archives.gov/ research_room/arc

an 3c, USN. Parents, Mr. and rs. Paul Smith Cook, Route 1, lobe.

NDALL, Rex F., Pfc, USMCR. ther, Mr. Floyd O. Crandall, Box , Litchfield Park.

MEENS, Louis Edward, Seaman , USN. Father, Mr. Stephen Ish- eal Cremeens, 1st St. and 19th ve, Yuma.

SBY, George Lorenzo, Pfc, SMCR. Mother, Florence G. Cros- , Walnut and Townley, Box 846, ute 6, Phoenix.

MINS, Harold Vernon, Seaman , USN. Father, Mr. I. O. Cum- ins, 137 Black Knob St., Warren.

RTIS, Herbert William, Aviation dio Technician 2c, USNR. Par- ts, Mr. and Mrs. Herbert Matthew rtis, 2608 E. Drackman St., Tuc- n.

RTIS, Lamar, Machinist's Mate 1c, SN. Parents, Mr. and Mrs. Platte, yman Curtis, 1105 E. Maple St., lobe.

D

RTER, James Roderick, Ensign, SN. Mother, Mrs. Nannie Mae arter, Casa Grande.

UTREMONT, Charles, Lt, (jg), SNR. Wife, Mrs. Ann Webster Autremont, Southern Arizona ank, Tucson.

VENPORT, Robert Elmer, Seaman , USNR. Brother, Mr. Maynard avenport, P. O. Box 551, Jerome.

ESCALANTE, Cipriano R., Pfc, USMCR. Parents, Mr. and Mrs. Manuel G. Escalante, Box 315, Tempe.

ESHELMAN, John William, Machinist's Mate 1c, USN. Father, Mr. Irvin H. Eshelman, Cave Creek.

ESTES, Rex G., Pfc, USMC. Father, Mr. James R. Estes, 362 No. 16th St., Phoenix.

EUSTACE, Milton Jack, Machinist's Mate 2c, USN. Parents, Mr. and Mrs. Lester Edward Eustace, 267 Orange Ave., Yuma.

F

FANCHETTE Robert Q., Pvt, USMCR. Wife, Mrs. Robert Q. Fanchette, R. F. D. 1, Box 795, Tucson.

FAUSSET, Eugene Raymond, Gunner's Mate 3c, USNR. Wife, Mrs. Roseleen Ellen Fausset, Gen. Del., Peoria.

FAUST, Joseph David, Coxswain, USCGR. Mother, Mrs. Ida Kathrine Faust, Box 1095, Buckeye.

FELTON, Russell B. Seaman 1c, USNR. Parents, Mr. and Mrs. Ben M. Felton, P. O. Box 1418, Winslow.

FIGUEROA, Frederick Bracamonte, Seaman 2c, USNR. Mother, Mrs. Rosa Bracamonte Cruz, 1510 W. Niagara St., Tucson.

FLYNN, Robert Morris, Lt, USNR. Brother, Thomas Flynn, Prescott.

FOSTER, Victor Wayne, Coxswain, USNR. Wife, Mrs. Betsy Lou Foster, Box 733, Bisbee.

FREITAG, Norman Richard, Cox-

haw, 950 E. Indian School Rd., Phoenix.

GUNASON, Robert W., Lt, (jg), USNR. Mother, Mrs. H. Meneley, Greenway Station, Tucson.

H

HADRA, Ernest, Gunner's Mate 3c, USN. Mother, Mrs. Minnie Linette Pool, Phoenix.

HALL, John Phillip, Aviation Ordnanceman 3c, USNR. Parents, Mr. and Mrs. Phillip Nick Hall, 21, W. Turney, Phoenix.

HALLMARK, Floyd V., Cpl, USMC. Parents, Mr. and Mrs. Floyd Hallmark, Tortilla Flat.

HAMBERLIN, Bernard M. Cpl, USMC. Mother, Mrs. Ercel Merkley, Box 371, Mesa.

HANDWERK, William Harold, Ensign, USNR. Parents, Mr. and Mrs. William Ambrose Handwerk, Apt. 06-D Alzona Park, Phoenix.

HARDING, William Ray, Seaman 1c, USNR. Parents, Mr. and Mrs. G. E. Harding, 4130 No. 17th St., Phoenix.

HARDY, George A., Pfc, USMCR. Parents, Mr. and Mrs. Warren E. Hardy, Route 5, Box 505, Tucson.

HARDY, John Ellis, Pharmacist's Mate 3c, USNR. Parents, Mr. and Mrs. Warren Ellis Hardy, Route 5, Box 505, Tucson.

HART, William Lester, Aviation Machinist's Mate 2c, USN. Father, Mr.

Since the obituary stated that John's brother also entered the service, I checked to see if he survived the war. He did not. The Navy Department's book listed both as killed in action and both have the same next of kin listed.

Internet Sources for WWII Casualties

The Internet's invention has made all research easier and shouldn't be overlooked when searching for historical information, especially for WWII casualties. Most large division associations and even smaller military organizations have put together websites listing historical information pertaining to their part in WWII. Most have some type of listing of those who were either killed or wounded from their division, unit or ship.

It can be a daunting task searching for a company web page, but I recommend starting at the Division or Ship level, such as the 101st Airborne Division or 3rd Army Division. Most of the larger division associations have a website with information on the history of the division and possible information on those who were part of the division, as well as listings of those who died from WWII.

Go to any Internet search engine such as *www.google.com, www.ask.com, www.dogpile.com* or *www.yahoo.com*. Type in name of the division or unit. Following is a sample of some of the websites that list historical information and casualties for WWII.

www.dday.org
The National D-Day Memorial Foundation is non-profit organization dedicated to the preservation of information regarding D-Day. They are putting together a database of those who participated and were killed in D-Day.

www.geocities.com/mbackstr2000/dead/dead.htm
Lists Marines that died at Iwo Jima, including name, rank, cause of death, place of death, division and branch of service. This listing is not yet complete.

www.nps.gov/usar/AZCas.html
Casualty listing for the USS Arizona. Lists name, rank, branch of service and home of record.

http://members.aol.com/dadswar/38deapho.htm
This site has photographs and descriptions of those killed during WWII from the 38th Armored Infantry Battalion in Europe.

www.haruth.com/29thCasualtyList.html
Casualties for the 29th Infantry Division. Lists name, rank and unit information.

www.94thinfdiv.com/94thCasualtyList.html
Lists casualties of 94th Infantry Division. Name, serial number, corps, cause of death, rank, date of death and unit information is given.

www.3ad.org/honor_roll
Complete casualty list for 3rd Armored Division. Name, rank, unit, cause of death, date of death are included.

www.10thmtndivassoc.org/hrunit.html
Listing of 997 men who died during WWII from the 10th Mountain Division. Listed by unit or alphabetically by last name. Name and unit are given, and if deceased is buried in an overseas cemetery, gives name of cemetery.

Military Reunion Associations

You can only find so much information from death listings, casualty reports and other military documents. Finding someone who served with your relative or talking with someone who was at a certain battle can provide much more detail about a situation. There are approximately 5,000 military reunions held every year in this country. The majority of the reunion groups are still WWII–era, but that is changing everyday.

The organization may have some casualty information or specific details relating to a casualty. Most reunion associations welcome relatives of a former comrade for membership or to attend reunions.

Another good source of information available from reunion associations is a printed or electronic newsletter. They normally allow either free or paid advertisements requesting information concerning a former member of their organization. A sample newsletter entry may read like the following:

> PFC Smith, John R. Died February 12, 1945 Searching for any information relating to his death or anyone that knew him during WWII. Please contact his cousin Fred Smith at (phone number) or (e-mail address).

There are many sources for military reunions. Most veterans or military magazines print a monthly listing of upcoming reunions. They may have archived reunions on their websites, but the most effective means is to check websites that have databases of military reunions.

Veterans Magazines

The American Legion Magazine
PO Box 1055
Indianapolis, IN 46206
www.legion.org

VFW Magazine
406 West 34th Street, Suite 523
Kansas City, MO 64111
www.vfw.org

DAV Magazine
PO Box 14301
Cincinnati, OH 45250-0301
www.dav.org

Internet sources that maintain databases of military reunions:

www.militaryusa.com
www.military.com
www.usmc.mil/reunins (for all branches)
www.fredsplace.org (Coast Guard)

If the reunion association has a website, it should be listed on the Internet reunion listing or check Internet search engines for a group web page. Check Appendix E (Military Reunion Associations).

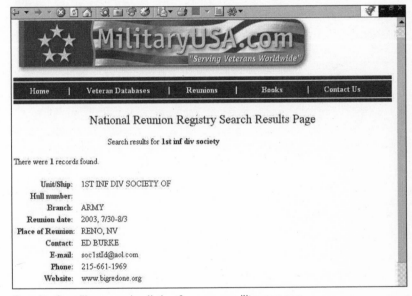

Sample of a military reunion listing from www.militaryusa.com

Children of WWII Casualties

Ann Bennett Mix founded the American WWII Orphans Network. Her father died in WWII and she started this organization as a support base for others who lost a parent in WWII.

American WWII Orphans Network
5745 Lee Road
Indianapolis, IN 46216
(540) 310-0750
www.awon.org

Death Index

WWII Casualties are not listed in today's Social Security Death Index. That database began around 1962 and doesn't contain any WWII deaths. I also checked on various state death listings, such as Texas, Illinois, and California, and they do not include the WWII casualties either. Unfortunately, that is not a source for date of birth or date of death of a WWII casualty.

Most state vital statistics offices that I spoke with said that they didn't receive copies of certificates of death for WWII killed. One exception is the Utah State Archives. Utah issued a death certificate for WWII killed overseas and were brought home for burial in a Utah cemetery. See Appendix A (State Records).

Chapter 5

WWII MEDALS

From the Revolution up to the Civil War the United States had no military medals. In 1861, Congress established the Medals of Honor for the Navy, followed in 1862 for the Army. For nearly 20 years, the Medal of Honor remained the sole American military award. In the 1880's the Navy and Marine Corps authorized the first Good Conduct Medals.

It was not until President Theodore Roosevelt took it upon himself to create military campaign medals to honor all of those who served in America's previous conflicts that America really developed a military awards program. In 1908 the United States authorized campaign medals, many retroactively, for the Civil War, Indian wars, War with Spain, the Philippine Insurrection and China Relief Expedition of 1900–1901. While the Army and the Navy used the same ribbon design, different medals were struck for each service. During the same time frame the custom of wearing service ribbons on the uniform was adopted with each service using different orders of precedence. Thus before World War I, the various services managed to establish the principal of independents in the creation and wearing of military awards that is virtually unchanged today.

When the United States entered World War I, the Medal of Honor, Certificate of Merit and the Navy and Marine Corps Good Conduct Medals were the only personal decorations available. Many were concerned that the Medal of Honor might be cheapened by being awarded too often or that other deeds of valor might go unrecognized. By 1918 the Army had created two new awards, the Army's Distinguished Service Cross and Distinguished Service Medal. In 1919 the Navy created the Navy Cross and its own Distinguished Service Medal for Navy and Marine Corps personnel.

At the end of World War I a Victory Medal was issued by each of the Allied countries. During this same time frame, the Army authorized a small silver star to go on medals ribbon to indicate a citation of gallantry during WW I or any previous campaign back to the Civil War. Officers and enlisted personnel awarded one of the small silver stars was also presented a Silver Star citation, which evolved into the Silver Star Medal in 1932.

After World War I, American troops were dispatched to such areas as Haiti, Nicaragua and China to put down rebellions and deal with civil unrest. Appropriate campaign medals were authorized to commemorate these events.

On September 8, 1939 in response to the growing threat of involvement in World War II, the President proclaimed a national emergency in order to increase this size of the United States military forces. For the first time, a peacetime service award, the American Defense Service Medal, was awarded to military personnel on active duty prior to the attack on Pearl Harbor, December 7, 1941.

The onset of American participation in World War II saw a significant increase in both personal decorations and campaign medals. Since United States forces were serving all over the world, a campaign medal was designed for each major (and carefully defined) area. The three campaign medals, the American Campaign Medal, the Asiatic-Pacific Campaign Medal and European-African-Middle Eastern Campaigns, encompassed the globe. However, the World War I practice of using campaign bars was discarded in favor of $3/_{16}$ inch bronze stars that could denote each subsequent military campaign, from a major invasion to a submarine war patrol. World War II also saw the first (and only) service medal unique to female military personnel. Known as the Women's Army Corps's service medal, it was authorized for service in both the WACs and its predecessor, the Women's Auxiliary Army Corps. In addition the large-scale award of foreign medals and decorations to American servicemen was authorized. The Philippine government authorized two medals to commemorate the defense and liberation of their island country. In the European theater, France and Belgium made many presentations of their war crosses (Croix de Guerre) to the U.S. military personnel.

American Campaign Medal, Asiatic-Pacific Campaign Medal and European-African-Middle Eastern Campaign Medal

Bronze Star Medal

Air Medal

Two personal decorations require special mention: the Bronze Star Medal and the Air Medal. The Air Medal was designed to recognize airmen of the Army, Navy, Marine Corps and Coast Guard who achieved a certain number of air combat missions. It was liberally awarded and considered a significant morale booster. The Bronze Star was also designed to be liberally awarded to ground troops in combat. However, due to the nature of combat and the lack of administrative support few Bronze Stars were awarded to combat ground forces compared to the number of Air Medals presented to airman. To correct this, the Army in 1947, authorized all military personnel who had received either the Combat Infantryman's Badge (CIB) or the Combat Medical Badge (CMB) from December 7, 1941 to September 2, 1945 be awarded the Bronze Star Medal for military merit. In addition, personnel who participated in defense of the Philippine Islands between December 7, 1941 and 1942 were awarded the Bronze Star Medal for their service.

What most Americans don't know is that when the veterans returned home after World War II there were no campaign medals issued because all brass production had been needed for ammunition. The only medals made during the war were personal decorations such as Bronze Stars, Air Medals and higher. The fourteen million American veterans returned home with only the ribbon bars on their uniform jackets. Their medals did not become available until years later and then required application to the National Personnel Records Center which unfortunately loss 80% of Army's WWII records in a fire in 1973.

Complete details on U.S. military awards presented during World War II can be found in *The Complete Guide to all United States Military Medals 1939 to Present*. Another excellent source is the superb video *The Medals of World War II*, both the video and the book are published by Medals of America Press and can be obtained by calling (800) 308-0849 or going to *www.usmedals.com* or *www.moapress.com*.

MEDAL OF HONOR ARMY

EFFECTIVE DATES: April 15, 1861 CRITERIA: Awarded for conspicuous gallantry and intrepidity at the risk of one's life, above and beyond the call of duty. This gallantry must be performed either while engaged in action against an enemy of the United States, while engaged in military operations involving conflict with an opposing foreign force, or, while serving with friendly foreign forces engaged in an armed conflict against an opposing armed force in which the United States is not a belligerent party. Recommendation must be submitted within three years of the act, and the medal must be awarded within five years of the act.

The Medal of Honor is a five-pointed gold-finished star (point down) with each point ending in a trefoil. Every point of the star has a green enamel oak leaf in its center, and a green enamel laurel wreath surrounds the center of the star, passing just below the trefoils. In the center of the star is a profile of the Goddess Minerva encircled by the inscription UNITED STATES OF AMERICA with a small shield at the bottom. The star is suspended by links from a bar inscribed VALOR. The back of the bar holding the star is engraved THE CONGRESS TO.

MEDAL OF HONOR NAVY

The Navy Medal of Honor arose from a Public Resolution signed into law by President Lincoln on 21 December 1861 authorizing the preparation of "200 medals of honor" to promote the efficiency of the Navy. It was followed by a Joint Resolution of Congress on July 12, 1862 (as amended) which actually approved the design and further defined the eligibility and required deeds of potential recipients.

CRITERIA: For conspicuous gallantry and intrepidity at the risk of life, above and beyond the call of duty, in action, involving actual conflict with an opposing armed force. The Medal of Honor is worn before all other decorations and medals and is the highest honor that can be conferred on a member of the Armed Forces. Since its inception, 3,427 Medals of Honor have been awarded to 3,408 individuals. A recommendation for the Navy Medal of Honor must be made within three years from the date of the deed upon which it depends and award of the medal must be made within five years after the date of the deed. A stipulation for the medal is that there must be a minimum of two witnesses to the deed, who swear separately that the event transpired as stated in the final citation.

Distinguished Service Cross

Service: Army
Instituted: 1918
Criteria: Extraordinary heroism in action against an enemy of the U.S. or while serving with friendly foreign forces.
Devices: Bronze, silver oak leaf cluster

Bronze   Silver

Note:100 copies of earlier design cross were issued with a European-style (unedged) ribbon.

Navy Cross

Instituted: 1919
Criteria: Extraordinary heroism in action against an enemy of the U.S. while engaged in military operations involving conflict with an opposing foreign force or while serving with friendly foreign forces.
Devices: Gold, silver star

Gold   Silver

Note: Originally issued with a 1–1/2" wide ribbon.

Distinguished Service Medal (Army)

Service: Army
Instituted:1918
Criteria: Exceptionally meritorious service to the United States Government in a duty of great responsibility.
Devices: Bronze, silver oak leaf cluster

Bronze   Silver

Distinguished Service Medal (Navy)

Instituted: 1919

Criteria: Exceptionally meritorious service to the U.S. Government in a duty of great responsibility.

Devices: Gold, silver star

Gold   Silver

Note: 107 copies of earlier medal design issued but later withdrawn. First ribbon design was 1 1/2" wide.

Silver Star

Service: All Services (originally Army only)

Instituted: 1932

Criteria: Gallantry in action against an armed enemy of the United States or while serving with friendly foreign forces.

Devices: Army/Air Force: bronze, silver oak leaf cluster; Navy/Marine Corps/Coast Guard: gold, silver star

Silver   Gold   Silver   Bronze

Note: Derived from the 3/16" silver "Citation Star" previously worn on Army campaign medals.

Legion Of Merit

Service: All Services

Instituted: 1942 retroactive to September 8, 1939

Criteria: Exceptionally meritorious conduct in the performance of outstanding services to the United States.

Devices: Army/Air Force: bronze, silver oak leaf cluster; Navy/Marine Corps/Coast Guard: bronze letter "V" (for valor), gold, silver star

Bronze   Silver   Gold   Silver   Bronze

Note: Issued in four degrees (Legionnaire, Officer, Commander & Chief Commander) to foreign nationals.

Distinguished Flying Cross

Service: All Services
Instituted: 1926 (Retroactive to 6 April 1917)
Criteria: Heroism or extraordinary achievement while participating in aerial flight.
Devices: Army/Air Force: bronze, silver oak leaf cluster; Navy/Marine Corps: bronze letter "V" (for valor), gold, silver star; Coast Guard: gold, silver star

Bronze　Silver　Gold

Silver　Bronze

Soldier's Medal

Service: Army
Instituted: 1926
Criteria: Heroism not involving actual conflict with an armed enemy of the United States.
Devices: Bronze, silver oak leaf cluster

Bronze　Silver

Navy And Marine Corps Medal

Instituted: 1942
Criteria: Heroism not involving actual conflict with an armed enemy of the United States.
Devices: Gold, silver star

Gold　Silver

Note: For acts of life-saving, action must be at great risk to one's own life.

Bronze Star Medal

Service: All Services
Instituted: 1944 retroactive to December 7, 1941.
Criteria: The Bronze Star Medal is awarded to individuals who, while serving in the United States Armed Forces in a combat theater, distinguish themselves by heroism, outstanding achievement, or by meritorious service not involving aerial flight.
Devices: All Services: bronze letter "V" (for Valor) Army/Air Force bronze, silver oak leaf cluster; Navy/Marine Corps/Coast Guard: gold, silver star

Bronze   Silver   Gold   Silver   Bronze

Note: Awarded for meritorious service to WWII holders of Army Combat Infantryman or Combat Medical Badge.

Purple Heart

Service: All Services (originally Army only)
Instituted:1932; The Purple Heart is retroactive to April 5, 1917; however, awards for qualifying prior to that date were made.
Criteria: Awarded to any member of the Armed Forces of the United States or to any civilian national of the United States who, while serving under competent authority in any capacity with one of the U.S. Armed Forces, since April 5, 1917 has been wounded, killed, or who has died or may die of wounds received from an opposing enemy force while in armed combat or as a result of an act of international terrorism or being a Prisoner of War.
Devices: Army/Air Force: bronze, silver oak leaf cluster; Navy/Marine Corps/Coast Guard:
gold, silver star

         Silver   Gold   Silver   Bronze

Air Medal

Service: All Services Silver   Bronze   Silver   Gold
Instituted: 1942 retroactive to September 8, 1939.
Criteria: Heroic actions or meritorious service while participating in aerial flight, but not of a degree that would justify an award of the Distinguished Flying Cross.
Devices: Army: bronze letter "V" (for valor) effective February 29, 1964, bronze numeral; Air Force: bronze, silver oak leaf cluster; Navy/Marine Corps: bronze letter "V" (for valor), bronze numeral, bronze star, gold, silver star ;
Coast Guard: gold, silver star

Note: During WWII, the Army Air Corps and US Army Air Forces employed bronze and silver oak leaf clusters as additional award devices on all decorations including the Air Medal. The same devices were used by the Army until the establishment of the bronze numeral as its unique additional award device for the Air Medal during the Vietnam War.

Army Commendation Medal

Service: Army
Instituted: 1945 (retroactive to 1941)
Criteria: Heroism, meritorious achievement or
meritorious service.
Devices: Bronze letter "V" (for valor), bronze, silver
oak leaf cluster

Bronze   Silver   Bronze

Note: Originally a ribbon-only award then designated
"Army Commendation Ribbon with Metal Pendant."
Redesignated: "Army Commendation Medal" in 1960.

Navy And Marine Corps Commendation Medal

Instituted: 1944/1950
Criteria: Meritorious service or achievement in a combat
or noncombat situation based on sustained performance
of a superlative nature.
Devices: Bronze letter "V" (for valor), gold,
silver star

Bronze   Silver   Gold

Note: Originally a ribbon-only award: "Secretary of
the Navy Commendation for Achievement Award with
Ribbon." Changed to present name in 1994.

 # Combat Action Ribbon

Criteria: Active participation in ground or air combat during specifically
listed military operations.
Devices: Gold, silver star

Gold   Silver

Note: This is the only Navy personal decoration which has no associated medal (a
"ribbon-only" award.)

*For active participation in specifically named ground or surface combat actions
subsequent to 1 March 1961, while in the grade of Colonel or below. The Combat Action
Ribbon is worn after the Navy and Marine Corps Achievement Medal and before the
Presidential Unit Citation in a ribbon display. It is worn as the senior ribbon on the right
breast when full-sized medals are worn on the left breast.*

*The Combat Action Ribbon was authorized by the Secretary of the Navy on 17
February 1969 and made retroactive to 6 December 1941. The principal requirement is
that the individual was engaged in combat during which time he/she was under enemy fire
and that his/her performance was satisfactory.*

*The Combat Action Ribbon is a ribbon only award. The ribbon is gold with thin
center stripes of red, white and blue and border stripes of dark blue on the left and red on
the right. Additional awards are authorized for each separate conflict/war and are
represented by five-sixteenth inch gold stars.*

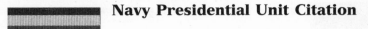 ## Navy Presidential Unit Citation

Service: Navy, Marine Corps
Instituted: 1942
Criteria: Awarded to Navy/Marine Corps units for extraordinary heroism in action against an armed enemy.
Devices: Bronze, silver star

                Bronze   Silver

 ## Prisoner Of War Medal

Instituted: 1985
Criteria: Awarded to any member of the U.S. Armed Forces taken prisoner during any armed conflict dating from World War I. Authorized for all U.S. military personnel taken prisoner during WWII.
Devices: Bronze, silver star

           Bronze   Silver

 ## Army Good Conduct Medal

Service: Army
Instituted: 1941
Criteria: Exemplary conduct, efficiency and fidelity during three years of active enlisted service with the U.S. Army (1 year during wartime).
Devices: Bronze, silver, gold knotted clasp

Gold, Silver or Bronze Clasp

Navy Good Conduct Medal

Service: Navy

Instituted: 1884

Criteria: Outstanding performance and conduct during three years of continuous active enlisted service in the U.S Navy.

Devices: Bronze, silver star replaced engraved clasps used through 1942.

Bronze   Silver

Note: After WWII the Navy replaced the "square" suspension ribbon and crossbar to attaching the medal directly to the ribbon by means of a suspension ring.

Marine Corps Good Conduct Medal

Instituted: 1896

Criteria: Outstanding performance and conduct during 3 years of continuous active enlisted service in the U.S Marine Corps.

Devices: Bronze, silver star

Bronze   Silver

Note: Earlier ribbon was 1¼" wide. Design changed after WWII, removing bar saying "U.S.Marine Corps" at the top.

Coast Guard Reserve Good Conduct Medal

Service: Coast Guard

Instituted: 1963

Criteria: Outstanding proficiency, leadership and conduct during 3 years of enlisted service in the Coast Guard Reserve.

Devices: Bronze, silver star (55, 61)

Bronze   Silver

Note: Originally a ribbon-only award-"Coast Guard Reserve Meritorious Service Ribbon." Current medal does not use the "square" suspension ribbon and bottom crossbar but is attached directly to the ribbon via a suspension ring.

Selected Marine Corps Reserve Medal

Instituted: 1939

Criteria: Outstanding performance and conduct during 4 years of service in the Marine Corps Selected Reserve.

Devices: Bronze, silver star

⭐ ⭐
Bronze   Silver

Note: Formerly "Organized Marine Corps Reserve Medal."

Navy Expeditionary Medal

Service: Navy   Instituted: 1936

Dates: 1936 to Present (retroactive to 1874)

Criteria: Landings on foreign territory and operations against armed opposition for which no specific campaign medal has been authorized.

Devices: Silver letter "W" (denotes bar below), bronze, silver star

W   ⭐   ⭐
Silver   Silver   Bronze

Bars: "Wake Island"   WAKE ISLAND

Note: This medal with Wake Island bar is rare.

Marine Corps Expeditionary Medal

Instituted: 1919/1921

Dates: 1919 to present (retroactive to 1874)

Criteria: Landings on foreign territory and operations against armed opposition for which no specific campaign medal has been authorized.

Devices: Silver letter "W", bronze, silver star

Bar: "Wake Island"

WAKE ISLAND   W   ⭐   ⭐
Silver   Silver   Bronze

. Note: Originally a "ribbon-only" award. This medal with Wake Island bar is rare.

China Service Medal

Instituted:1940

Dates: 1937–39, 1945–57

Criteria: Service ashore in China or on-board naval vessels during either of the above periods.

Devices: Bronze star

Bronze

Note: Medal was reinstituted in 1947 for extended service during dates shown above.

American Defense Service Medal

Service: All Services   Instituted:1941   Dates:1939–41

Criteria: Army: 12 months of active duty service during the above period.

Devices: All Services: bronze star (denotes bars above), bronze letter "A"

Bars: Army: FOREIGN SERVICE for service outside the continental United States (CONUS); Navy/Marine Corps: FLEET for service on the high seas and BASE for service at bases outside CONUS; Coast Guard: SEA for service on the high seas.

Bronze Bronze

FLEET
Navy

BASE
Navy

 FOREIGN SERVICE
Army

SEA
Coast Guard

Women's Army Corps Service Medal

Service: Army

Instituted: 1943

Dates: 1941–46

Criteria: Service with both the Women's Army Auxiliary Corps and Women's Army Corps during the above period

Devices: None

Note: Only U.S. award authorized for women only.

American Campaign Medal

Instituted: 1942
Dates: 1941-46
Criteria: Service outside the U.S. in the American theater for 30 days, or within the continental United States (CONUS) for one year.
Devices: All Services: Bronze star

Bronze

Asiatic-Pacific Campaign Medal

Service: All Services
Instituted: 1942
Dates: 7 December 1941 to 2 March 1946
Criteria: Service in the Asiatic-Pacific theater for 30 days or receipt of any combat decoration in theater
Devices: All Services: bronze, silver star; Army/Air Force: bronze arrowhead; Navy: bronze Marine Corps device

Silver   Bronze

European-African-Middle Eastern Campaign Medal

Service: All Services
Instituted: 1942
Dates: 7 December 1941 to 2 March 1946
Criteria: Service in the European-African-Middle Eastern theater for 30 days or receipt of any combat decoration
Devices: All Services: bronze, silver star;
Army/Air Force: bronze arrowhead;
Navy: bronze Marine Corps device

Silver   Bronze

World War II Victory Medal

Service: All Services
Instituted: 1945
Dates: 7 December 1941 to 31 December 1946
Criteria: Awarded for service in the U.S. Armed
Forces during the above period.
Devices: None

Army Of Occupation Medal

Service: Army/Air Force
Instituted: 1946
Dates: 1945–55 (Berlin: 1945–90)
Criteria: 30 consecutive days of service in occupied
territories of former enemies during above period.
Devices: Gold airplane for Berlin airlift
Bars: "Germany", "Japan"

 Gold Airplane

Germany Clasp   Japan Clasp

Note: Many WWII Veterans qualify for this medal but never knew about it since it did
not come in until a year after the war.

Navy Occupation Service Medal

Service: Navy, Marine Corps, Coast Guard
Instituted: 1948
Dates: 1945–55 (Berlin: 1945–90)
Criteria: 30 consecutive days of service in occupied
territories of former enemies during above period.
Devices: Gold airplane for Berlin Airlift
Bars: "Europe", "Asia"  Gold Airplane

EUROPE   ASIA

Europe Clasp   Asia Clasp

Note: Many WWII Veterans qualify for this medal but never knew about it since it did not
come in until a year after the war.

Army Presidential Unit Citation

Service: Army   Instituted: 1942, redesignated 1966
Criteria: Awarded to Army units for extraordinary
heroism in action against an armed enemy.
Devices: Bronze, silver oak leaf cluster   Bronze   Silver
Note: Original designation: Distinguished Unit Citation. Redesignated
to present name in 1966.

 Philippine Republic Presidential Unit Citation

Country: Republic of the Philippines   Instituted:1948
Criteria: Awarded to units of the U.S. Armed Forces for service in the war
against Japan and/or for 1970 and 1972 disaster relief.

Different Forms of a Military Medal

Enamel Lapel Pin

Basic Ribbon Bar

Hat Pin

Full Size Medal

Miniature Medal

Reverse of Medal

Ribbon Bar With Appropriate Devices

All World War II veterans and their families are encouraged by the United
States Government to wear and display their full size or miniature medals on
civilian suits or shirts on appropriate occasions such as Memorial Day and
Armed Forces Day. Other events that call for the wear of military medals by
veterans are military funerals, memorial services, and inaugurals. Patriotic
parades on national holidays, social functions of a military nature and formal
functions requiring black or white tie.

Medals of America
114 Southchase Blvd,
Fountain Inn, SC 29644
(800) 308-0849, *www.usmedals.com*

Examples of World War II Medal Displays

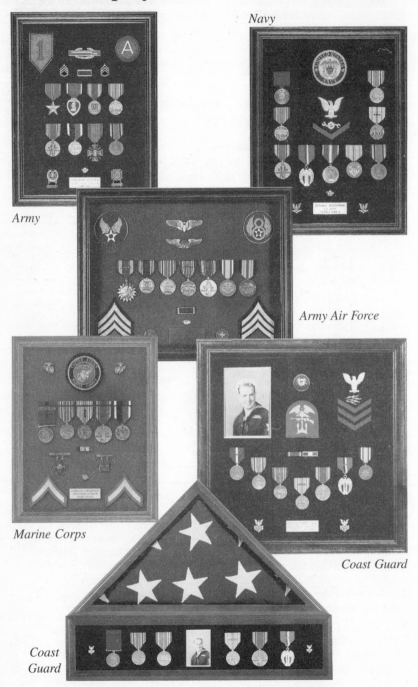

Navy

Army

Army Air Force

Marine Corps

Coast Guard

Coast Guard

Chapter 6

VETERAN'S DEATH RECORDS

This chapter details how to obtain death information for veterans who survived the war and have since died. Unfortunately, WWII veterans are dying by the thousands each day. In this section are resources to help you find out the veteran's date of birth, date of death, proof of death, burial location, military serial number, rank and branch of service. This information is needed when requesting the military records of a deceased veteran.

The *complete military records* of a relative that served in the military are not releasable unless the veteran is deceased. If the veteran is still living, the complete military records can be obtained only by the veteran's request. But anyone can request records citing the Freedom of Information Act. See Chapter One (Individual Military Records).

If a veteran is deceased and you are next of kin or the only living relative, it is required to show proof of death of the veteran when requesting the military records. It will be necessary to include the veteran's military serial number, date of birth, branch of service, date of death and proof of death with the records request.

> Proof of death can be a copy of a death certificate, an obituary, or a print out from the Social Security Death Index, state death index or a grave listing.

The Social Security Death Index does not contain information about a person's military service. A veteran's death index similar to the Social Security Administration's death listing does not exist.

Department of Veterans Affairs

The Department of Veterans Affairs is allowed to release a report of death on a veteran. Once a person (veteran) has died, he no longer has a right to privacy and basic information can be released such as date of death, place of burial, branch of service and dates of service. You must be able to supply at least enough information for the Department of Veterans Affairs (VA) office to be able to identify the right person in its files. That information can include name, branch of service, military serial number or Social Security number.

During WWII, the military member was issued a military serial number as a means of identification. If the veteran used benefits with the VA after Social Security numbers were implemented, the VA office is able to search for a record based on a name and Social Security number.

Not every veteran used VA benefits and not all deceased veterans are listed with the VA. But this avenue should not be overlooked.

The VA does offer benefits available to deceased veterans such as a burial allotment. Most funeral homes report a veteran's death to the VA.

The Veterans Affairs office can use any of the following identifying information to check its files:

- Name only (if unique)
- Name and complete date of birth
- Name and military serial number
- Name and Social Security number
- Veterans Affairs claim number

A VA claim number is a number prefixed by the letter "C". When a claim is made, the VA issues this number to a veteran

Social Security Death Index

Most researchers are familiar with the Social Security Administration's listing of deaths since 1962. It lists the person's first name, last name and just recently includes the middle initial, date of birth, date of death, Social Security number, what state the Social Security number was issued from and, if available, place the death payment was sent. There is no indication on this database if the person was a veteran. But there are ways to check if the person listed served in the military. One way is to use the information obtained from the Social Security Death Index and ask the VA if this person served in the military. Be sure to state that you are a relative and that the veteran is deceased. Mention that you are trying to research his military background and need information such as military serial number, branch of service and dates of service.

Here is a sample entry from the Social Security Death Index. It makes no indication that the person is a veteran.

Leonard Dahlquist
SSN: 197-16-XXXX
Issued from Pennsylvania
Date of birth: 03/13/1926
Date of death: 09/20/1990
Death payment sent to: Escondido, California 92027

Internet sites for the Social Security Death Index
www.ancestry.com
http://ssdi.genealogy.rootsweb.com

Department of Veterans Affairs National Cemeteries

The VA maintains a database of burials for the national cemeteries. The database can be found on the Internet at *www.findagrave.com* or *www.interment.net*. Not every burial in the national cemeteries is a veteran; spouses and dependents are entitled to burial as well. The burial listing gives name, rank, branch of service, date of birth, date of death and place of burial. Usually the cemetery will have additional information not available on the Internet. Contact the cemetery directly for all available information concerning your relative. See Appendix D (Department of Veterans Affairs National Cemeteries).

In some cases, rubbings or photographs of gravestones are available from the individual cemetery.

Leonard A Dahlquist

Birth: Mar. 13, 1926

Death: Sep. 20, 1990

NM, US NAVY

Burial:

<u>Riverside National Cemetery</u>

Riverside (Riverside County)

Riverside County

California, USA

Plot: 27, 0, 1703

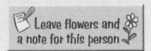

Record added: Feb 25 2000

www.findagrave.com

Based on the information obtained from the Social Security Death Index, a check also was made using the national cemetery database. This shows that he was a veteran who served in the Navy.

www.findagrave.com
Click on 3.8 million non-famous graves. Search by name or by cemetery.

www.interment.net
Listed under the United States and then by state

The VA cemetery listings do not contain military serial numbers or Social Security numbers. Searches have to be made based on name only, or name and date of birth. By matching the two databases, you have quite a bit of information: name, Social Security number, state the Social Security number was issued from, date of birth, date of death, last known residence, branch of service, rank or rating and place of burial. Dates of service are missing and may be obtained from either the VA directly or the cemetery.

State death databases also can provide more information about a deceased person. But, again, it does *not* indicate if the decedent is a veteran. Not every state has a separate state death index but some states such as California, Texas and Illinois have more information than that available on the Social Security Death Index.

Information from the California Death Index:
Leonard
Arnold
Dahlquist
SSN: 19716XXXX
Date of birth: 03/13/1926
Date of death: 09/20/1990
County resided in: San Diego
County died: San Diego
Mother's maiden name: Folk
Race: Caucasian
Place of birth: Pennsylvania

Now, we even have more information concerning this veteran, including where he was born, and his mother's maiden name.

State Death Indexes

Alabama. 1908–1959
www.ancestry.com Fee charged

California. 1940–1997
http://searches.rootsweb.com Free search

Connecticut. 1949–1996
www.ancestry.com Fee charged

Florida. 1936–1998
www.ancestry.com Fee charged

Georgia. 1919–1998
www.ancestry.com Fee charged

Illinois. 1916–1950
www.cyberdriveillinois.com/departments/archives/
databases.html   Free search

Kentucky. 1911–2000
http://ukcc.uky.edu/~vitalrec   Free search
http://searches.rootsweb.com   Free search

Maine. 1960–1997
http://searches.rootsweb.com   Free search

Minnesota. 1908–1966
http://people.mnhs.org/dci/Search.cfm   Free search

Michigan. 1971–1996
www.ancestry.com   Fee charged

Montana. 1989–1998
www.ancestry.com   Fee charged

North Carolina. 1968–1996
www.ancestry.com   Fee charged

Ohio. 1958–1991
www.ancestry.com   Fee charged

Oregon. 1903–1998
www.ancestry.com   Fee charged

Texas. 1964–1998
http://searches.rootsweb.com   Free search

Vermont. 1989–1996
www.ancestry.com   Fee charged

There are many county death index databases available. Because of the volume, it is not feasible to list them in this publication. If the name you're searching for isn't listed on the state index or if the county database may have more information, do a simple Internet search at *www.google.com* or www.*ask.com* for that specific county's death index.

Obituaries

An obituary for a deceased veteran may include information about his military service such as time period of service, rank and awards received. More recent obituaries are becoming available on the Internet either from the newspaper or from genealogical sites.

Chapter 7

LOCATING
VETERANS

A ctually finding someone that served with your relative is well worth the effort. But this can be quite a challenge. This section gives guidance on how to find a retired military member as well as veterans. Use the information provided from the unit or ship records that list others in the same unit at the same time period. Due to the advancing age of WWII veterans, the best method would be to start with the youngest of the groups. This may be the lower ranks such as private, private first class and the lower ranking Officers. Unfortunately, the older commanding Officers have since died. Even if a veteran has passed away, his spouse or children may have some information that may assist you in with your research.

Retired Military

A retired military member is a person who has completed 20 or more years of duty in any of the military components and is receiving retired pay (there are some exceptions to the 20–year service period). He may be retired from active duty or from a reserve component. A member of a reserve component is not eligible for retired pay until he reaches age 60. A military member may also retire from active duty for disability due to injury or illness, with less than 20 years of active service.

Each branch of the service except the Army has a Retired Locator. The armed forces Retired Locators will forward a letter to retired members. However, they are prohibited from releasing addresses. All branches also have retired pay centers that may forward a letter in the same manner as the Retired Locator. This includes anyone who retired from active duty, the reserve, or National Guard.

To use the Retired Locators, you must have enough information for the locator to identify the person being sought. Information could include the name (no nicknames), rank, Social Security number (not all require this), previous duty assignments, date of birth or age, date of retirement, etc. If you wish to have a letter forwarded, plce the letter in a seal,ed stamped envelope. Put your name and return address in the upper left–hand corner. In the center of the envelope, put the rank and the full name of the person you are trying to locate. Then write the available identifying information on a separate sheet of paper. Include everything known about the person so the locator can identify the correct person. Then place your letter in another larger envelope and address it to the appropriate Retired Locator. Don't forget to enclose the search fee. The check should be made payable to the U.S. Treasury unless it's for the Air Force.

Army

The army is no longer operating a retired locator. Try alternate sources for locating a retired Army veteran, such as the Department of Veterans Affairs (VA), veterans associations, the Defense Finance and Accounting Service (see below) or a private researcher.

Air Force

U.S. Air Force World–Wide Locator
AFPC–MSIMDL
550 "C" Street West, Suite 50
Randolph AFB, TX 78150-4752
($3.50 fee) Hours: 7:30 am to 4:30 pm, Central Time.
Make check payable to DAO–DE RAFB.

> Even though the Air Force did not exist during WWII, a person may have switched services after the Air Force was established.

Coast Guard

Coast Guard Human Resources Service & Information Center
444 SE Quincy Street
Topeka, KS 66683-3591
(785) 357-3415, (785) 295-2639 Fax
(No fee) Hours: 6:30 am to 5:00 pm, Central Time.

Marine Corps
HQ U.S. Marine Corps
Manpower & Reserve Affairs (MMSR-6)
3280 Russell Road
Quantico, VA 22134-5103
(703) 784-9310, (703) 784-9434 Fax
(No fee) Hours: 7:30 am to 4:30 pm, Eastern Time.

Navy
Commanding Officer
Naval Reserve Personnel Center
4400 Dauphine Street
New Orleans, LA 70149-7800
(504) 678-5400, (800) 535-2699, (504) 678-6934 Fax
($3.50 fee, made payable to U.S. Treasurer)
Hours: 7:00 am to 3:30 pm, Central Time.
*Do not put return address on letter to be forwarded.

Defense Finance and Accounting Services

The Defense Finance and Accounting Office maintains files of all retired military members (active duty, reserve and National Guard), and Survivor Benefit Plan annuitants (widows, widowers and some dependent children.) They will forward a letter in a manner similar to that of the retired locators. Identifying information is necessary to locate the right person, such as name, date of birth or Social Security number. No fees charged.

Air Force, Army, Marine Corps & Navy Retired Military
Defense Finance and Accounting Services
PO Box 99191
Cleveland, OH 44199-1126
(800) 321-1080, (216) 522-5955, (800) 469-6559 Fax

Air Force, Army, Marine Corps & Navy Retired Military

(Survivor Benefit Plan Annuitants)
Defense Finance and Accounting Services
6760 E Irvington Place
Denver, CO 80279-6000
(800) 435-3396, (303) 676-6552, (800) 982-8459 Fax

Coast Guard Retired Military

Human Resources and Information Center
Retiree and Annuitant Services
444 S.E. Quincy Street
Topeka, KS 66683-3591
(800) 772-8724, (785) 295-2639 Fax

Armed Forces Retirement Homes

There are two military retirement homes: the U.S. Naval Home and the U.S. Soldier's and Airmen's Home. A person must either be retired or have met the military requirements to reside in these two facilities.

U.S. Naval Home
1800 Beach Drive
Gulfport, MS 39507-1587
(800) 332-3527, (601) 228-4013 Fax
www.afrh.com
500 residents

U.S. Soldier's and Airmen's Home
3700 N. Capitol Street, N.W.
Washington, DC 20317-0001
(800) 422-9988, (202) 722-3492 Fax
www.afrh.com
1,000 residents

Retirement Service Officers

Retirement Service Officers handle retirement affairs for military installations. They usually have a mailing list of the retired military that are living in their surrounding area. It's the Officer's job to notify retirees of upcoming events, and give them updates on retiree issues. Some may send out newsletters. The Army has paid staff retirement service Officers for most of the large Army installations in the United States and overseas. Other branches have volunteers that handle these duties. Contact the retirement service officer in the area that you believe the military member retired. Because of privacy issues, they only will forward a letter.

Locating Veterans

A veteran is a person who, at one time, served on active duty in one or more branches of the armed forces. During WWII, the vast majority of those who served fall under this category.

The Department of Veterans Affairs

The Department of Veterans Affairs is normally cooperative in providing assistance in locating veterans. But be aware that privacy laws apply and counselors are not allowed to give out addresses and information over the telephone. They will forward a letter to a veteran, if they can identify the person in their files and if they have a current address. They can release report of death if the veteran is deceased. When a person dies, they no longer have the right to privacy and therefore information such as date of death, place of burial, branch of service and dates of service can be released to the public. They will not release a Social Security number. They should be able to release a military serial number, since that is not protected under the privacy act.

You must supply enough information to the Department of Veterans Affairs office so that they can identify the right person. This can be name only (if unique), name and serial number, name and date of birth or name and Social Security number. To have a letter forwarded, place your their

correspondence in an unsealed, stamped envelope with a
return address. Put the veteran's name and (other
identifying information) on the front of the envelope. Next,
prepare a short fact sheet and state that you're requesting
that the VA forward this letter to the veteran indicated on
the sheet. Place the letter and fact sheet in a larger envelope
and mail to the nearest Department of Veterans Affairs
Regional Office. See Appendix A (State Records). If they are
unable to identify the veteran, they will return your letter.
This process may take several months.

> The Department of Veterans Affairs does not have ev-
> ery veteran listed in their computers, only those WWII–
> era veterans that at some time applied for benefits.

You may also try the Department of Veterans Affairs
Insurance Office.

Department of Veterans Affairs
PO Box 8079
Philadelphia, PA 19101
(800) 669-8477

Military Reunion Associations

A great source of information may come from the
reunion association for the division or ship that your relative
served with. They may have a master roll of all who were in
that outfit during the War. Since they have a reunion every
year or two, they actively search for people that were
assigned to their unit. They may have information on the
person or, if they are deceased, their date of death. Check
the military reunion databases on the Internet at
www.militaryusa.com, www.military.com, www.usmc.mil/
reunions (all branches). Check Appendix E (Military
Reunion Associations).

Military & Patriotic Organizations

Thousands of veterans and retired military maintain
membership in one or more military or patriotic
organizations. They will normally forward a letter to one of

members. Several have magazines and print a section entitled "In Search Of" as a means to find a veteran. Listed below are some of the largest of the organizations. Due to privacy, they will only forward a letter but check with the organization directly for their policy.

The American Legion
PO Box 1055
Indianapolis, IN 46206
(317) 630-1200
www.legion.org

American Veterans of WWII, Korea and Vietnam
AMVETS
4647 Forbes Blvd
Lanham, MD 20706-4380
www.amvets.org

Association of the United States Army
2425 Wilson Blvd.
Arlington, VA 22201
(800) 336-4570, (703) 841-4300
www.ausa.org

Disabled American Veterans
PO Box 14301
Cincinnati, OH 45250-0301
(606) 441-7300
www.dav.org

Association of Graduates of the U.S. Military Academy
West Point, NY 10996-1611
(914) 938-4600
www.aog.usma.edu

Non–Commissioned Officers Association
10635 IH 35 North
San Antonio, TX 78233
(210) 653-6161
www.ncoausa.org

The Retired Officer's Association
201 N. Washington Street
Alexandria, VA 22314-2539
(703) 549-2311
www.troa.org

U.S. Naval Academy Alumni Assn
247 King George St
Annapolis, MD 21402-5068
www.usna.com

U.S. Coast Guard Alumni Services
U.S. Coast Guard Academy
47 Mohegan Avenue
New London, CT 06320-8111
(860) 444-8237
www.uscgaaa.onlinecommunity.com

Veterans of Foreign Wars
406 West 34th Street
Kansas City, MO 64111
(816) 756-3390
www.vfw.org

Women in Military Service for America Memorial
Foundation, Inc.
Dept. 560
Washington, DC 20042-0560
(800) 222-2294, (703) 533-1155
http://womensmemorial.org
Lists maiden name and hometown of women veterans.

Internet Sources for Locating Veterans
www.hullnumber.org
This is a site dedicated to help veterans keep in touch. It includes a listing by name of vessel and then has a ship's log listing by the year the person was aboard, rank or rating, first name, last name, hometown and state, and e-mail address.

www.military.com
Military.com is one of the largest websites for the military and veteran community. Search by veteran's name or by list of units or ships.

Private Researchers
There are many private investigators or private researchers that handle military or veterans cases. Check with them directly before paying any fees and find out if they offer a guarantee on finding the right person. You may want to check death records first due to the age of the WWII veterans. See Chapter Six (Veteran's Death Records).

Military Information Ent, Inc.
PO Box 17118
Spartanburg, SC 29301
(800) 937-2133
www.militaryusa.com

U.S. Locator Service
PO Box 140194
St. Louis, MO 63114-0194
(314) 423-0860 Phone/Fax
uslocator@earthlink.net

For more information about locating veterans please refer to *How To Locate Anyone Who Is or Has Been in the Military: Armed Forces Locator Guide.*

Story

Some time ago, I received a letter from the daughter of a recently deceased WWII soldier. After her father's death, she was going through his belongings when she stumbled upon his box of mementos from his WWII military service. She found his WWII Victory Medal, copy of his discharge certificate and an old photograph of two men in uniform. She recognized one of the men in the photo as her father but didn't know who the other person was. In the very bottom of the box was an item with a name and some other information. It was a dog tag that belonged to another soldier, not her father's. It listed his name and serial number.

Since her father never spoke about his military service, she had no idea who this person could be. She wondered if the photograph of the unknown soldier and the dog tag could be the same person, maybe a good friend of her father's during the war. She began her search by contacting the Department of Veterans Affairs. They informed her that they did not have a report of death and could forward a letter to the veteran. This took several months; but proved to be the right avenue. After receiving her letter, he quickly contacted the daughter of his war-time buddy. He confirmed that they were good friends and he was the other person in the photograph taken on leave during their time in Italy. He answered many questions about her father's service during the war.

PRESERVING THE PAST

N ow that your work is completed, take advantage of the avenues available to preserve the work that has been done. Do your best to make sure that your relative's service is not forgotten! There are many avenues and sources to keep memories alive. Many companies specialize in military memorabilia such as military insignia, medal replacement and cases, photograph restoration, and even offer reproductions of WWII era uniforms.

Museums or memorials spend time and resources to find those that served in a particular unit, ship, battle or campaign and would value information from a family member. If your relative participated in D-Day, make sure that the D-Day Foundation has his information. For female veterans, contact the Women in Military Service for America. Many states now have a separate WWII Memorial either completed or in progress.

Here are some of the programs and resources that should be contacted. If there is a military museum that may have some interest in your relative's service or copy of an award, contact the museum historian. Check Appendix C (Military Museums) for specialized museums. State archives or university libraries may also have an interest in receiving copies of a veteran's WWII military history.

WWII Memorial
National World War II Memorial
2300 Clarendon Boulevard, Suite 501
Arlington, VA 22201
(800) 639-4WW2
www.wwiimemorial.com

The World War II Registry of Remembrances allows families or veterans to register a veteran who served. Once completed, it will allow for searches either online or at the memorial. All branches of the military as well as civilians may register.

U.S. Navy Memorial Foundation
www.lonesailor.org
The Navy Log commemorates veterans of Naval service.
The log includes the veteran's name, branch of service, rate
or rank, dates of service, date and place of birth, duty
stations, awards and a photograph. The Navy log is
available at the foundation or online.

Quartermaster Roll Call, Quartermaster Museum
OQMG USA Quartermaster Center
1201 22nd Street
Fort Lee, VA 23801-1601
www.qmfound.com/rollcall.htm
Lists the past and present men and women who served
or are serving in the quartermaster corps. It is available only
in the Quartermaster Museum at Ft. Lee, Virginia. Donation
is required.

Department of the Army
U.S. Army Military History Institute
Carlisle Barracks, PA 17013-5008
http://carlisle-www.army.mil/usamhi/index.html
Provides questionnaires for veterans of WWII to fill out
and submit.

Women In Military Service for America Memorial
Dept. 560
Washington, DC 20042-0560
(800) 222-2294
www.womensmemorial.org
Lists women of all eras that served in the military;
includes female veterans' maiden name and hometown.

National D-Day Memorial Foundation
PO Box 77
Bedford, VA 24523
(800) 351-DDAY
Project goal is to list all those who participated in the D-Day campaign.

Airborne & Special Operations Roll Call
Airborne & Special Operations Museum
PO Box 89
Fayetteville, NC 28302-0089
(910) 483-3003
www.asomf.org/rollcall/index.htm
Registers veterans of Airborne and Special Operations. Roll Call database is available online.

Preserving Your Research

Now that you have completed your research, make sure to preserve it for future generations. Some examples of preservation might include:
• Obtaining all of the medals and having the medals encased in a frame
• Putting together a scrapbook of items from a relative's military service
• Storing photographs and documents on a CD-Rom program
• Building a web page dedicated to the veteran's service
• Framing important items from their military service: flight jacket, helmet or boots.

WWII Military Reproductions

Part of the preservation/memorial may include obtaining the medals and having them framed. You might like to frame a specific medal with a copy of the citation, obtain a replica of a flight jacket, boots or hat, or incorporate the military insignia in a scrapbook or digital photo album. Here are some sources for WWII military memorabilia.

Military Insignia
H J Saunders
US Military Insignia
5025 Tamiami Trail East
Naples, FL 34113-4126
(941) 775-2100
www.saundersinsignia.com

Medals & Display Cases
Medals of America
114 Southchase Boulevard
Fountain Inn, SC 29644
(800) 308-0849
www.usmedals.com

WWII Military Uniforms
World War Two Impressions
11814 Woodruff Avenue
Downey, CA 90241
(562) 803-6080. (562) 803-8812 Fax
www.wwiiimpressions.com

Dogtags
http://web.ndak.net/~colt45

Scrapbooks and Albums
Scrapbooking has become a popular trend in recent years. Military scrapbooks provide a wonderful place to display your research. Many styles and accessories are available for military–only books. Scrapbooks are available with the branch of service engraved on the outside with impressive branch insignia, or simply use the color of the branch such as Navy Blue.
www.memoriesinuniform.com

Digital Scrapbooks
Create a digital scrapbook on computer or CD. Create for a web page or copy the CD for all family members.

Postscript

I have enjoyed this enormous research project, which has taken more than three years to complete. It is my sincere hope that I have supplied you with a comprehensive and valuable tool to begin your search into the past, allowing you to take a glimpse into the life of a WWII veteran that served to protect our freedom, family and way of life.

—Debra Johnson Knox

STATE RECORDS

This section of the book describes the detailed records held by each state. State records are an important source for additional information pertaining to a veteran's military service during WWII. State held records might be an alternate source:

- if federal military records were destroyed in the NPRC fire
- for a veteran's military serial number
- for additional information on a WWII casualty
- to obtain National Guard personnel records

State Archives

This state office may have records pertaining to individuals who served in WWII from their state. The archives may be the repository for records from the state Veterans Affairs office or the state Adjutant General, which may have WWII bonus records or National Guard records. In some states, records held by the archives submitted by these agencies are still restricted and only available to family members, while other states provide full access.

State Library or University Library

In many states the state library houses historical data concerning WWII as well as newspaper holdings for those years. The service record books may be found at most state libraries along with the casualty books for the War Department and the Navy Department. Large university libraries that are also federal depository libraries can be an additional source for personal papers, military publications and county service books. University libraries may also be a source for officer registers published during WWII.

State Historical and Genealogical Societies

The historical/genealogical societies may have additional resources for military service history such as county records. Although I tried to list as many of the county books as possible there are some that are not cataloged in libraries and may only be available from county historical and genealogical societies.

State Adjutant General

This top state military office usually maintains records for National Guard personnel, before being called to federal service in 1940. Some maintain discharge records for veterans from their state. These records are not public and are protected under the Privacy Act. Therefore, all requests have to come from the veteran, if living, or if the veteran is deceased, the next of kin is entitled. They require proof of death and proof of relationship with all requests.

State Department of Veterans Affairs

The majority of state VA offices do not maintain records. But this varies by state. Records maintained by state agencies are protected under the Privacy Act.

Department of Veterans Affairs

This office is a federal agency, which has at least one regional office per state. The VA may have additional information concerning a WWII veteran and should not be overlooked as a source.

Alabama

WWII Bonus Records: NO

Alabama Department of Archives and History
PO Box 300100
624 Washington Avenue
Montgomery, AL 36130-0100
(334) 242-4435
www.archives.state.al.us
Click on "For Genealogists and Historians" and then click
on "Military Records"

US Marine Corps Releases from Alabama.
   Contains press releases from the US Marine Corps about
Alabama Marines. This series is not a complete list, but has
only 3 folders.

NEWS
OF THE
UNITED STATES MARINES

DISTRIBUTED BY:
PUBLIC RELATIONS SECTION
U. S. MARINE CORPS
SOUTHERN PROCUREMENT DIVISION
ATLANTA NATIONAL BUILDING
50 WHITEHALL STREET
ATLANTA 3, GA.

Marine Corps Base, San Diego, California, April OO......
   Heavily-ladened Marine Private First Class William W.
Gray, Munford, Alabama, who saw the Okinawa campaign through
the turrent-slits of an amphibious tractor, recently arrived
at San Diego on the USS WAKEFIELD, bound for processing here
prior to discharge from the Marine Corps.
   Veteran of the Okinawa campaign with the 9th Amphibious
Tractor Battalion, Gray's service to the Marine Corps has been
in keeping with it's highest traditions.
   Pfc. Gray enlisted in the Marine Corps September 1,
1943, at Birmingham, Alabama and left for overseas duty in
October, 1944. After six months of training on Guadalcanal,
he landed on Okinawa Easter Day, April 1, 1945. Grey spent
82 days on the blood-soaked island. After another 10 months
on Guam, he returned to the United States.
   Pfc. Gray is the son of Mrs. Charlice and the Reverand
Hudson A. Gray of the Methodist Church in Munford, A labama.

*US Marine Press Releases from Alabama. Alabama Department of Archives and
History, Montgomery, Alabama.*

WWII Dental Military.

The Alabama Dental Association compiled a book in 1947 listing the military service of Alabama dentists who served during WWII.

Military Absentee Ballots 1942–1944.

Montgomery county only. Information includes military member's name, military address, hometown and precinct. Ballots were only sent to personnel who requested them.

World War II Honor List of Dead and Missing Army and Army Air Forces Personnel. State of Alabama, War Department, 1946.

Auburn University Libraries
231 Mell Street
Auburn University, AL 36849-5606
(334) 844-1738
www.lib.auburn.edu

Service Record Book of Men and Women of Eufaula, Alabama, and Community, VFW Post 5850, 194?

World War II Bullock County Veterans: The War Years, 1941–1945, Union Springs, AL, 1996.

The Valley in World War II, Lanett Bleachery and Dye Works, 1947.

Limestone County during World War II, Limestone County Historical Society, 1983.

Alabama Historical Association
PO Box 870380
Tuscaloosa, AL 35487-0380
www.archives.state.al.us/aha/aha.html

Alabama Genealogical Society
800 Lakeshore Drive
Birmingham, AL 35229
(205) 870-2749

The Adjutant General of Alabama
State Military Department
ATTN: Retired Records
PO Box 3711
Montgomery, AL 36109-0711
(334) 271-7200, (334) 213-7703 Fax

National Guard records for WWII. Request records by full
name and military serial number. The privacy act does
apply.

State Department of Veterans Affairs
PO Box 1509
Montgomery, AL 36102
(334) 242-5077, (334) 242-5102 Fax

The state of Alabama has the majority of discharge
certificates for WWII veterans. Please supply name, date of
birth, military serial number, branch of service, dates of
service (if known). Privacy issues apply.

Veterans Affairs Regional Office
345 Perry Hill Rd
Montgomery, AL 36109
(800) 827-1000

Alaska

WWII Bonus Records: NO

State of Alaska
Alaska State Archives
141 Willoughby Ave
Juneau, AK 99801
(907) 465-2270, (907) 465-2465 Fax
www.archives.state.ak.us

Territorial Governor's Correspondence File 1934–1954.
   Miscellaneous information pertaining to the war such as
telegrams, reports and newspaper articles. Contains lists of
casualties with newspapers clippings.

Alaska Historical Collections, Alaska State Library
PO Box 110571
Juneau, AK 99811-0571
(907) 465-2925, (907) 465-2990 Fax
www.library.state.ak.us/hist/hist.html

Newspapers for WWII years.

University of Alaska Fairbanks
Elmer E Rasmuson Library
310 Tanana Drive
Fairbanks, AK 99775-6800
(907) 474-7224
www.uaf.edu

STATE GROUP **16** { IDAHO / OREGON / WASHINGTON / ALASKA

MORNING NEWSPAPERS
HOLD FOR RELEASE
Not for use by press or radio before

OWI Serial No. 115
Navy No. 424

PAGE 1   7 PM, EWT, WEDNESDAY, JULY 25, 1945

Navy War Casualties Report

It is requested that all communications concerning change of status in casualty lists be addressed directly to the Office of Public Information, Navy Department, Washington 25, D. C.

All these reports are based on prior notification to next of kin. In case of divergence between this list and information sent to the next of kin, the last Navy Department telegram or letter to the next of kin is always the appropriate final authority.

NOTE TO EDITORS: The Navy Department states that there will be a temporary lapse of several days between this and its next casualty report. This means that for a brief period you will receive no report from OWI. Resumption of reports will make proper allowance in scheduled release dates. The next report will carry OWI Serial No. 116.

TOTAL NAVAL CASUALTIES TO JULY 25, 1945

The Navy Department announces for the United States as a whole 1,010 casualties for July 25, 1945, of the U. S. Naval Forces (Navy, Marine Corps, and Coast Guard) not heretofore released on Navy Department total casualty lists, consisting of 602 dead, 391 wounded, and 17 missing. These casualties bring the total reported to next of kin and released for publication since December 7, 1941, to July 25, 1945, to 138,822, classified as follows:

	Dead	Wounded	Missing	Prisoners of War	Totals
United States Navy	31,317	22,704	10,666	2,039	66,588
United States Marine Corps	19,094	49,069	918	1,720	70,816
United States Coast Guard	908	212	95		1,116
Total casualties	51,319	72,066	11,978	3,759	138,622

IDAHO

NAVY DEAD

ALMOND, William Francis, Pharmacist's mate 3c, USNR. Sister, Mrs. Theda Almond Zollinger, Sublett.

FERRIN, Floyd Thaddeus, Pvt., USMCR. Parents, Mr. and Mrs. Clovis Ferrin, Acequia.

GARDNER, Stephen Junior, Pvt., USMC. Parents, Mr. and Mrs. Steve J. Gardner, Sugar City.

JONES, Arvill Lamar, Pvt., USMCR. Parents, Mr. and Mrs. David M. Jones, Rigby.

PINKSTON, John Perry, Pvt., USMC. Parents, Mr. and Mrs. Perry P. Pinkston, Orofino.

NAVY WOUNDED

LEWIS, Garth Arthur, Lt. (jg), USNR. Parents, Mr. and Mrs. George A. Lewis, 175 E. 18th St., Idaho Falls.

WALKER, James Oliver, Sgt., USMCR. Mother, Mrs. Amy Walker, Idaho Falls.

WEITZEL, Douglas George, Pfc., USMCR. Parents, Mr. and Mrs. George Weitzel, Weiser.

OREGON

NAVY DEAD

GARY, Marvin Lee, Aviation machinist's mate 3c, USNR. (Previously reported missing.) Parents, Mr. and Mrs. John Wood Gary, 1123 NE. Couch, Portland.

HANDSHUH, Harold Leo, Ensign, USNR. (Previously reported missing.) Wife, Mrs. Virginia Grass Handshuh, 6836 N. Atlantic Ave., Portland.

JONES, Lloyd Merle, Cpl., USMCR. Father, Chasius A. Jones, Oakridge.

LEONARD, James Gordon, Lt., USNR. (Previously reported missing.) Mother, Mrs. Martha Leonard, Island City.

MEYERS, Harold Charles, Pfc., USMC. Mother, Mrs. Creta G. Meyers, 2055 Everett St., Portland.

ROGERS, John Duane, Cpl., USMCR. Father, John K. Rogers, 905 NE. 44th Ave., Portland.

SAUER, Paul John, Pvt., USMCR. Parents, Mr. and Mrs. Alvin A. Sauer, 4413 Freida St., Klamath Falls.

SMITH, Gerald Eugene, Cpl., USMCR. Wife, Mrs. Eleanor W. Smith, 1710 NE. Tillamook, Portland.

WELLS, Earl Huston, Pvt., USMCR. Wife, Mrs. Augusta M. Wells, c/o Horst Co., Independence.

WILLIAMS, John Harold, Cpl., USMCR. Parents, Mr. and Mrs. Thomas J. Williams, 601 N. Knott St., Portland.

NAVY WOUNDED

JOHNSON, Reuben Clarence, Pharmacist's mate 3c, USNR. Parents, Mr. and Mrs. John O. Johnson, Carlton.

SEMMLER, Clifford Martin, Pfc., USMCR. Parents, Mr. and Mrs. George H. Semmler, 3241 NE. 73d Ave., Portland.

TERNYIK, Wilbur Earl, Pvt., USMCR. Mother, Mrs. Adella B. Brown, Warrenton.

WOLFE, Harold William, Pfc., USMCR. Parents, Mr. and Mrs. Ervin M. Wolfe, Blachly.

WASHINGTON

NAVY DEAD

BARNESS, Maynard Cleon, Cpl., USMCR. Father, Melvin Barness, Nord Hotel, 212 S. 1st St., Seattle.

GLENN, Robert Theodore, Pvt., USMC. Parents, Mr. and Mrs. Harry D. Glenn, 9350 55th Ave. S., Seattle.

LUCENFIE, Louis Michael, Pfc., USMC. Wife, Mrs. Helen M. Lucente, 2923 E. Wabash St., Spokane.

MARTENS, Bernard Wesley, Aviation ordnanceman 3c, USNR. (Previously reported missing.) Parents, Mr. and Mrs. Lisle Bernard Martens, 2226 W. 99th, Seattle.

MITCHELL, Bruce Allen, Pvt., USMC. Mother, Mrs. Isabel Westgarth, 2322 Hallack Ave., Seattle.

MITCHELL, Loren LeRoy, Pvt., USMC. Mother, Mrs. Ellis Mitchell, 2105 W. 4th St., Spokane.

NIELSEN, Roy Gerhardt, Pvt., USMCR. Mother, Mrs. Hildur Nielsen, 4101 Greenwood Ave., Seattle.

RAYMOND, George Glenn, Pfc., USMCR. Wife, Mrs. June M. Raymond, 1230 157th SW., Seattle.

STROWBRIDGE, Clarence John, Pvt., USMC. Wife, Mrs. Viola J. Strowbridge, 3435 Pacific Way, Longview.

TAYLOR, Kenneth R. C., Pvt., USMC. Father, Charles J. Taylor, 4072 26th Ave. SW., Seattle.

NAVY WOUNDED

PAINTER, Brian Edward, Pfc., USMC. Parents, Mr. and Mrs. Edward Painter, E. 208 Liberty Ave., Spokane.

ROOT, Robert R., Pvt., USMCR. Mrs. Tressa Maine, Newport.

RUBLE, William Ray, Pfc., USMC. Mother, Mrs. Georgia M. Ruble, Prescott.

SCHIMMER, Marland Paul, Pfc., USMC. Parents, Mr. and Mrs. Paul Schimmer, 9300 E. Marginal Way, Seattle.

SEAL, Ernest Howard, Jr., Pvt., USMCR. Parents, Mr. and Mrs. Ernest H. Seal, Sr., 4652 Sunnyside, Seattle.

WALLACE, Ralph Raymond, Pfc., USMCR. Wife, Mrs. Ethel M. Wallace, 1720 W. Augusta Ave., Spokane.

WILSON, Milton Hubbard, Sgt., USMCR. Wife, Mrs. Rae M. Wilson, 1125 N. 77th St., Seattle.

WOLF, Philip Richard, Pfc., USMCR. Parents, Mr. and Mrs. Christopher C. Wolf, Pomeroy.

NAVY MISSING

LA GROW, Merle Donald, Jr., Pfc., USMCR. Parents, Mr. and Mrs. Merle N. La Grow, Prosser.

ALASKA

NAVY DEAD

JONES, Otis Clark, Pfc., USMCR. Mother, Mrs. LaRee C. Arend, Fairbanks.

NOTE TO EDITORS.—If you have a question relating to failure to receive a casualty list on time, or if you lose it, wire or write to the Office of War Information, Casualty Division, Room 9260, Social Security Building, Washington 25, D. C. Inquiry concerning individual names of casualties should be sent directly to the Office of Public Information, Navy Department, Washington 25, D. C. No back copies of these lists will be available, but a master list will be maintained by the Office of War Information, Washington 25, D. C.

US Navy Casualties Report, July 25, 1945, Territorial Governor's Correspondence File. Courtesy of Alaska State Archives.

The World War II Black Regiment that built the Alaska Military Highway: A Photographic History, Griggs, William E.

The Capture of Attu: A WWII Battle as told by the Men that fought there. By Mitchell, Robert J.

Kodiak Military History Museum
1623 Mill Bay Road
Kodiak, AK 99615
(907) 486-7015, (907) 486-5541 Fax
www.kadiak.org

Alaska Historical Society
PO Box 100299
Anchorage, AK 99510
(907) 276-1596
www.alaskahistoricalsociety.org

Alaska Genealogical Society
7030 Dickerson Drive
Anchorage, AK 99504

Alaska Department of Military & Veterans Affairs
PO Box 5800
Ft Richardson, AK 99505-0800
(907) 428-6030

300 served from the territory of Alaska during WWII. Check with their office for information concerning WWII veterans from Alaska.

Veterans Affairs Regional Office
2925 DeBarr Road
Anchorage, AK 99508-2989
(800) 827-1000

Alaska was an American territory during WWII. Some documents will be under the state territories section, such as the WWII casualty books for the War Department and the Navy Department.

Arizona

WWII Bonus Records: NO

Department of Library, Archives and Public Records
History and Archives Division
1700 West Washington, 3ʳᵈ Floor
Phoenix, AZ 85007
(602) 542-4159, (602) 542-4402 Fax
www.dlapr.lib.az.us

Discharge certificates for WWII veterans for Yuma County only. This file is not a complete list of veterans.

Obituary Index.
    This includes some WWII veterans that died during the war. The obituary is listed only if someone submitted it.

World War II Honor List of Dead and Missing Army and Army Air Forces Personnel. State of Arizona, War Department, 1946.

Newspapers for WWII years.

Arizona State University Libraries
Box 871006
Tempe AZ 85287-1006
(480) 965-6164
www.asu.edu/lib/hayden

Tucsonans who Died in Military Service during World War II, William Bigglestone, 1994.

Arizona Historical Society
949 East Second Street
Tucson, AZ 85719
(602) 628-5774
www.ahs.state.az.us

Arizona State Genealogical Society
PO Box 42075
Tucson, AZ 85733-2075
(520) 275-2747
www.rootsweb.com/~asgs

The Adjutant General of Arizona
5636 East McDowell Road
Phoenix, AZ 85008-3495
(602) 267-2710, (602) 267-2715 Fax

National Guard records for WWII. Submit request giving
the veteran's name and serial number.

Arizona Department of Veterans' Services
3225 North Central Avenue, #910
Phoenix, AZ 85012
(602) 255-3373

No WWII records.

Veterans Affairs Regional Office
3225 N Central Avenue
Phoenix, AZ 85012
(800) 827-1000

Arkansas

WWII Bonus Records: NO

Arkansas History Commission
One Capitol Mall
Little Rock, AR 72201
(501) 682-6900
www.ark-ives.com

Arkansas National Guard Personnel Reocrds, 1920–1958.
   Individual National Guard records. Include the vetean's
name, serial number and time period of discharge to
request records.

The only records specifically dealing with WWII are newspapers holdings. The newspapers are not indexed and have to be searched in person. If an article is listed in the newspaper it may have a photograph. Information contained in the newspapers include enlistments, discharges, casualty notices, awards and obituaries.

The *Arkansas Legionnaire* published by the American Legion contain enlistments.

Fighting Men of Arkansas–1946.
   Biographies of Arkansas servicemen. Names of servicemen who were included by their families. Contains over 1,000 pages.

Men and Women in the Armed Forces from Drew County.
   Biographies of Drew County, Arkansas servicemen and women. Includes the veteran's name, rank, next of kin, schools attended, military serivce, awards, photograph, if casualty lists date of death and place of casualty.

University of Arkansas Libraries
365 N Ozark Avenue
Fayetteville, AR 72701-4002
(479) 575-4101
http://libinfo.uark.edu

We Were There: Clark Countians in World War II, Clark County Historical Assn, 1995.

State Summary of War Casualties from World War II for Navy, Marine Corps, and Coast Guard Personnel from Arkansas. Navy Department, 1946.

Arkansas National Guard Museum
Camp J T Robinson
N Little Rock, AR 72118
(501) 212-5215
www.arngmuseum.com

Muster rolls of National Guard units from Arkansas that were activated during WWII. Includes name, rank and serial number.

Arkansas Genealogical Society
PO Box 908
Hot Springs, AR 71902-0908
www.rootsweb.com/~args

The Adjutant General of Arkansas
Camp J T Robinson
N Little Rock, AR 72118-2200
(501) 212-4014

Records for WWII National Guard turned over to the History Commission.

Arkansas Department of Veterans' Affairs
PO Box 1280
North Little Rock, AR 72115
(501) 370-3820

No WWII records.

Veterans Affairs Regional Office
PO Box 1280
Little Rock, AR 72115
(800) 827-1000

California

WWII Bonus Records: NO

California State Archives
1020 O Street
Sacramento, CA 95814
(916) 653-7715
www.ss.ca.gov/archives/archives_e.htm

Has only records pertaining to the California State Militia and National Guard up to 1941. Records are organized by unit.

Newspapers for WWII years.

San Francisco Public Library
100 Larkin Street (at Grove)
San Francisco, CA 94102-4733
(415) 557-4400
http://sfpl.lib.ca.us

San Francisco Roll of Honor, World War II.
    San Francisco News, Printed at the Grabhorn Press, 1942.
Handwritten. Contains list of all San Francisco residents
that served in Army, Navy, Marine, Air Force, Merchant
Marines, and Coast Guard. Lists the person's name, branch
of service, name of parents, wife or husband, and address.
Stars by names of those who died, lists where they were
killed.

Naval Non-Combat Dead, World War II, Navy Department, 1946.

Combat Connected Naval Casualties, World War II, Navy
Department, 1946.

*World War II Honor List of Dead and Missing Army and
Army Air Forces Personnel. State of California,* War
Department, 1946.

Los Angeles Public Library
630 West 5th Street
Los Angeles, CA 90071
(213) 228-7000
www.lapl.org

*Honor roll of the husbands, sons, daughters, son-in-law,
daughters-in-law, brothers, sisters, nephews, nieces of the
California members of the Daughters of the American
Revolution.* DAR, California State Society, 1946. Contain
listing of WWII veterans from California.

*State Summary of War Casualties from World War II for
Navy, Marine Corps, and Coast Guard Personnel from
California,* Navy Department, 1946.

Roster of Officers and Enlisted men, 84th Infantry Division, European Theatre of Operations, World War II, Viking Press, 1946.

Roster 35th Infantry Division, POE to POE, 1945.

Roster of the 44th Infantry Division,
    September 4, 1944–July 20, 1945.

Wilson Men: Service Records, World War II, Woodrow Wilson High School, 1949. (Available from the Woodrow Wilson High School or from the Wisconsin Historical Society Library, *www.wisconsinhistory.org*)

California Historical Society
678 Mission Street
San Francisco, CA 94105
(415) 357-1848
www.californiahistoricalsociety.org

California Genealogical Society
1611 Telegraph Avenue, Suite 100
Oakland, CA 94612-2154
(510) 663-1358
www.calgensoc.org

The Adjutant General of California
9800 S Goethe Road
Sacramento, CA 95826-9101
(916) 854-3500, (916) 854-3671 Fax

National Guard records.
    Submit a SF 180 when making a records request. California Military Benefit Index Cards 1940–1964. NPRC received a copy of these cards on microfiche and are labeled as "QTD." Some of the California records were destroyed by fire.

California Department of Veterans' Affairs
Veteran Services Division
1227 "O" Street, Suite 101
Sacramento, CA 95814
(916) 653-2573, (800) 952-5626

No WWII records.

Veterans Affairs Regional Office – Oakland
1301 Clay Street
Oakland, CA 94612
(800) 827-1000

Veterans Affairs Regional Office – Los Angeles
Federal Building
11000 Wilshire Blvd
Los Angeles, CA 90024
(800) 827-1000

Veterans Affairs Regional Office – San Diego
8810 Rio San Diego Drive
San Diego, CA 92108
(800) 827-1000

Colorado

WWII Bonus Records: NO

Colorado State Archives
Room 1-B20, 1313 Sherman Street
Denver, CO 80203
(303) 866-2358, (303) 866-2257 Fax
www.archives.state.co.us

Photographs and Surveys of Casualties from World War II
in Colorado.

In 1947 Colorado began a project to collect information
on the men who served in WWII from their state. It includes
photographs, survey sheets which lists information on the
veteran's family, military service history, education, employment, and circumstances of death. The index is on the
Internet: *www.archives.state.co.us/wwcod/wwIIdex.htm*

Julius W. Kraft, Identification Card Booklet, KIA, Courtesty Colorado State Archives, www.archives.state.co.us/wwcod/wwiihp.htm

World War II Honor List of Dead and Missing Army and Army Air Forces Personnel. State of Colorado, War Department, 1946.

Summary of War Casualties from World War II for Navy, Marine Corps, and Coast Guard Personnel from Colorado, Navy Department, 1946.

Colorado Historical Society
1300 Broadway
Denver, CO 80203-2137
(303) 866-2305
www.coloradohistory.org

The Fighting Men of Colorado, Byrnes, 1948.

Induction Roster, Colorado National Guard: World War no. II, 1940–1941, Office of the Adjutant General.

Colorado Genealogical Society
PO Box 9218
Denver, CO 80209-0218
(303) 571-1535
www.rootsweb.com/~cocgs

The Adjutant General of Colorado
6848 South Revere Parkway
Englewood, CO 80112-6703
(303) 677-8801, (303) 677-8811 Fax

National Guard personnel files for WWII.

Department of Military and Veterans Affairs
Division of Veterans Affairs Office
789 Sherman Street, #260
Denver, CO 80203
(303) 894-7474

If the veteran applied for benefits the office may have a record.

Veterans Affairs Regional Office
155 Van Gordon Street
Denver, CO 80225
(800) 827-1000

Connecticut

WWII Bonus Records: YES

Connecticut State Library
231 Capitol Ave
Hartford, CT 06106
(860) 757-6595, (860) 757-6542 Fax
www.cslib.org

The state of Connecticut paid a bonus to veterans of WWII. If a veteran applied for the bonus payment the Connecticut State Library has a copy of their discharge certificate. When requesting a bonus record give the veteran's name, branch of service, serial number and city of enlistment, if known. Since the records contain discharge certificates privacy issues apply. The records were put on microfilm and may be poor quality.

Veterans' Deaths Index: American Revolution–Vietnam.

Divided into three sections, Connecticut Veterans' Deaths–alphabetically by the veteran's last name. Connecticut Veterans' Burials–by town. Out of state Burials of Connecticut Veterans– Organized by war then by name.

Lists of WWII and Korean War Dead returned on Funeral Ships.

Gold Star Lists 1940–1945.

The family of the deceased veteran filled out a service record card. This group is organized by Connecticut town and includes name of the deceased, serial number, address, date of birth, place of birth, next of kin and relationship, address of next of kin, when and where entered the service, awards and decorations, branch and section of service, date and place casualty and cause of death. Information varies by card.

Card list of World War II dead, 1940–1945.

Includes name, address, age, rank, date and place of death, next of kin, and serial number.

World War II Honor Roll 1945–1946.

Photographs of plaques that listed names of veterans that served from a town. Casualties are also included on these plaques. The photograph of the plaque lists the veteran's name, town and possibly a rank. Arranged by town.

Service Records, 1940–1945.

Information available on this card collection includes name, address, next of kin and address, occupation and employer before entering the service, enlistment and discharge information, awards, assignments, promotions etc. Arranged by county and then by name of veteran. Not a complete list-only those that responded are included.

List of State Employees in Military Service.

Information on state employees that entered the military. Arranged by name and department.

Military Discharge Certificates, 1898–1956.

Discharge certificates for WWII and later years. Information contains name, address, school and military background. Listed alphabetically by last name. This is not a complete list. Check with the archives for privacy issues.

Photographs 1898–1950.

This photograph collection consists of five boxes for photograph from WWII servicemen. Arranged alphabetically by last name.

World War II Honor List of Dead and Missing Army and Army Air Forces Personnel. State of Connecticut, War Department, 1946.

State Summary of War Casualties from World War II for Navy, Marine Corps, and Coast Guard Personnel from Connecticut, Navy Department, 1946.

This History of the 304th Infantry, Brugel, 1946.

Unit photographs and listing of names of members with information on the commanding officers.

History of the Twelfth Infantry Regiment in World War II. Johnson, 1947.

Includes a list of all who served in the unit.

Yale Men who died in the Second World War: A Memorial Volume of Biographical Sketches, Yale University Press, 1951.

Bristol, Connecticut, in World War II, depicting the part played by our brave men and women who dedicated their services to their country, as well as the mobilization of our home life and industries in support of the war effort, 1939–1946, World War II Historical Committee, 1947.

World War II history of Manchester, Connecticut, Archie Kilpatrick, 1946.

New Canaan Library
151 Main Street
New Canaan, CT 06840
(203) 594-5000
http://newcanaanlibrary.org

New Canaan War Veterans Speak. War Records Committee
of the Town of New Canaan/New Canaan Historical Society,
1946–1951.

The Connecticut Historical Society
1 Elizabeth Street at Asylum Avenue
Hartford, CT 06105
(203) 236-5621, (203) 236-2664 Fax
www.chs.org

The Adjutant General of Connecticut
National Guard Armory
360 Broad Street
Hartford, CT 06105-3795
(860) 524-4953

National Guard records. Request should include the
veteran's name, service number and date of birth.

Department of Veterans' Affairs
287 West Street
Rocky Hill, CT 06067
(860) 529-2571

No WWII records.

Veterans Affairs Regional Office
450 Main Street
Hartford, CT 06103
(800) 827-1000

Delaware

WWII Bonus Records: YES

Delaware Public Archives
Hall of Records
121 Duke of York Street
Dover, DE 19901
(302) 744-5000
www.state.de.us/sos/dpa

WWII bonus records held by Delaware Public Archives are available to the veteran. If the veteran is deceased, contact the archives for releasable information. Discharge certificates are not public information and are restricted. The highest amount paid for the WWII bonus was $300.

WWII Bonus Records.

Cash bonus claims paid. 1949–1951.

Index to Paid and rejected claims for bonuses for WWII Veterans 1955–1958.

Applications for WWII bonus payments denied by the veterans military pay commission 1949–1951.

Separation and Discharge Papers 1941–1947.
These records were microfilmed and furnished to the National Personnel Records Center in St. Louis, Missouri. Access restricted.

Enlistment Cards 1941–1946.

Delaware Soldiers and Sailors in WWII.

WWII News Clippings, 1940–1947.

News Releases: 1946–1947

Fort DuPont *Flashes.* 1942–1943. Post newspapers published by Fort DuPont.

Delaware's Role in World War II, 1940–1946.
Book published by the archives detailing Delaware's participation in WWII. Contains rosters and biographical information.

Delaware's Role in World War II Photograph collection, 1940-1946. Photographs that were used in the publication *Delaware's Role in World War II.*

Memorial Volume, 1944–1949.
    Commemorative volume by the Public Archives Commission of Delawareans who died in WWII. Includes the veteran's name, rank, unit, residence, names of parents and spouse (if married), dates of service, and awards. Alphabetical by last name.

Record of Delawareans Who Died in WWII, 1944–1946.
    Information used for the Memorial Volume. A photograph may be available, if obtained. Alphabetical by last name.

Historical Society of Delaware
505 Market Street
Wilmington, DE 19801
(302) 655-7161
www.hsd.org

Delaware Genealogical Society
http://delgensoc.org

The Adjutant General of Delaware
First Regiment Road
Wilmington, DE 19808-2191
(302) 326-7001

Records turned over to the Archives.

Delaware Commission Of Veterans Affairs
PO Box 1401
Old State House - The Green
Dover, DE 19903
(302) 739-2792

This office maintains copies of discharge certificates for WWII veterans, if the veteran registered. Privacy issues apply to records. Provide name, branch of service, time period of service, serial number when requesting records.

Veterans Affairs Regional Office
1601 Kirkwood Highway
Wilmington, DE 19805
(800) 827-1000

☆ **BASTOGNE** ☆ **GERMANY** ☆ **PHILIPPINES** ☆

JOSEPH A. ACKERMAN, Aviation Cadet, U. S. Navy Air Corps, of 1320 West Street, Wilmington, Delaware, son of Ignatius A. and Anna L. Ackerman. Died September 4, 1945, in the U. S. Naval Hospital, Brooklyn, New York, of internal injuries received in a plane crash while on a training flight at Pensacola, Florida. He was an aerial photographer and served two years, four months.

ADAM STANLEY ADAMOWICZ, Private, U. S. Army, of 1031 West Second Street, Wilmington, Delaware, son of John and Teofila Adamowicz. Killed in action June 4, 1944, at Rocca Priord, Italy, while serving with Company B, 760th Tank Battalion of the Fifth Army. He served for one year, six months, and was decorated with a citation for the African Campaign in 1944 and awarded the Purple heart for wounds received at death.

JOHN ERNEST ADAMS, JR., Private First Class, U. S. Army, of Laurel, Delaware, son of John Ernest, Sr. and Bertha E. (Morris) Adams. Killed September 7, 1944, in the sinking of a Japanese Prison of War ship (freighter) while being transported from Bataan to Japan. He was taken prisoner in the capture of the Philippines in December of 1941 and served four years, two months.

LORAN CHARLES ADAMS, Technician Fourth Grade, U. S. Army, of R. D. 1, Felton, Delaware, son of Charles Cannon and Mamie (Still) Adams. Killed in action on June 2, 1944, in the battle around Cassino in the midst of the great drive for Rome, Italy, by a low-level German plane while excavating wounded with the Medical Detachment of the First Battalion, 339th Regiment of the 85th Division of the Fifth Army. He served for eleven months and was decorated with the European-African-Middle Eastern Campaign Ribbon with one bronze battle star, the Bronze Star Medal and the Purple Heart.

RALPH E. ADAMS, Private First Class, U. S. Army, of 95 South Chapel Street, Newark, Delaware, son of Lawrence E. and Lillian (Buckingham) Adams. Killed in action June 29, 1944, in an anti-tank assault with the Infantry in Normandy, France. He served nine months.

CHESTER ADKINS, Second Lieutenant, U. S. Army Air Corps, of Maple Street, Holly Oak, Delaware, son of George William and Jennie (Rankins) Adkins. Died from wounds received November 26, 1944, when his plane was shot down over Germany while serving with the 854th Squadron, 491st Group, Eighth Air Force, at Station AAF-143A. He served two years, one month, and received the Air Medal and Purple Heart.

☆ **SICILY** ☆ **CASSINO** ☆ **NORMANDY** ☆ **ANZIO** ☆

Delaware WWII Memorial Volume, Delaware State Archives

District of Columbia

WWII Bonus Records: NO

District of Columbia Archives
1300 Naylor Court
Washington, DC 20001-4225
(202) 671-1107 (archivist)
http://os.dc.gov/info/pubrec/pubrec.shtm

Historical Society of Washington DC
1307 New Hampshire Ave, NW
Washington, DC 20036-1507
(202) 785-2068
http://hswdc.org

The Library of Congress
101 Independence Ave, SE
Washington, DC 20540
(202) 707-5000
www.loc.gov

Veterans Affairs Regional Office
1120 Vermont Ave, NW
Washington, DC 20421
(800) 827-1000

The War Department and the Navy each printed a book for
the District of Columbia casualties of WWII. No information
on those who served from the District of Columbia.

Florida

WWII Bonus Records: NO

Florida State Archives
R A Gray Building
500 South Bronough Street
Tallahassee, FL 32399-0250
(850) 245-6700
http://dlis.dos.state.fl.us/barm/index.html

Soldiers and Sailors Discharges.
  Listed by county. Not all counties have these records.
Local records collection.

Florida Photograph Collection.
  Contains photographs from WWII.
http://fpc.dos.state.fl.us/memory

WWII Casualty Card Files.
  Lists Floridians who died during the war, were missing in
action or taken prisoner of war. Arranged by county and
then by last name.

Florida State Library
500 S Bronough Street
Tallahassee, FL 32399
(850) 245-6600
http://dlis.dos.state.fl.us/stlib

Patriots of Florida: World War 2, American Publishers, 19—.

*Roster of officers, warrant officers and enlisted men, active
and inactive national guard, inducted into active military
service: World War II with the national guard units.* Florida
National Guard alphabetical mobilization roster, 25
November 1940. (FSU)

Florida National Guard Killed or Died: World War II
biographical/service abstracts.

*World War II Honor List of Dead and Missing Army and
Army Air Forces. State of Florida,* War Department, 1946.

*State Summary of War Casualties from World War II for
Navy, Marine Corps, and Coast Guard Personnel. State of
Florida,* Navy Department, 1946.

Newspapers for WWII years.

The Florida Historical Society
1320 Highland Avenue
Melbourne, FL 32935
(321) 254-9855
www.florida-historical-soc.org

Florida State Genealogical Society, Inc.
PO Box 10249
Tallahassee, FL 32302-2249
www.rootsweb.com/~flsgs

The Adjutant General of Florida
PO Box 1008
St Augustine, FL 32085-1008
(904) 823-0100

National Guard records for WWII. For those who were
called to active duty their records may contain a discharge
certificate. Request records by full name, date of birth and
serial number (if known). The privacy act does apply.

Florida Dept of Veterans' Affairs
Mary Grizzle Bldg, Room 311-K
11351 Ulmerton Road
Largo, FL 33778-1630
www.floridavets.org

No WWII records.

Florida's World War II Memorial, *www.floridawwii.com*
According to the website approximately 248,000 Floridians
served during WWII.

Veterans Affairs Regional Office
144 First Avenue, South
St. Petersburg, FL 33701
(800) 827-1000

Georgia

WWII Bonus Records: NO

Georgia Department of Archives and History
5800 Jonesboro Road
Morrow, GA 30260-1101
(404) 656-2393, Reference (404) 656-2350
www.sos.state.ga.us/archives

Georgia Department of Defense. Special Orders to the Army
National Guard. 1941–1945. (22-1-21)
 Orders include resignations, promotions, discharges,
awards, commendations, the granting of leave, temporary
and permanent duty assignments and appointments to
service schools. Chronological.

National Guard Field Training and Morning Report Files.
 Attendance and activity reports for each company. Arranged by date of report and then by unit.

Military Discharges.
 Copies of discharge certificates that were filed by the
veteran at the county office. Arranged by county. Has very
good coverage for WWII discharges. Privacy act applies to
these records. Microfilmed records.

Private Papers Collection
 The private papers collection includes scrapbooks, photo-
graphs, letters, obituaries, etc. Of particular interest in the
WWII collection is the Cofer, Mrs. C. J. Scrapbooks and
Ball, Lamar Q family collections.

State Summary of War Casualties from World War II for
Navy, Marine Corps, and Coast Guard Personnel from
Georgia, Navy Department, 1946.

World War II Honor List of Dead and Missing Army and
Army Air Forces Personnel. State of Georgia, War
Department, 1946.

Georgia Historical Society
501 Whitaker Street
Savannah, GA 31401
(912) 651-2125
www.georgiahistory.com

Georgia Newspaper Project
University of Georgia Libraries
Athens, GA 30602-1641
(706) 542-2131
www.libs.uga.edu/gnp

Resource for Georgia newspaper holdings.

Georgia Genealogical Society
PO Box 54575
Atlanta, GA 30308-0575
www.gagensociety.org

The Adjutant General of Georgia
Georgia Department of Defense
PO Box 17965
Atlanta, GA 30316-0965
(404) 624-6001

No WWII records.

Georgia Department of Veteran Service
1700 Clairmont Road, NE
Decatur, GA 30033-4032
(404) 929-5345

No WWII records.

Veterans Affairs Regional Office
730 Peachtree Street NE
Atlanta, GA 30365
(800) 827-1000

Hawaii

WWII Bonus Records: YES*

Hawaii State Archives
Kekauluohi Building, Iolani Palace Grounds
Honolulu, HI 96813
(808) 586-0329, (808) 586-0330 Fax
http://kumu.icsd.hawaii.gov/dags/archives/welcome.html

Hawaii Holocaust Project
   Interviews with Holocaust survivors who live in Hawaii
and Hawaii veterans who participated in the liberation of
Dachua.

*Japanese Eyes, American heart: Personal Reflections of
Hawaii's World War II Nisei soldiers.* Brief history and
interviews.

Hawaii's War Records Depository
University of Hawaii at Manoa Library
2550 The Mall
Honolulu, HI 96822
(808) 956-8264, (808) 956-5968 Fax
*http://libweb.hawaii.edu/hwrd/HWRD_html/HWRD_
welcome.htm*

*In Freedom's Cause: A Record of the Men of Hawaii Who
Died in the Second World War,* University of Hawaii Press,
1949.
   Photographs and biographies of those who died from
Hawaii in WWII. Information includes name, date of birth,
serial number, date of death, cause of death and next of kin.

Aloha to Those who Served, U.S. Navy, 1941–1945, US Navy,
14th District, 1945.

Various books describing history of the major units from
Hawaii 100th and the 442nd. Include rosters.

Newspapers for WWII years.

ARAKAWA, JENTOKU HAROLD, Pfc. b. Puunene, Maui, Nov. 9, 1915. s. Saburo and Kama (Shinsato) Arakawa. Educ. Paia Sch., Maui High Sch., Maui. Clerk, Hawaiian Pineapple Co., Ltd., Honolulu.

Ind. Army, Dec. 9, 1940, Honolulu. s.n., 30100270. Trained, Schofield Bks., Oahu; Cp. McCoy, Wis.; Cp. Shelby, Miss. Served, 100th Inf. Bn.; Hawaiian Islands, USA, Algeria, Italy. Awards: PH, AD, AP, A, EAME, WW II V. Killed in action, Leonardo, near Piedimonte d'Alife, Italy, Oct. 21, 1943.

ARITA, HIROAKI, Pvt. b. Paauilo, Hawaii, Sept. 12, 1919. s. Tomeichi and Tsuru (Sakamoto) Arita. Educ. Paauilo Elem. and Inter. Sch., Hawaii. Laborer, Hamakua Mill Co., Hawaii.

Ind. Army, Dec. 10, 1940, Paauilo, Hawaii. s.n., 30100483. Trained, Schofield Bks., Oahu; Cp. McCoy, Wis.; Cp. Shelby, Miss. Served, 299th Inf. Regt., 100th Inf. Bn.; Hawaiian Islands, USA, Algeria, Italy. Awards: BS, PH, CIB, AD, AP, EAME, A, WW II V. Killed in action, Castelnuovo, near Coili, Italy, Nov. 30, 1943.

ARNOLD, ALFRED LESTON, III, 1st Lt. b. Owosso, Mich., Dec. 20, 1922. s. Alfred Leston and Hulda Zylpha (Smith) Arnold. Educ. Punahou Sch., Oahu; grade and high sch., Mich.; St. John's Mil. Acad., Wis.; Univ. of Mich. Student at time of enlistment.

Enl. Army Air Corps, Mar. 23, 1942, Mich. s.n., 0674541, after commission, Mar. 20, 1943, Lubbock Field, Tex. Trained, Grider Field, Ark.; Kelly Field, Perrin Field, Tex.; Columbia Air Base, S.C. Served, North Africa, Italy, Egypt, India. Awards: AM, A, EAME, AP, WW II V. Died, non-battle, China-Burma area, May 7, 1944.

ASADA, TATSUMI, Pfc. b. Puunene, Maui, July 18, 1926. s. Tomizo and Asano (Matsuno) Asada. Educ. Iao Sch., Wailuku Elem. Sch., Maui; Honolulu Voc. Sch. Laborer, Wailuku Sugar Co., Maui.

Ind. Army, July 12, 1945, Maui. s.n., 30120418. Trained, Schofield Bks., Oahu. Served, Inf.; Germany, Austria. Awards: AP, EAME, WW II V, AO. Died, non-battle, Austria, May 21, 1946.

ASAI, RALPH YUKIO, Pfc. b. Honolulu, Apr. 29, 1919. s. Hanshiro and Tokiyo (Kuroiwa) Asai. Educ. Palolo Sch., Liliuokalani Inter. Sch., McKinley High Sch., Oahu. Stevedore, McCabe, Hamilton & Renny, Honolulu.

Ind. Army, Nov. 15, 1941, Schofield Bks., Oahu. s.n., 30102360. Trained, Schofield Bks., Oahu; Cp. McCoy, Wis.; Cp. Shelby, Miss. Served, 298th Inf. Regt., 100th Inf. Bn.; Hawaiian Islands, USA, Algeria, Italy. Awards: PH, CIB, AP, A, EAME, WW II V. Killed in action, Santa Maria Oliveto, Italy, Nov. 7, 1943.

In Freedom's Cause, University of Hawaii at Manoa
(Photographs not included)

Hawaiian Historical Society
560 Kawaiahao Street
Honolulu, HI 96813
(808) 537-6271
www.hawaiianhistory.org

The Adjutant General of Hawaii
3949 Diamond Head Road
Honolulu, HI 96816-4495
(808) 733-4132

Veterans Affairs Regional Office
PO Box 50188
Honolulu, HI 96850-0188
(800) 827-1000

*The bonus records for Hawaii WWII veterans are held by each island's Veterans Affairs offices.

Hawaii was an American territory during WWII. Some documents will be under the state territories section, such as the WWII casualty books for the War Department and the Navy Department.

Idaho

WWII Bonus Records: NO

Idaho State Historical Society Library & Archives
450 N 4th Street
Boise, ID 83702
(208) 334-2620 Archives, (208) 334-3198 Fax
www.idahohistory.net/library_archives.html

Honoring Camas County Veterans of World War II, Fairfield, Idaho, Camas County Courier.
   Information pertaining to WWII veterans of Camas County. Includes photographs, military service and biographical information.

World War II Honor List of Dead and Missing Army and Army Air Forces Personnel. State of Idaho. War Department, 1946.

State Summary of War Casualties from World War II for Navy, Marine Corps, and Coast Guard Personnel from Idaho. Navy Department, 1946.

Idaho. World War II Military Records. Pocatello & Surrounding Areas. (microfilm collection)
Card file on veterans from those areas that contain some basic military service data.

USS Boise.
Manuscript collection of USS Boise reunions. May contain a list of crewmembers.

World War II Commemorative Collector's Edition, South Idaho Press, 1995.
Alphabetically lists of Minidoka and Cassia county WWII veterans with biographical information.

Newspapers for WWII years.

University of Idaho Library
PO Box 442351
Moscow, ID 83844-2351
(208) 885-7951
www.lib.uidaho.edu

War Records Committee—Military Personnel Files, 1941–1956.
Information about men and women connected with the University of Idaho who served in the military during WWII. Majority of the collection consists of newspaper articles, letters, address cards, and photographs.

Regimental Histories.
1st Cavalry Division, 494th Bombardment Group (H), 761st Tank Battalion, 361st Infantry Regiment, 65th Infantry Division (50th Anniversary)

*State Summary of War Casualties from World War II for
Navy, Marine Corps, and Coast Guard Personnel from Idaho,*
Navy Department, 1946.

Idaho Military History Museum
4040 West Guard Street
Boise, ID 83705-5004
(208) 422-4841
http://inghro.state.id.us/museum

Rosters of National Guard units. Selective Service records
that may contain information about service and medals
received.

Idaho State Historical Society
1109 Main Street, Suite 250
Boise, ID 83702
(208) 334-2682, (208) 334-2774
www.idahohistory.net

Idaho Genealogical Society
PO Box 1854
Boise, ID 83701-1854
(208) 384-0542
www.lili.org/idahogenealogy/index.htm

The Adjutant General of Idaho
4040 West Guard Street
Boise, ID 83705-5004
(208) 422-5242

National Guard records for WWII.

Idaho Division of Veterans Services
805 West Franklin Street
Boise, ID 83702-5560
(208) 334-1245

No WWII records.

Veterans Affairs Regional Office
805 West Franklin Street
Boise, ID 83702
(800) 827-1000

Illinois

WWII Bonus Records: YES

Illinois State Archives
Norton Building, Capitol Complex
Springfield, IL 62756
(217) 782-4682, (217) 524-3930 Fax
www.sos.state.il.us/departments/archives/archives.html

WWII Bonus records are available from the Department of
Veterans Affairs (see below). They are protected under the
privacy act. Types of bonus records maintained:

WWII Bonus Applications from Veterans, 1947–1953.

World War II Bonus Applications from Beneficiaries of
Deceased Veterans, 1947–1953.

Abstract of World War II Bonus Applications, 1947–1953.

Bonus Applications from Veterans referred to the board of
review, 1947–1953.

Board of Review Actions on Questionable Claims, 1948–1952.

War Veterans' Burials, *The Honor Roll of Veterans Buried in
Illinois* (Springfield 1956) (1774–1955).
    Listings of veterans buried in Illinois cemeteries. Infor-
mation includes the veteran's name, rank, branch of service,
unit or organization, date of death, name and location of
cemetery and may also list the grave location. The *Honor
Roll* includes the years 1899–1955 and is arranged by county
and then alphabetically by last name of veteran. Gives the
veteran's name, rank, time period of service and date of
death.

Illinois Veterans' Home Residents
   Information pertaining to veterans who resided in the
Illinois Veterans Home. Information may include veteran's
military service, pension, discharge or death.

University of Illinois Archives
Room 19 Library (MC-522)
1408 W Gregory Drive
Urbana, IL 61801
(217) 333-0798
http://web.library.uiuc.edu/index.html

The University of Illinois has a collection of records for the
Third Armored Division Association. These holdings
include division history, unit diaries, after action reports,
scrapbooks, newspaper clippings, photographs,
correspondence and association documents. *http://
web.library.uiuc.edu/ahx/ead/ua/2620076/2620076f.html*

Harvey Public Library
15441 Turlington Ave
Harvey, IL 60426
(708) 331-0757, (708) 331-2835 Fax

*Harvey, Illinois during World War II: Extraction from the
Harvey tribune, the Gold star Honor Roll, and letters to the
Behind-The-Lines committee,* Robert Pierre Roach, 2001.

Evanston Historical Society
225 Greenwood Street
Evanston, IL 60201
(847) 475-3410
www.evanstonhistorical.org

RESTRICTED

HEADQUARTERS THIRTY SIXTH ARMORED INFANTRY REGIMENT
APO 253, U S ARMY

31 March 1945

SUBJECT: Action against Enemy, Reports After/After Action Reports.

TO   : THE ADJUTANT GENERAL
       Washington, D.C.   (thru channels)

(a) Original Unit: No change

(b) Changes in Organizations:

(1) Regtl Hq., Hq Co and Ser Co., 36th AIR were a part of Combat Command "R" throughout the period.

(2) The 1st Bn., 36th AIR was attached to Combat Command "A" throughout the period.

(3) The 2nd Bn., 36th AIR was attached to Combat Command "B" throughout the period.

(4) The 3rd Bn., 36th AIR was attached to Combat Command "R" throughout the period.

(c) Strength:

Date	Officers	Warrant Officers	Enlisted Men
1 Mar 1945	113	4	2482
31 Mar 1945	109	4	2344
Net loss	4	0	138

(d) Stations: No change

(e) Marches: Marches same as Battle Narrative shown in paragraph (g) this report.

(f) Campaigns: None designated since last report.

- 1 -

RESTRICTED

Classification changed per authority WD ltr 17 Aug 1945 Subj: Downgrading of Classified Records.

An Inventory of 3rd Armored Division Assn. Records at the University of Illinois Archives. http://web.library.uiuc.edu/ahx/ead/ua/2620076/2620076f.html

Gold Star Veterans, 1920–1970.

Records created by the American Legion Evanston Post 42. Includes a list of veterans of WWII with listings of killed in action and captured prisoners returned alive.

Illinois State Historical Library
Reference Department, Old State Capitol
Springfield, IL 62701
(217) 782-4836
www.state.il.us/hpa/lib

Illinois Newspaper Project: Maintains newspapers from all counties dating back to World War II, however newspapers are not indexed.

World War II Honor List of Dead and Missing Army and Army Air Forces Personnel. State of Illinois, War Department, 1946.

Illinois State Genealogical Society
PO Box 10195
Springfield, IL 62791-0195
(630) 355-4370
www.rootsweb.com/~ilsgs

The Adjutant General of Illinois
1301 N MacArthur Blvd
Springfield, IL 62702-2399
(217) 761-3500

National Guard records only.

Illinois Department of Veterans Affairs
833 S Spring Street
Springfield, IL 62706
(217) 782-4652
www.state.il.us/agency/dva

Maintain records for those veterans who applied for benefits or bonus payments. Records are protected under the privacy act. The only information available as public record is veteran's branch and dates of service.

Veterans Affairs Regional Office
536 S Clark Street
Chicago, IL 60680
(800) 827-1000

The WWII Illinois Veterans Memorial
PO Box 5652
Springfield, IL 62705-5652
(866) 992-4145
www.springfield-il.com/ww2Memorial/index.shtml

Indiana

WWII Bonus Records: YES

Indiana State Archives
State Library Bldg, 140 N Senate Ave
Indianapolis, IN 46204-2215
(317) 591-5222
www.in.gov/icpr/archives

Veterans' Graves Registration File.
    Card file collection of veterans' graves in about half of the
Indiana counties. Card usually lists the veteran's name,
cemetery name and location, time period of service. Only
some cards contain the veteran's date of birth, dates of
death and next of kin.

Indiana World War II Discharge Certificates, 1941–1945.
    Maintains the discharge certificates of Indiana veterans
who applied for the WWII bonus. Request records by
veteran's name, date of birth and branch. Privacy issues
apply to these records. Include proof of death of the
veterans as well as proof of relationship.

US Army and Navy Casualties, World War II, 1941–1945.
    Card file of Army and Navy casualties from Indiana.
Cards includes the veteran's name, rank, may include date
of death, address of next of kin and military theater. A
separate list if available fro Marion County casualties.

Indiana State Library
140 N Senate Avenue
Indianapolis, IN 46204
(317) 232-3675, (317) 232-3728 Fax
www.statelib.lib.in.us

Indiana World War II Servicemen Database.

   This database consists of a card file index created by
Indiana Division librarians from 1942-1946, librarians indexed the three major Indianapolis daily newspapers,
(News, Star, and Times) for mentions of WWII casualties,
missing, prisoners, and decorations or awards. This database is available online and has 26,058 names entered.
Includes the veteran's name, date of article, newspaper
name and article location, branch of service, veteran's
hometown and remark (casualty, prisoner, etc).
http://199.8.200.90:591/wwii.html

Newspapers for WWII years.

USS Indianapolis (CA-35): The Final Sailing List, July 1945,
Moore, Katherine D

*World War II Honor List of Dead and Missing Army and
Army Air Forces Personnel. State of Indiana,* War
Department, 1946.

Veterans' record cards of Spanish–American, World War I
and World War II veterans, DeKalb County, Indiana.

Mishawaka-Penn-Harris Public Library
209 Lincoln Way East
Mishawaka, IN 46544
(574) 259-5277

World War II Service notes of Mishawaka, Indiana
residents. Newspaper clippings.

Allen County Public Library
PO Box 2270
Fort Wayne, IN 46801-2270
(260) 421-1200

World War II Honor Roll, Mary Penrose Wayne Chapter
DAR, Fort Wayne, IN.

Indiana Historical Society
450 W Ohio Street
Indianapolis, IN 46202
(317) 234-0321
www.indianahistory.org

*Service Record Book of Men and Women of Attica, Indiana
and Community,* Attica, IN, 19??

*Owen County Indiana Honors its Men and Women in the
Armed Forces: fourth war loan: nineteen hundred forty–four,*
Spencer, IN, 1944?

Jefferson County in World War II, 1941–1945, Jefferson
County Historical Society, 1947.

Shelby County in World War II, Montgomery, Hortense,
1946. (Includes Honor Roll and casualties).

Indiana Genealogical Society
PO Box 10507
Fort Wayne, IN 46852-0507
www.indgensoc.org

The Adjutant General of Indiana
ATTN: MDI-AG
2002 South Holt Road
Indianapolis, IN 46241-4839
(317) 247-3559

National Guard records.

Indiana Department of Veterans' Affairs
302 W Washington Street, Room E120
Indianapolis, IN 46204-2738
(317) 232-3910, (800) 400-4520

No WWII records.

Veterans Affairs Regional Office
575 N Pennsylvania Street
Indianapolis, IN 46202
(800) 827-1000

Iowa

WWII Bonus Records: YES

State Historical Society of Iowa
600 East Locust
Des Moines, IA 50319-0290
(515) 281-5111
www.iowahistory.org/archives

WWII Bonus Case Files.
  Contains applications for WWII Bonuses paid from Iowa.
These applications were submitted by the veteran or next of
kin of a deceased veteran. Application includes the name of
applicant, address, legal residence before entering the
military, date and place of birth, serial number, military
service information, status of discharge, claim number,
warrant number and bonus earned. The series is arranged
by claim number. The alphabetical name index lists the
claim number.

WWII Casualty Files.
  Files for Iowans who died in WWII. This collection includes an Honor Roll form that the deceased's next of kin
submitted. The form contains the veteran's name, home
address, date and place of birth, parents, married (spouse's
names and when), children names, education, civilian
occupation, induction information, branch and unit assignments, overseas information, date of death and circumstances of death, citations, decoration or awards and

information pertaining to the person who filled out the form. A photograph of the deceased veteran is also in the file. Arranged alphabetically by name.

Armed Forces Grave Registrations.

Grave listings of over 270,000 veterans buried in Iowa. Information contained in the registrations includes the veteran's name, date and place of birth, names of parents, spouse or other family member, military service, burial information, and name and location of cemetery.

Newspapers for WWII years.

Iowa Genealogical Society
PO Box 7735
Des Moines, IA 50322-7735
(515) 276-0287
www.iowagenealogy.org

Iowa Gold Star Museum
7700 Northwest Beaver Drive
Johnston, IA 50131-1902
(515) 252-4531

Iowa Adjutant General's Report of 1941. Contains rosters of all National Guard units called to active duty. Book published in 1944.

Museum has a large reference library containing detailed information pertaining to the 34th Infantry Division, which includes morning reports and rosters.

Iowa Commission of Veterans Affairs
Camp Dodge
7700 NW Beaver Drive
Johnston, IA 50131-1902
(515) 242-5331

All of their records were transferred to the archives.

Veterans Affairs Regional Office
210 Walnut Street
Des Moines, IA 50309
(800) 827-1000

Kansas

WWII Bonus Records: NO

Kansas State Historical Society/State Archives
6425 SW Sixth Avenue
Topeka, KS 66615
(785) 272-8681, (785) 272-8682 Fax
www.kshs.org

Newspaper clippings from Kansas newspapers mentioning WWII veterans. Arranged by last name.

US Naval Air Station, Hutchinson, Kansas. Roster of Officers, February 1, 1944.

Fort Hays Kansas State College. Alumni, Former Students, and Faculty in the Armed Services, World War II (as listed up to April 11, 1945).

WWII War Letters Project
www.kshs.org/ms/warletters

Their Record: Pratt County, World War II. VFW Post 1362. 195?

Military Records of Saline County, Kansas, 1861–1991, Mary Maley, 1998.

Men and Women in the Armed Forces from Shawnee County. Myers & Co, 1947.

Men and Women in the Armed Forces from Douglas County, Myers and Co, 1947.

Those Who Served in World War II...from Harvey County, Kansas, Jewell Sage, 1947.

Honor Roll of Kansas Marines who gave "their last full measure of devotion." Walter, Marine Corps League, 2001?

World War II Honor List of Dead and Missing Army and Army Air Forces Personnel. State of Kansas, War Department, 1946.

State Summary of War Casualties from World War II for Navy, Marine Corps, and Coast Guard Personnel from Kansas, Navy Department, 1946.

War Memorial Album of World War II, Finney County, Kansas.

Their Record: A Memorial of the Services and Sacrifices of the 8,346 Reno county Men and Women in the Armed Forces in World War II, VFW Post 1361, 1947.

Memorial Day: Where Jackson County's Honored dead are buried. Microfilm collection. Includes WWII veterans.

Kansas Council of Genealogical Society
PO Box 103
Dodge City, KS 67801
www.dodgecity.net/kgs

The Adjutant General of Kansas
2800 SW Topeka Boulevard
Topeka, KS 66611-1287
(785) 274-1192

Maintains discharge certificates for WWII veterans that served from Kansas. Will issue a statement of service, which includes the veteran's name, serial number, dates of service, character of service, medals and awards, unit and rank. Submit a standard form 180. They do not have National Guard personnel records.

Kansas Veterans Commission
700 SW Jackson Street
Topeka, KS 66603-3150
(785) 296-3976

No WWII records.

Veterans Affairs Regional Office
5500 East Kellogg
Wichita, KS 67211
(800) 827-1000

Kentucky

WWII Bonus Records: YES

Kentucky Department for Libraries and Archives
300 Coffee Tree Road, PO Box 537
Frankfort, KY 40602-0537
(502) 564-8300, (502) 564-5773 Fax
www.kdla.state.ky.us

After Action Reports, 1944–1945.
5th Armored Division Records.

After Action Reports, 1942–1953.
Includes various armored divisions and tank battalions during WWII. Main areas covered are the Pacific and European theaters.

United States Army Armor School World War II historical documents collection.
This collection consists of unit histories, intelligence reports, plans, after action reports, journals, and war diaries of several armored and infantry units.

General Index to Veteran's Discharges, 1922–1978.

Discharges records for Estill County Kentucky.

Newspapers for WWII years.

University of Kentucky
500 S Limestone
Lexington, KY 40506-0456
(859) 257-0500, (859) 257-0505 Fax
www.uky.edu/Libraries

Hardin County and Her part in World War II, WM Boling, 1948.

Bourbon County Men and Women who Served in World War Two, Bourbon County Woman's Club, Paris, KY.

Majority of newspapers for World War II years.

Photographs and personal accounts.

The Filson Historical Society
1310 S Third Street
Louisville, KY 40208
(502) 635-5083, (502) 635-5086 Fax
www.filsonhistorical.org

USS LST 1097 WWII Association.
    Documents from the associations, including histories, some biographical information, correspondence and person papers.

State Summary of War Casualties from World War II for Navy, Marine Corps, and Coast Guard Personnel from Kentucky. Navy Department, 1946.

Patriots of Kentucky: World War II.
    Scrapbook containing newspaper clippings from WWII years.

Service Record Book of Men and Women of Kuttawa, Kentucky and Community, Lyon County VFW Post 5458, 1947.
    List of veterans from that area with service information.

Kentucky Historical Society
100 W Broadway
Frankfort, KY 40601
(502) 564-1792
www.kyhistory.org

State Summary of War Casualties from World War II for Navy, Marine Corps, and Coast Guard Personnel from Kentucky. Navy Department, 1946.

World War II Honor List of Dead and Missing Army and Army Air Forces Personnel. State of Kansas. War Department, 1946.

Service Record Book of Men and Women of Paintsville, Kentucky and community. Paintsville, KY, 1947.

The Heroes of McLean County, Kentucky, 1941-1945, World War II. Lacefield, William Bryant, 2001.

Heroes World War II, Calloway County, Kentucky: supplement to The Ledger and Times. Ledger and Times, 1946.

Kentucky Genealogical Society
PO Box 153
Frankfort, KY 40602
www.kygs.org

Kentucky Department of Military Affairs
Military Records and Research Branch
1121 Louisville Road
Frankfort, KY 40601
(502) 564-4883, (502) 564-4437 Fax
www.dma.state.ky.us

Discharges and Bonus Applications, World War II.
  The WWII Bonus was implemented in 1960. Request records by veteran's name, Social Security number or serial number. Privacy act applies.

National Guard Records on Microfilm.
Alphabetically by last name and date of birth. Privacy act applies.

Casualty Lists, 1860–1992.
Listings of military casualties from World War II. The information contained in these records includes the name, date of death, cause of death, area of residence, and occasionally, the next of kin, birth date, rank, and branch of service.

38th Infantry Division. Yearbook, Ohio, Indiana, Kentucky.
Lists members of the division.

Military Unit Histories, 1880–1989.
Some histories contain muster rolls.

Veterans Affairs Regional Office
545 S Third Street
Louisville, KY 40202
(800) 827-1000

Louisiana

WWII Bonus Records: YES

Louisiana State Archives
3851 Essen Lane
Baton Rouge, LA 70809-2137
(225) 922-1000
www.sec.state.la.us/archives

Bonuses Given to World War II Veterans.
WWII bonus records contain the veteran's name, bonus number, copy of discharge certificate and date the check was mailed. Arranged by bonus number. See bonus record index.

Bonus Record Index.
Arranged by last name. Contains the bonus number needed to search the WWII bonus record.

State Library of Louisiana
701 North 4th Street
Baton Rouge, LA 70802
(225) 342-4923, (225) 219-4804 Fax
www.state.lib.la.us

Fighting Men of Louisiana and a History of World War II,
Louisiana Historical Institute, 1946. By parish.

*Index to the Fighting Men of Louisiana: From the book by the
Louisiana Historical Institute,* J. Riffel, 1981.

Fighting Men of Louisiana: Index (v.2), compiled by
Ferguson, 1986.

In Defense of a Nation: Servicewomen in World War II,
Holm, 1998.

Louisiana War Casualties –1994. Casualties from WWI –
Desert Storm.

*Combat Connected Naval Casualties, World War II, by States.
1946.* Navy Department, 1946.

Louisiana State University
Middleton Library
Baton Rouge, LA 70806
(225) 578-5652, (225) 578-9432 Fax
www.lib.lsu.edu

*State Summary of War Casualties from World War II for
Navy, Marine Corps, and Coast Guard Personnel from
Louisiana.* Navy Department, 1946.

*World War II Honor List of Dead and Missing Army and
Army Air Forces Personnel. State of Louisiana.* War
Department, 1946

*Honor Roll of St Landry Parish (Louisiana) Men and Women
Serving in the Armed Forces of the United States of America,*
Daily World, 1944.

Newspapers for WWII years.

Louisiana Historical Society
5801 St Charles Avenue
New Orleans, LA 70115
(504) 866-3049
www.louisianahistoricalsociety.org

Louisiana Genealogical and Historical Society
PO Box 82060
Baton Rouge, LA 70884-2060
www.rootsweb.com/~la-lghs

The Adjutant General of Louisiana
ATTN: Separated Records
Headquarters Bldg, Jackson Barracks
New Orleans, LA 70146-0330
(504) 278-8211

National Guard records.
   Include the veteran's full name, serial number or Social
Security number, approximate discharge date and date of
birth with requests.

Department of Veterans Affairs
PO Box 94095, Capitol Station
Baton Rouge, LA 70804-9095
(225) 922-0500, (225) 922-0511 Fax

Discharges certificates maintained by parish. Parish list
available online, *www.ldva.org/cap.html*

Veterans Affairs Regional Office
701 Loyola Avenue
New Orleans, LA 70113
(800) 827-1000

Maine

WWII Bonus Records: NO

Maine State Archives
84 State House Station
Augusta, ME 04333-0084
(207) 287-5795, (207) 287-5739 Fax
www.state.me.us/sos/arc

Requests for restricted records held by the state archives should contact the state agency that supplied the records. For military records, contact either the Adjutant General or Maine veterans' services.

Index of Veterans.
 Information on veterans includes name, address, enlistment date, date of discharge, physical description and time period of service. Access restricted.

Casualties.
 Contains the veterans name, type of casualty, next of kin, decorations, citations, and military history. Access restricted.

Women in Service Since World War II.
 Card collection including includes veteran's name, place of birth, place and date of enlistment, marital status, place and date of discharge, rank and time period of service. Access restricted.

University of Maine
5729 Fogler Library
Orono, ME 04469
(207) 581-1110
www.library.umaine.edu

Majority of newspapers for WWII years.

The Maine State Library
230 State Street
State House Station # 64
Augusta, ME 04333
(207) 287-5600, (207) 287-5615
www.state.me.us/msl

World War II: A Tribute to Pepperell People in the Service.
Pepperell Manufacturing Company, 1946. A book containing information about the veterans who served during that war that were employed in Pepperell mills in Maine, Georgia, Alabama and Massachusetts. Included photographs.

State Summary of War Casualties from World War II for Navy, Marine Corps, and Coast Guard Personnel from Maine. Navy Department, 1946.

http://ursus.maine.edu
Online catalog system for the University of Maine, Bangor Public Library, Maine State Library and the Maine State Law and Legislative Reference Library. They have a large selection of regimental histories.

Waldoboro Public Library
PO Box 768
Waldoboro, ME 04572
www.waldoborolibrary.org

Waldoboro Honor Roll World War II December 7, 1941 to September 2, 1945, Genthner, Cooney, 1948.

The Maine Historical Society
489 Congress Street
Portland, ME 04101
(207) 774-1822
www.mainehistory.org

Maine National Guard Roster of Officers.

Maine Genealogical Society
PO Box 221
Farmington, ME 40938-0221
www.rootsweb.com/~megs/MaineGS.htm

The Adjutant General of Maine
Military Bureau, Camp Keyes
Augusta, ME 04333-0033
(207) 626-4353

National Guard records. Request records by veteran's name
and town lived in at the time of service. Records are
categorized by unit.

Maine Veterans' Services
SHS 117
Augusta, ME 04333-0117
(207) 626-4464

Discharge Certificates for WWII.
   Include the veteran's name and date of birth with records
request. Privacy Act applies to these records.

Veterans Affairs Regional Office
Route 17 East
Togus, ME 04330
(800) 827-1000

Maryland

WWII Bonus Records: NO

Maryland State Archives
350 Rowe Boulevard
Annapolis, MD 21401
(410) 260-6400, (410) 974-3895 Fax
www.mdarchives.state.md.us

Jewish War Records of World War II (From: Compiling Jewish War Records of World War II), Kohs, 1946.

Jews in the Armed Forces (From: Compiling Jewish War Records of World War II), Kraft, Louis, 1946.

Maryland in World War II: Register of Service Personnel, War Records Division, Maryland Historical Society, 1965.

Maryland in World War II, Vol I: Gold Star Honor Roll, Maryland Historical Society, 1956.

Newspapers for WWII years.

University of Maryland at College Park
McKeldin Library
College Park, MD 20742-7011
(301) 405-0800
www.lib.umd.edu

Baltimore in World War II: As originally printed in the pages of The Baltimore News-Post, Historical Briefs, 1992.

State Summary of War Casualties from World War II for Navy, Marine Corps, and Coast Guard Personnel from Maryland, Navy Department, 1946.

Maryland Historical Society
201 W Monument Street
Baltimore, MD 21201-4674
(410) 685-3750, (410) 385-2105 Fax
www.mdhs.org

Maryland World War II Records, 1945–1965.

A collection of records from the Maryland War Records Division, which covers all aspects of WWII in Maryland. Information was used from this collection for the WWII service personnel books printed in 1965.

Honor roll of Hampden, Roland Avenue and Thirty-Fourth Street, Baltimore, Maryland, Robert Hayes, Jr, 1946.

Marylanders in Italy, James Wingate, 1945.

Answering their Country's Call: Marylanders in World War II, Johns Hopkins University Press, 2002.

We Live Among Heroes. A Commemorative of Wicomico County's World War Two Veterans, Sylvia Bradley, 1996.

Maryland National Guard Museum
5th Reg Armory, 29th Division St
Baltimore, MD 21201
(410) 576-6160
www.mdmilitaryhistory.org

Books for the 175th Infantry Regiment, 115th Infantry Regiment and the 110th Field Artillery Regiment, includes rosters. Records for the 29th Infantry Division during WWII.

Maryland National Guard Historical Society, Inc.
29th Division Street
Baltimore, MD 21201-2288
(410) 576-6160

Maryland Genealogical Society
201 West Monument Street
Baltimore, MD 21201
www.mdgensoc.org

Maryland National Guard
29th Division Street
ATTN: Military Archives
Baltimore, MD 21201
(410) 576-6097

National Guards records. Contact their office for the
necessary form.

Maryland Veterans Commission
Federal Building, Room 110
31 Hopkins Plaza
Baltimore, MD 21201
(410) 962-4700, (410) 333-1071 Fax

WWII book.
  Lists veteran's name, serial number & residence at time of
entry.

Veterans Affairs Regional Office
31 Hopkins Plaza Federal Bldg.
Baltimore, MD 21201
(800) 827-1000

Massachusetts

WWII Bonus Records: YES

Massachusetts Archives
220 Morrissey Blvd
Boston, MA 02125
(617) 727-2816, (617) 288-8429 Fax
www.state.ma.us/sec/arc/arcidx.htm

Index of Military Casualties in WWII, 1941–1945.
  Casualty information contains the veteran's name, rank,
race, residence, branch of service, date of death, next of kin,
cause of death, and theater of operations.

*World War II Honor List of Dead and Missing Army and
Army Air Forces Personnel. State of Massachusetts,* War
Department, 1946.

The State Library of Massachusetts
George Fingold Library
State House Room 341
Boston, MA 02133
(617) 727-2590, (617) 727-5819
www.state.ma.us/lib

Wenham in World War II: War service of Wenham Men and Women and Civilian Services of Wenham People, Historical Assn, 1948.

Newspapers for WWII years.

Massachusetts Historical Society
1154 Boylston Street
Boston, MA 02215
(617) 536-1608, (617) 859-0074 Fax
www.masshist.org

Collection of personal papers from WWII veterans.

National Guard Military Museum & Archives
44 Salisbury Street
Worcester, MA 01609
(508) 797-0334

National Guard rosters and WWII bonus cards.

Military Records Branch
239 Causeway Street, Ste 130
Boston, MA 02114
(617) 727-2964

Discharge certificates for WWII. Include the veteran's name, date of birth and home of record at the time of service with request.

Veterans Affairs Regional Office
JFK Federal Bldg. Govt Center
Boston, MA 02114
(800) 827-1000

Michigan

WWII Bonus Records: YES

The Michigan Department of History, Arts & Libraries
PO Box 30740
Lansing, MI 48909-8240
(517) 373-1408–Archives, (517) 373-1300–Library
www.michigan.gov/hal

Archives

Administrative Records of the Michigan Department of
Military Affairs Personnel Division, 1897–1971.

Includes personnel lists for 1940–1949; directories that list
personnel, 1937–1971; and also contains documentation of
those who were called to federal service during WWII.

Library

*The Hy-lighter Honor Roll of Michigan State Highway
Department Men and Women in the Armed Services,*
Michigan State Highway Department, 1944.

*Rural Manistee County in World War II: Cleon-Marilla-
Springdale.*
Contains service rolls of Cleon Township, Marilla Town-
ship and Springdale, 1946.

*Service Record Book of Men and Women of Roscommon
County: World War I and II veterans,* American Legion Post
326, 19??

*Service Record Book of Men and Women of Elkton, Mich,
and Community,* VFW Post 6013, 19??

*Service Record Book of Men and Women of Bergland,
Michigan and Community,* American Legion Auxiliary Post
562, 19??

*United States Army Air Corps Veterans of World War II from
Three Rivers, Michigan,* Crose, 1993.

State Summary of War Casualties from World War II for Navy, Marine Corps, and Coast Guard Personnel from Michigan, Navy Department, 1946.

World War II Honor List of Dead and Missing Army and Army Air Forces Personnel. State of Michigan, War Department, 1946.

Newspapers for WWII years.

Bentley Historical Library, UOM
1150 Beal Avenue
Ann Arbor, MI 48109-2113
(734) 764-3482, (734) 936-1333 Fax
www.umich.edu/~bhl

*Service Record Book of Men and Women of West Branch, Michigan and Ogemaw County,*VFW Post 5680, 1950?

The program of the victory reunion and one hundred second commencement of the University of Michigan: June 20–22, 1946, The University, 1946.

A Tribute–to the Men and Women of Pleasant Ridge in the World War, 1941–1945, World War II Memorial Committtee, Pleasant Ridge, MI, 1947.

Historical Society of Michigan
1305 Abbot Rd
East Lansing, MI 48823
(517) 324-1828
www.hsmichigan.org

Michigan Genealogical Council
PO Box 80953
Lansing, MI 48908-0953
www.rootsweb.com/~mimgc

The Adjutant General of Michigan
2500 South Washington Ave
Lansing, MI 48913-5101
(517) 483-5507 702-5137

National Guard records for WWII.
   Include the veteran's name, dates of service and serial
number when requesting records.

Michigan Veterans Trust Fund
7109 West Saginaw Highway
Lansing, MI 48913
(517) 335-1636, (517) 335-1631 Fax

WWII bonus records.
   The bonus records includes a copy of the veteran's discharge certificate. Privacy issues apply to these records. If
the veteran is decased next of kin can fax a request to their
office. Include the veteran's name, branch of service, date of
birth, date of death, proof of death, relationship and a phone
number.

Veterans Affairs Regional Office
477 Michigan Avenue
Detroit, MI 48226
(800) 827-1000

Minnesota

WWII Bonus Records: YES

Minnesota Historical Society
345 Kellogg Boulevard W
St Paul, MN 55102-1906
(651) 296-6126
www.mnhs.org

World War II Bonus Records, 1950s, (microform), Minnesota
Dept of Veterans Affairs, 1970s.
   Collection consists of applications for the Minnesota
WWII bonus payment. Information includes personal data,

military service history, proof of residence, and proof of honorable discharge, which is normally a copy of the discharge certificate. Some may be of illegible.

World War II Bonus Index, 1950s.
Index card to the WWII bonus records. Card lists the veteran's name, serial number, and the bonus claim number. Use the claim number to access the bonus records.

Military Service Record Cards, (microfilm), Minnesota Dept of Veterans Affairs, 1971.
Card for those who entered federal service from the Minnesota National Guard. Information contained on the cards includes name, serial number, age or date of birth, place of birth, next of kin, enrollment information and history of military service. Civil War–WWII.

Soldier's and Sailor's Discharge Record, 1919–1960, (microform),
Genealogical Society of Utah, 1993. Discharge records for Martin County only.

War Memorial Committee records, 1945–1948.
Information from the War Memorial Committee used for the roster of war dead for Hennepin County. Includes a list of Minnesota WWII dead.

Death Certificate Search.
Online database of death certificates from Minnesota. Years 1908–1996. *http://people.mnhs.org/dci*

Service Record Book of Men and Women of Clinton, Minnesota, and Community, American Legion Post, 1947.

Service Record Book of Men and Women of Wells and Community, American Legion Post 210, 1950.

Service Record Book of Men and Women of Edgerton, Minnesota, and Community, American Legion Post 42, 1948?

Service Record book of Men and Women of World War II, Martin County, American Legion, VFW and DAV, 1950?

Service Record Book of Men and Women of Adrian, Minnesota, and Community, VFW Post 8775, 1946.

Victory Album. Dedicated to the Men and Women of Freeborn County who are serving in the Armed Forces of the United States, Albert Lea, MN, 1943.

Men and Women in the Armed Services from Hamline Methodist Church, 1940–1945, 1945.

Fulda folks in Service, Christmas 1943, Fulda, MN, 1943.

Gold Star Boys: Adrian, Nobles County, Minnesota: World War I, World War II, Korea, Vietnam, Vaselaar, 2001.

We Honor our Fallen Comrades–in–Arms: Jackson County, Minnesota, H. Ed Carlson. 1989.
   Includes casualties from WWI – Vietnam.

Minnesota's World War II Army Dead, Park Genealogical Books, 1994.

State Summary of War Casualties from World War II for Navy, Marine Corps, and Coast Guard Personnel from Minnesota, Navy Department, 1946.

World War II Honor List of Dead and Missing Army and Army Air Forces Personnel. State of Minnesota, War Department, 1946.

Newspapers for WWII years.

Minnesota Genealogical Society
5768 Olson Memorial Highway
Golden Valley, MN 55422
(763) 595-9347
www.mngs.org

Veterans Service Bldg
ATTN: Retirement Services
20 West 12th St, 1st Floor
St Paul, MN 55155

National Guard enlistment cards only.
    Records are organized by year of discharge and name.
Privacy issues apply.

Minnesota Department of Veterans Affairs
20 W 12th Street
St Paul, MN 55155
(651) 296-2562

WWII Bonus Records.
    Does include military service history. Include veteran's
name, time period of service, where entered from, serial
number (if known). Privacy act applies.

Veterans Affairs Regional Office
1 Federal Drive
St. Paul, MN 55111
(800) 827-1000

Mississippi

WWII Bonus Records: NO

Mississippi Department of Archives and History
Archives and Library Division
PO Box 571
Jackson, MS 39205-0571
(601) 359-6850, (601) 359-6975 Fax
www.mdah.state.ms.us

Discharge Records.
    Copies of discharge certificates, if filed with the county
clerk's office. Microfilm.

Roster of Co B, 155th Infantry Regiment January, 1940.
    National Guard unit.

Returns of Deceased Servicemen, WWII
    Includes deceased veterans that were killed in overseas theaters and their remains were sent home for burial in Mississippi. Contains veteran's burial information, information about the next of kin.

World War II Honor List of Dead and Missing Army and Army Air Forces Personnel. State of Mississippi, War Department, 1946.

State Summary of War Casualties from World War II for Navy, Marine Corps, and Coast Guard Personnel from Mississippi, Navy Department, 1946.

Newspapers for WWII years.

Mississippi State University Library
PO Box 5408
Mississippi State, MS 39762
http://library.msstate.edu/index.asp

Army Administration Officer Candidate School, no. 4, State College, Mississippi, 1943.

Valor Remembered: War Dead of the State of Mississippi, Sullivan/Hughes, 1996.

"On the beam": West Point–Clay County, Mississippi, 1941-1945. Coleman, 1985?

Armed Forces Museum
Bldg 850
Camp Shelby, MS 39407-5500
(601) 558-2757
www.ngms.state.ms.us/campshelby/Museum

Detailed information about the 65th, 69th, 31st, 37th, 38th, and the 442nd Infantry Divisions. Collection consists of partial casualty lists for the 69th, yearbooks, rosters and histories of these units.

Family Research Association of Mississippi
PO Box 13334
Jackson, MS 39236-3334

The Adjutant General of Mississippi
PO Box 5027
Jackson, MS 39296-5027
(601) 313-6232

WWII National Guard records. Request records by name,
serial number and discharge date.

Mississippi Veterans Affairs Board
PO Box 5947
Pearl, MS 39288-5946
(601) 576-4850
www.vab.state.ms.us

WWII records that contain date of entry, discharge date,
branch of service, type of discharge received, county and
serial number. Request records by veteran's name and date
of birth.

Veterans Affairs Regional Office
100 West Capitol Street
Jackson, MS 39269
(800) 827-1000

Missouri

WWII Bonus Records: NO

Missouri State Archives
600 W Main, PO Box 1747
Jefferson City, MO 65102
(573) 751-3280
www.sos.state.mo.us/archives

Discharge Records.
   Maintains veteran's discharge certificates on microfilm, if filed with the county recorder of deeds. Most counties have an index of discharges.

Casualty Card Index.
   Card file that lists name, serial number, rank, branch, type of casualty and county of Missouri casualties. Alphabetical.

Death Index
   List of casualties includes dead and wounded. Contains the veteran's name, rank, next of kin, relationship, address, place of casualty, date of release or date of death. Alphabetical.

Ellis Library
University of Missouri-Columbia
Columbia, MO 65201
(573) 882-3362
http://web.missouri.edu/~elliswww/ellis.html

Madison County Veterans World War II, Historic Madison County, MO, 1998.

Concordia Area Veterans who Served in World War II, Mel Bockelman, 1996.

The Pursuit of a Ruptured Duck: When Kansas Citians Went to War ...by Edward T. Matheny, Jr. 2001.

Unit Citation and Campaign Participation Credit Register, The Army, 1961.

State Historical Society of Missouri
1020 Lowry Street
Columbia, MO 65201-7298
(573) 882-7083, (573) 884-4950 Fax
http://system.missouri.edu/shs/newspaper.html

Benton County People in World War II: Those who served at home, those who served away from home, Kathleen White Miles, 1972.

Henry County People in World War II: A scrapbook of articles which appeared during the war years in the Clinton eye and the Henry County Democrat, compiled-Miles, 1972.

Men and Women in the Armed Forces from Newton County, Roll of Honor Publishing Co, 1944.

Nodaway County, Missouri Veterans: Civil War, WW I, WW II, Korean & Vietnam Conflict, compiled Lawnick, Northwest Missouri Genealogy Society, 198?

World War II Rushville, Missouri Service Men: Taken from the book compiled by the Rushville, Missouri Community, Northwest Missouri Genealogy Society, 198?

World War II Honor List of Dead and Missing Army and Army Air Forces Personnel. State of Missouri, War Department, 1946.

State Summary of War Casualties from World War II for Navy, Marine Corps, and Coast Guard Personnel from Missouri, Navy Department, 1946.

Newspapers for WWII years.

Missouri State Genealogical Association
PO Box 833
Columbia, MO 65205-0833
www.mosga.org

The Adjutant General of Missouri
2302 Militia Drive
Jefferson City, MO 65101-1203
(573) 638-9710

Discharge certificates for WWII veterans. When requesting records please supply as much information as possible.

Please supply the veteran's name, serial number, date of birth, branch, and dates of service.

Missouri Veterans Commission
PO Drawer 147
Jefferson City, MO 65102
(573) 751-3779

No WWII records.

Veterans Affairs Regional Office
400 South 18th Street
St. Louis, MO 63103
(800) 827-1000

Montana

WWII Bonus Records: YES*

Montana Historical Society Library and Archives
PO Box 201201, 225 North Roberts
Helena, MT 59620-1201
(406) 444-2681
www.his.state.mt.us

Montana Adjutant General's Office Records 1889–1959.

Card file of enlistments for the years 1898–1945.

Information includes the veteran's name, date and location of enlistment, rank, serial number, military service history and date of discharge. Arranged by branch and contains dishonorable discharges and enemy aliens.

The War Years, Prairie County, Montana, Curtis Media Corp, 1993. A 50th anniversary volume.

American Legion. Post No. 39 Service Book of Men and Women of Rosebud County, 1949.

Includes entry date, name, branch of service, rank, discharge date and a photograph of WWI and WWII veterans of Rosebud County.

Men and Women from Sanders County, MT, Who Served during World War 1 & World War II (also several peace time service personnel), 1917–1949, by Ann Miller, 2001.

List of Montanans Killed or Missing in Action: World War I, World War II, Korean War, Vietnam War, Montana. Dept of Military Affairs, Veteran Affairs Division, 1989.

Montana G.I.'s Lost in World War II, Sharp, Bill
   Lists of casualties and POWs from Montana. Includes the list of losses of the 163rd Infantry Regiment.

World War II Honor List of Dead and Missing Army and Army Air Forces Personnel. State of Montana, War Department, 1946.

Newspapers for WWII years.

Montana Military Museum
PO Box 125
Ft Harrison, MT 59636-0125
(406) 324-3550
www.montanaguard.com/museum.htm

The National Guard of the United States, Historical and Pictorial Review, National Guard of the State of Montana 1940, Army & Navy Publishing Co, LA.

Directory of the Organizations and Units of the Montana National Guard–1943 State of Montana, Office of the Adjutant General, April 1, 1943.
   Book includes roster of personnel for the 163rd Infantry Regiment of the 41st Infantry Division when called to federal service in 1940. Lists hometown, name, rank and serial number.

Montana Directory of Public Affairs, 1864–1960, Ralph Owens, 1960.
   Contains the most complete list of Montana casualties.

Montana State Genealogical Society
PO Box 989
Boulder, MT 59632-0989
www.rootsweb.com/~mtmsgs

Department of Military Affairs
PO Box 4789
Helena, MT 59604-4789
(406) 324-3010

National Guard records.

Montana Veterans Affairs Division
PO Box 5715
Helena, MT 59804
(406) 324-3740

No WWII records.

Veterans Affairs Regional Office
Williams Street & Hwy 12 West
Ft Harrison, MT 59636
(800) 827-1000

*Montana did pay a bonus to WWII Veterans but have been
unable to locate those records.

Nebraska

WWII Bonus Records: NO

Nebraska State Historical Society
PO Box 82554, 1500 R Street
Lincoln, NE 68501
www.nebraskahistory.org

Nebraska Servicemen Who Fought in World War II.
    Index cards with information pertaining WWII veterans
from Nebraska. The source of information was Nebraska
newspapers. The cards contain the veteran's name, newspaper source and date of article and may include other infor-

mation about the veteran. This project began in December, 1941 and ended in November, 1942. Arranged by veteran's last name.

"Nebraska and Nebraskans in World War II", Armstrong, Robert McDowell, *Nebraska History* 24, (July–Sept./Nov, 1943): pages 174–180.

"Hitchcock County, Nebraska Records" Riley, Paul Davis, 1978.

Nebraskans in the Service (1942), Nebraska State Historical Society.
    Card file collection consisting of reference to newspapers mentioning WWII veterans from Nebraska. Original data was from scrapbooks put together by the WPA in the early 1940's.

World War II Service Record, Gosper County, Nebraska.

World War II Honor List of Dead and Missing Army and Army Air Forces Personnel. State of Nebraska, War Department, 1946.

State Summary of War Casualties from World War II for Navy, Marine Corps, and Coast Guard Personnel from Nebraska, Navy Department, 1946.

Newspapers for WWII years.

Oral history project of WWII veterans from Nebraska and personal papers collection.

Beatrice Public Library
100 North 16th Street
Beatrice, NE 68310
(402) 223-3584
www.ci.beatrice.ne.us/library

World War II and the People of Cherry County, Mildred Gates, 1993.

World War II and the People of Dundy County: A 50th Anniversary Album, 1992.

Nebraska State Genealogical Society
PO Box 5608
Lincoln, NE 68505-0608
www.rootsweb.com/~nesgs

Nebraska Military Department
1300 Military Road
Lincoln, NE 68508
(402) 309-7210

National Guard records. Request records giving the veteran's name and date of birth.

Nebraska Department of Veterans Affairs
PO Box 95083
Lincoln, NE 68509-5083
(402) 471-2458, (402) 471-2491 Fax

Discharge certificates of Nebraska veterans and veteran grave cards. When requesting the records please supply as much information as known about the veteran.

Veterans Affairs Regional Office
5631 S 48th Street
Lincoln, NE 68516
(800) 827-1000

Jefferson County, Nebraska, in World War II, The Stilwell Printery, 1946. This book is in the Library of Congress catalog but apparently not part of any Nebraska Library collection.

Nevada

WWII Bonus Records: NO

The Nevada State Library and Archives
100 North Stewart Street
Carson City, NV 89701-4285
(775) 684-3310–Archives, (775) 684-3360–Library
http://dmla.clan.lib.nv.us/docs/nsla

Archives

Statement of Service World War II.

The Adjutant General's office prepared service cards on Nevada WWII veterans. The service card includes the veteran's name, serial number, residence, date of birth, place of birth, race, sex, branch of service, type of enlistment (enlisted, inducted or commissioned), date of entry into the service, date of discharge, rank or grade, type of discharge received (honorable, presumed dead, transferred to reserve) battles and campaigns, decorations and awards, foreign service or sea service (dates), remarks and date card was prepared. Also includes if the veteran registered with the Selective Service and if so which board. Alphabetical by veteran's last name. Request records by name only or name and date of birth. Records open to the public.

Adjutant Generals Report 1945–1946.

Contains a list of Nevada WWII casualties.

Library:

Newspapers for WWII years.

Nevada Historical Society
1650 North Virginia Street
Reno, NV 89503
(775) 688-1190, (775) 688-2917 Fax
http://dmla.clan.lib.nv.us/docs/museums/reno/his-soc.htm

Nevada State Genealogical Society
PO Box 20666
Reno, NV 89515-0666
www.rootsweb.com/~nvsgs

The Adjutant General of Nevada
Nevada Military Department
2525 S Carson Drive
Carson City, NV 89701-5502
(775) 887-7302

National Guard records. Supply as much information as
known about the veteran when requesting records.

Nevada Office of Veterans' Services
1201 Terminal Way, Room 108
Reno, NV 89520
(775) 688-1653, (775) 688-1656 Fax

No WWII records.

Veterans Affairs Regional Office
1201 Terminal Way
Reno, NV 89520
(800) 827-1000

11776

1. LAST NAME—FIRST NAME—MIDDLE NAME OR INITIAL	2. SERVICE SERIAL NO.		
3. RESIDENCE: (Number and street, or RFD number, town, city, county, and State) **Las Vegas, Nevada**	4. SELECTIVE SERVICE LOCAL BOARD **#1 Clark County**		
5. DATE OF BIRTH (Day—Month—Year)	6. PLACE OF BIRTH (Town, city, and State) **Dell Rapids, So. Dak.**	7. RACE **white**	8. SEX Male [x] Female [ ]
9. REGISTERED Yes [x] No [ ]	10. SERVICE IN Coast Guard [ ] Army [x] Navy [ ] Marine Corps [ ]	11. ENTERED SERVICE BY Enlistment [ ] Induction [x] Commission [ ]	
12. DATE OF ENLISTMENT—INDUCTION—COMMISSION (Day—Month—Year) **29 October 1942**	13. DATE OF ENTRY INTO ACTIVE DUTY (Day—Month—Year) **29 October 1942**	14. DATE OF RELEASE FROM ACTIVE DUTY (Day—Month—Year) **1 April 1943**	
15. GRADE OR RATING AT SEPARATION **Pvt**	16. HIGHEST GRADE OR RATING HELD **Pvt**	17. CHARACTER OR TYPE OF SEPARATION OR DISCHARGE **Honorable**	
18. BATTLES AND CAMPAIGNS **NA**			
19. DECORATIONS AND CITATIONS **NA**			
20. FOREIGN AND/OR SEA SERVICE (Years—Months—Days) Yes [ ] No [ ] **NA**			
21. REMARKS			
¹For nonregistrant's home address at time of entrance into service.	**STATEMENT OF SERVICE WORLD WAR II**	Date prepared: (Day—Month—Year) **16 November 1948**	

O. S. S. R. Form 4—Budget Bureau Approval No. 33-4703.   16—54116-2

Statement of Service Card, Nevada State Library and Archives
(For privacy, personal information is deleted from the sample)

New Hampshire

WWII Bonus Records: YES

New Hampshire State Library
20 Park Street
Concord, NH 03301
(603) 271-2392, (603) 271-6826 Fax
http://webster.state.nh.us/nhsl

State Summary of War Casualties from World War II for Navy, Marine Corps, and Coast Guard Personnel from New Hampshire, Navy Department, 1946.

The Honor Roll of Peterborough Slip, Sliptown, Striptown, Sharon, New Hampshire, 1775–1945, King, 1945.

Newspapers for WWII years.

New Hampshire Historical Society
30 Park Street
Concord, NH 03301-6384
(603) 228-6688, (603) 224-0463 Fax
www.nhhistory.org/index.html

A Directory of New Hampshire Ex-POWs, *Dr. F Douglas, Bowles, 1997.*

Amherst in World War I, 1917–1918, and in World War II, 1941–1945, Cabinet Press, 1947.

Tamworth in World War II, Marjory Gane Harkness.

Milford in World War II, 1939–1945, Cabinet Press, 1949.

St Paul's School in the Second World War, Edmonds, Alumni Assn of St Paul's School, 1950.

Honor Roll of Those Who Served in the Armed Forces of the United States of America, World War II, 1941–1946, Town of Northwood, NH.

New Hampshire Society of Genealogists
PO Box 2316
Concord, NH 03302-2316
(603) 225-3381
http://nhsog.org

The Adjutant General of New Hampshire
State Military Reservation, 4 Pembroke Road
Concord, NH 03301-5652
(603) 225-1200, (603) 225-1257

WWII Bonus Records.
   If veteran applied for the New Hampshire bonus the record would contain their military service information. Include the veteran's name, serial and year of discharge with request. Their office also has casualty information.

New Hampshire State Veterans Council
275 Chestnut Street, Room 321
Manchester, NH 03101-2411
(603) 624-9230

No WWII records.

Veterans Affairs Regional Office
275 Chestnut Street
Manchester, NH 03101
(800) 827-1000

New Jersey

WWII Bonus Records: NO

New Jersey State Library
185 West State St, PO Box 520
Trenton, NJ 08625-0520
(609) 292-6220
www.njstatelib.org

Berlin Borough, Camden County, New Jersey in the Second World War, 1941–1945. Microfilm

Bayonne in the World Wars. [Scrapbooks] Microfilm collection.

Includes a list of servicemen and servicewomen who served in the military from Bayonne, New Jersey. The source of information came from newspaper clippings.

WWII—Deaths.

A card index listing casualties that were brought back to be buried in New Jersey. Includes the veteran's name, branch, rank, next of kin, and county.

Historic Morris County: An informal story of men and events beginning with the discovery of iron in the colonial period. The National Iron Bank of Morristown, 1943.

Includes honor roll of Morristown and community.

Combat Connected Naval Casualties World War II, Navy Department, 1946.

Newark Public Library
5 Washington Street
Newark, NJ 07101
(973) 733-7784
www.npl.org

Newark Evening News Index to New Jersey Servicemen 1941–1945; 1950–1953.

The WWII section is missing surnames beginning with E-O. These names can still be researched from the newspapers. Includes name, rank, branch and town from, and information mentioned in the newspaper, which may include military service or awards.

World War II Honor List of Dead and Missing Army and Army Air Forces Personnel. State of New Jersey, War Department, 1946.

Newspapers for WWII years.

New Jersey Historical Society
52 Park Place
Newark, NJ 07102
(973) 596-8500, (973) 596-6957 Fax
www.jerseyhistory.org

The Genealogical Society of New Jersey
PO Box 1291
New Brunswick, NJ 08903
www.rootsweb.com/~njgsnj

Department of Military and Veterans Affairs
PO Box 340
Trenton, NJ   08625-0340
(800) 624-0508

National Guard records for WWII. Request records giving the veteran's name, date of birth, serial number and other available information.

Veterans Affairs Regional Office
20 Washington Place
Newark, NJ 07102
(800) 827-1000

New Mexico

WWII Bonus Records: YES

New Mexico Commission of Public Records
Archives and Historical Services
1205 Camino Carlos Rey
Santa Fe, NM 87505
(505) 476-7908, (505) 476-7909 Fax
www.nmcpr.state.nm.us

Records of the Adjutant General.

Index to WWII Enlistments & Discharges. 1945–1947.

Selective Service–Separations. 1945–1946. By county.

WWII Service Records. 1945–1946. By last name.

Military Discharges. 1945–1947. By last name.

Veterans Graves–Albuquerque 1945

Deserter and Absentee lists, WWII 1943

Newspaper Clippings on WWII Servicemen, 1944–1947

Bataan Death March Casualty List. Cain, Memory H, 1942.

The New Mexico State Library
1209 Camino Carlos Rey
Santa Fe, NM 87507
(505) 476-9700, (505) 476-9701 Fax
www.stlib.state.nm.us

Newspapers for WWII years.

It tolled for New Mexico: New Mexicans Captured by the Japanese, 1941–1945, by Eva Jane Matson.

Service Record Book of Men and Women of Hidalgo County, VFW Post 3099, 1949. (Available from the Arizona State University Library, *http://library.lib.asu.edu*)

Bataan Memorial Military Museum & Library
1050 Old Pecos Trail
Santa Fe, NM 87505
(505) 474-1670, (505) 474-1671 Fax
www.nmculture.org

Historical Society of New Mexico
PO Box 1912
Santa Fe, NM 87504
www.hsnm.org

New Mexico Genealogical Society
PO Box 8283
Albuquerque, NM 87198-8283
www.nmgs.org

Department of Military Affairs
NMAG-APA-RO
47 Bataan Boulevard
Santa Fe, NM 87508
(505) 474-1202

National Guard records.
   Supply the veteran's name, date of birth, serial number
and date of discharge with records request.

New Mexico Veterans Service Commission
PO Box 2324
Santa Fe, NM 87504
(505) 827-6300

WWII Bonus Records.
   Veterans from New Mexico were given a tax exemption
as a bonus. Records exist for those veterans who applied for
the exemption.

Veterans Affairs Regional Office
500 Gold Avenue, SW
Albuquerque, NM 87102
(800) 827-1000

New York

WWII Bonus Records: YES

New York State Library
Cultural Education Ctr, Empire State Plaza
Albany, NY 12230
(518) 474-5355
www.nysl.nysed.gov

Genesee County World War II: Gold Star Memorial Book,
1953.

Yale Men who died in the Second World War, Yale University
Press, 1951.

Book of Honor, World War II, New Rochelle, NY, 1948.

American Jews in World War II, Dial Press, 1947.

Armenian-American Veterans of World War II, New York, 1951.

Andover's Part in World War II: A Pictorial Record of young Men and Women who served and are serving in the United States Forces from Andover and vicinity, George Wereley, 1946.

The town of St. Armand Honors the Veterans in the Celebration of the 50th Anniversary of World War II: Proudly They Served, Mary Gonyea, town of St. Armand historian, 1995.

A pictorial rememberance of the flag raisings & honor rolls dedicated to the men & women from the City of Albany, New York who served in World War II, J. Don Riley, American Legion Post 30, 2002.

Combat Connected Naval Casualties, World War II, Navy Department, 1946.

World War II Honor List of Dead and Missing Army and Army Air Forces Personnel. State of New York, War Department, 1946.

Union Club World War II Records, 1940–1947, New York, 1947. (This book is available from Auburn University Library, *www.lib.auburn.edu)*

New York State Newspaper Project
New York State Library, Cultural Education Center
Albany, NY 12230
(518) 474-7491
www.nysl.nysed.gov/nysnp

Newspapers for WWII years.

The New York Genealogical & Biographical Society
122 East 58th Street
New York, NY 10022-1939
(212) 755-8532
www.nygbs.org

The Adjutant General/Commander of New York
330 Old Niskayuna Road
Latham, NY 12110-2224
(518) 786-4600

No WWII records.

New York State Division of Veterans Affairs
5 Empire State Plaza #2836
Albany, NY 12223-1551
www.dmna.state.ny.us

World War II Bonus Records.
   Information on WWII bonus payments to New York
veterans includes their name, or next of kin, address of
person who received the bonus, serial number and amount
of payment. Please send request by E-mail or in writing.

Veterans Affairs Regional Office – Buffalo
111 West Huron Street
Buffalo, NY 14202
(800) 827-1000

Veterans Affairs Regional Office – New York
245 W Houston St.
New York, NY 10014
(800) 827-1000

North Carolina

WWII Bonus Records: NO

North Carolina State Archives
Public Services Branch
4614 Mail Service Center
Raleigh, NC 27699-4614
(919) 733-3952, (919) 733-1354 Fax
www.ah.dcr.state.nc.us

Military Personnel Records in the North Carolina State
Archives, 1918–1964.
    Discharge records. Organized by servicemen who regis-
tered with Selective Service and arranged by county and
then by name. Non-registrants are filed by last name.

Enlisted Men of the National Guard Commissioned and
Inducted Into Active Federal Service, 1940.
    Lists the name, war vacancy assignment, and enlistment
status.

Discharge Records by County.
    Copies of discharge certificates, if the veteran filed a copy
with the county clerk's office. Access is restricted, and is
only available to next of kin.

USS North Carolina.
    Ship's Diary 1941–1947; Battleship history file 1942–1945;
Honor Roll file, 1941–1945; Photographs of ship, officers and
crew.

Jackson County Heroes of WWII, The Sylva Herald.

*Roster of Franklin County Servicemen who Participated in all
wars to the Present,* April, 1945.

*Young American Patriots, The Youth of North Carolina in
WWII,* 1948.

*Service Record Book of Men and Women of WWII –
Yanceyville and Community,* VFW Post 7316, 1950.

Historical Annual, National Guard of the State of North Carolina, 1938.

Honor Roll of Cleveland County, North Carolina Men and Women serving in the Armed Forces of the United States, 1944.

World War II Honor List of Dead and Missing Army and Army Air Forces Personnel. State of North Carolina, War Department, 1946.

State Summary of War Casualties from World War II for Navy, Marine Corps, and Coast Guard Personnel from North Carolina, Navy Department, 1946.

Newspapers for WWII years.

North Carolina Genealogical Society
PO Box 22
Greenville, NC 27835-0022
www.ncgenealogy.org

The Adjutant General of North Carolina
4105 Reedy Creek Road
Raleigh, NC 27607-6410
(919) 664-6101

National Guard records for WWII.
    Request records by veteran's name, date of birth or serial number.

NC Division of Veterans Affairs
325 North Salisbury Street
Albemarle Building, #1065
Raleigh, NC 27603
(919) 733-3851

Casualty records only.

Veterans Affairs Regional Office
251 North Main Street
Winston-Salem, NC 27155
(800) 827-1000

North Dakota

WWII Bonus Records: YES

State Archives and Library (historical/genealogical)
612 East Boulevard Avenue
Bismarck, ND 58505-0830
(701) 328-2091, (701) 328-2650
www.state.nd.us/hist//sal.htm

North Dakotans in the Military Services, World War II:
Clippings, 1942–1946.
Collection contains copies of newspaper clippings con-
cerning North Dakotans serving in the military during
WWII. Information may include notice of marriages, deaths,
discharges from service, injuries, etc. Not indexed.

*Register of North Dakota Veterans, World War II, 1941–1945,
and Korean Conflict, 1950–1953.* 1968.
Lists North Dakota veterans of WWII and Korean War
and also includes National Guard.

*Report of Mobilization of the North Dakota National Guard,
World War II.* Office of the Adjutant General, 1942.
Rosters included with name, service number and rank.

*Service Record Book of Men and Women of Mountrail
County, North Dakota,* VFW Post 2707, 1947.

*Service Record Book of Men and Women of Valley City,
North Dakota, and Community.* Frank Henry Post 2764,
1947.

History of the 47th Infantry Regiment (in World War II).
United States Army 47th Infantry Regiment, 1947.

State Summary of War Casualties from World War II for Navy, Marine Corps, and Coast Guard Personnel from North Dakota, Navy Department, 1946.

World War II Honor List of Dead and Missing Army and Army Air Forces Personnel. State of North Dakota, War Department, 1946.

Newspapers for WWII years.

University of North Dakota, Chester Fritz Library
Department of Special Collections
PO Box 9000
Grand Forks, ND 58202
(701) 777-4625, (701) 777-3319 Fax
www.und.edu/dept/library/Collections/spk.html

164th Infantry Association Records. (Bulk 1941–1945).
    Contents include daily journals, battle reports, killed in action reports, missing in action reports, military awards and orders. Most of the collection is from the years 1943–1945.

North Dakota Prisoner of War Reports.
    Collection consists of questionnaires that were completed by North Dakota POWs and includes photographs, letters and telegrams.

The Adjutant General of North Dakota
PO Box 5511
Bismarck, ND 58506-5511
(701) 333-2001

National Guard records. Includes the veteran's name, date of birth and dates of service. *Citizens as Soldiers,* Book listing all WWII veterans from North Dakota. Please use the information request available on their website
www.guard.bismarck.nd.us

Department of Veterans Affairs
PO Box 9003
Fargo, ND 58106-9003
(701) 239-7165, (866) 634-8387

WWII Bonus Records.
   Bonus records include veteran's name, dates of service,
residence and serial number. Request records by name, date
of birth and year of discharge.

Veterans Affairs Regional Office
2101 Elm Street
Fargo, ND 58102
(800) 827-1000

Ohio

WWII Bonus Records: YES

The Ohio Historical Society
1982 Velma Avenue
Columbus, OH 43211
(614) 297-2300,
www.ohiohistory.org

Compensation Fund, Pensions, and Discharges.
   Records that consists of Ohio veterans that applied for
and received WWII bonus payments. This file also contains
discharge records. The records are in four sub series:
compensation fund alphabetical files (CR), next of kin
pension files (NFKP), next of kin compensation applications
(NFK-CA), and discharge records (P). Please request records
by veteran's name or other identifying information. Most
bonus applications were made in 1948.

Young American Patriots: The Youth of Ohio in World War II.
   Biographies of Ohioans who served in WWII. Contains
the veteran's name, rank, branch, date of birth, religion,
date entered the service, medals and next of kin name and
address. A photograph is included for most.

Photographs of the 37th Infantry Division. Six series.

Graves Registration File.
   Includes most veterans buried in Ohio up to 1967. May include date and place of birth and death, cause of death, and next of kin. Arranged alphabetically by last name.

Honor List, World War II
   Names of those missing—Army, Air Force, Navy, Marines and Coast Guard.

State Library of Ohio
274 East First Avenue
Columbus, OH 43201
(614) 644-7061
http://winslo.state.oh.us

Muskingum County Men and Women in World War II, Zanesville Publishing Co, 1947.

The Veterans of World War II: Morgan County, Ohio, Elmer Gerlach, 1986.

Ohio Genealogical Society
713 S Main Street
Mansfield, OH 44907-1644
www.ogs.org

The Adjutant General of Ohio
ATTN: Library
2825 West Dublin Granville Road
Columbus, OH 43235-2789
(614) 336-7070
www.ohionationalguard.com

National Guard records for WWII. Records organized by year of discharge and alphabetically by last name.

Governor's Office of Veterans' Affairs
77 South High Street
Columbus, OH 43215
(614) 664-0898

WWII Bonus Records.

Records for WWII veterans that applied for the Ohio WWII bonus. These records are restricted and not available. Only information releasable is a certificate of discharge, which is basic service information. This is only done on a limited basis.

Veterans Affairs Regional Office
A J Celebrezze Federal Building
1240 East 9th Street
Cleveland, OH 44199
(800) 827-1000

Adams ☆ ☆ YOUNG AMERICAN PATRIOTS ☆ ☆ 49

ALLEN, LEONARD C.
Cpl., U. S. Army. Born Sept. 12, 1917. Entered service Dec. 21, 1942, Camp Tyson, Tenn.; Sicily; Italy; France. Awarded 4 Battle Stars, Good Conduct Medal. Attended Manchester H. S. Protestant. Son of Mr. and Mrs. H. R. Allen, Manchester, Ohio. Husband of Mrs. Dorothy Barbour Allen, 205 E. 7th St., Manchester, Ohio.

ALMAND, HUBERT L.
Cpl., U. S. Army. Born Feb. 17, 1917. Entered service Dec. 3, 1942, Camp Van Dorn, Miss.; St. Paul, Minn.; Sioux Falls, S. Dak. Attended Withrow H. S. Protestant. Son of Mrs. Hazil Almand, Dayton, Ohio. Husband of Mrs. Leola Roush Almand, 207 W. 8th St., Manchester, Ohio.

ANDERSON, ROBERT HARRY
RT 1/c, U. S. Navy. Born Nov. 4, 1920. Entered service Oct. 13, 1943, Great Lakes, Ill.; Panama C. Z.; Hawaii; Philippines; Japan. Awarded Good Conduct Medal. Attended Cincinnati H. S. Methodist. Son of the late Mr. and Mrs. Harry Anderson, Cincinnati, Ohio. Husband of Mrs. Marie Haag Anderson, Box 212, West Union, Ohio.

AREY, EDWARD F.
T/5, U. S. Army. Born Sept. 11, 1917. Entered service Mar. 8, 1944, Camp Robinson, Ark.; Philippines; Okinawa; Japan. Awarded Good Conduct Medal. Attended Peebles H. S. Church of Christ. Son of Mr. and Mrs. Charles Arey, Lawshe, Ohio. Husband of Mrs. Kathleen Nichols Arey, Lawshe, Ohio.

AREY, RAY
Pfc., U. S. Army. Born Mar. 27, 1920. Entered service Oct. 16, 1941, Ft. Sill, Okla.; Ft. Thomas, Ky.; Aleutians. Awarded Battle Star, Good Conduct Medal. Attended Peebles H. S. Christian Church. Son of Mr. and Mrs. Charley A. Arey, Lawshe, Ohio. Husband of Mrs. Eva Frost Arey, Peebles, Ohio.

ATKINS, EARL
Cpl., U. S. Army. Born Apr. 26, 1913. Entered service Oct. 5, 1942, Ft. Thomas, Camp Breckinridge, Ky. Awarded Good Conduct Medal. Attended Argo and Phelps School. Presbyterian. Son of Mr. and Mrs. Luther Atkins, Lawshe, Ohio. Husband of Mrs. Rose McNeil Atkins, Lawshe, Ohio.

AUSTIN, DONALD WILBUR
S/Sgt., U. S. Army. Born Oct. 1, 1923. Entered service Feb. 15, 1943, Ft. Thomas, Ky.; Camp Swift, Tex. Awarded Good Conduct Medal. Attended Peebles H. S. Church of God. Son of Mr. and Mrs. Ross Austin, Peebles, Ohio. Husband of Mrs. Velma Samalley Austin, Peebles, Ohio.

AYERS, THOMAS M.
T/4, U. S. Army. Born June 9, 1921. Entered service Aug. 3, 1942, Fts. Thomas, Ky., Rosecrans, Calif.; Aleutian Isles. Awarded Good Conduct Medal. Attended Wayne Twp. H. S. United Presbyterian Church. Son of Mr. and Mrs. Grant Ayers, Cherry Fork, Ohio. Husband of Mrs. Ardonna Johnson Ayers, Cherry Fork, Ohio.

BEIGHLE, RALPH E.
Sgt., U. S. Army. Born Apr. 10, 1919. Entered service July 7, 1941, Patterson Field, Ohio; Stout Field, Ind. Awarded Good Conduct Medal. Attended Russellville H. S. Protestant. Son of Mr. and Mrs. W. H. Beighle, Winchester, Ohio. Husband of Mrs. Dorothy Moore Beighle, Rt. 1, Winchester, Ohio.

BERRY, GEORGE, JR.
S/Sgt., U. S. Army. Born June 16, 1920. Entered service Jan. 20, 1941, Camp Shelby, Miss.; England; Scotland; Ireland; N. Africa; Sicily; France; Belgium. Awarded Purple Heart, Pres. Unit Cit. with Cluster, 6 Battle Stars, Bronze Star with Cluster, Good Conduct Medal. Attended Wayne Twp. H. S. Protestant. Son of the late Mr. and Mrs. George Berry Sr., Cherry Fork, Ohio.

Young American Patriots: The Youth of Ohio in World War II, Ohio Historical Society

Oklahoma

WWII Bonus Records: NO

Oklahoma Historical Society
2100 North Lincoln Blvd
Oklahoma City, OK 73105-4997
(405) 522-5223
www.ok-history.mus.ok.us

Oklahoma Army Honor Roll of WWII Casualties.
   Notices of casualties taken from the *Daily Oklahoman* newspapers. Includes the veteran's Last name, rank and casualty type.

Fighting Men of Oklahoma: History of Oklahoma Warriors. Volume II.
   Information includes the veteran's name, serial number and date of birth, branch of service, rank, relatives, place of birth and education. Some entries include a photograph. Index of the book is available online at *www.rootsweb.com/ ~okgenweb/books/fight/fight-ab.html*

Service Records WWII, 1941–1945.
   This collection originates from the records of the Oklahoma Daughters of the American Revolution. Questionnaires sent to members of the DAR to have them fill out concerning a relative's WWII service. These documents include the veteran's name, branch, date of birth, place of birth, relatives, military service information, spouse's name and children.

Newspapers for WWII years.

Oklahoma Department of Libraries
200 NE 18th St
Oklahoma City, OK 73105-3298
(405) 521-2502, (405) 525-7804 Fax
www.odl.state.ok.us

The Homefront: Monthly news and gossip from, to, and between the service men and the folks at home, Jefferson, OK, 1943–1945.

World War II Honor List of Dead and Missing Army and Army Air Forces Personnel. State of Oklahoma, War Department, 1946.

State Summary of War Casualties from World War II for Navy, Marine Corps, and Coast Guard Personnel from Oklahoma, Navy Department, 1946.

Oklahoma Genealogical Society
PO Box 12986
Oklahoma City, OK 73157
www.rootsweb.com/~okgs

The Adjutant General of Oklahoma
3501 Military Circle, NE
Oklahoma City, OK 73111-4398
(405) 228-5320,

No WWII records.

Oklahoma Department of Veterans Affairs
2311 N Central Ave
Oklahoma City, OK 73150
(405) 521-3684, (405) 521-6533 Fax

No WWII records.

Veterans Affairs Regional Office
125 S Main Street
Muskogee, OK 74401
(800) 827-1000

Oregon

WWII Bonus Records: YES

Oregon State Archives
800 Summer St NE
Salem, OR 97310
(503) 373-0701, (503) 373-0953
http://arcweb.sos.state.or.us

Statement of Service Cards 1917–1919; 1941–1945.
Information taken from military service records of the U.S. Army, Navy and Marine Corps. Information includes veteran's name, residence, place of birth, age or date of birth, organizations served with and discharge date. Arranged by war, then by branch and alphabetically by veteran's last name.

Enlistment and Service Records 1847–1920, 1930–1977.
Documents included in this collection consist of enlistment statements, recruit examinations and declarations, assignment cards, oaths of office, physical descriptions, appointments, correspondence, reenlistment applications, vaccination register, fingerprint cards and parental consent forms. Alphabetically by last name. Privacy Act applies to records. Once the veteran is deceased, authorized person can request records.

Military Unit Records 1917–1948.
Consists of information concerning military reserve units. Units included are the 41st Div, 116th Med Reg, 82nd Brig, 186th Inf Reg, 162nd Inf Reg. Information includes efficiency reports on officers, station lists of units, organizational charts, and drill attendance.

Morning Reports 1855–1949.
National Guard units. Includes unit name, location, number of men on duty, rank, remarks, and record of events.

Non-Resident Service Records Extracts 1941–1944.

Contains the veteran's name, home address, age, pay rate, rank, unit name, induction date and location, data concerning prior service (if any). Name beginning with "O" through "Z" are missing. Alphabetical by last name.

World War II Honor List of Dead and Missing Army and Army Air Forces Personnel. State of Oregon, War Department, 1946.

Oregon Historical Society
1200 SW Park Avenue
Portland, OR 97205-2483
(503) 222-1741, (503) 221-2035 Fax
www.ohs.org

Oregon Genealogical Society
PO Box 10306
Eugene, OR 97440-2306
(541) 345-0399
www.rootsweb.com/~orlncogs/ogsinfo.htm

The Adjutant General of Oregon
Oregon Military Dept, PO Box 14350
Salem, OR 97309-5047
(503) 584-3980

Maintains National Guard records. Submit request in writing with proof of death and relationship. Include the veteran's name, service number and time period of service.

Oregon Department of Veterans' Affairs
700 Summer St NE
Salem, OR 97301-1285
(503) 373-2388, (503) 373-2362 Fax

Their office maintains a card file of Oregon veterans that applied for the state's WWII bonus. The card contains the veteran's name, serial number and address the bonus was mailed to. If veteran was deceased, then next of kin may have requested the bonus. The Oregon WWII bonus began in 1950. Privacy Act applies. Alphabetical.

Veterans Affairs Regional Office
1220 SW 3rd Avenue
Portland, OR 97204
(800) 827-1000

Pennsylvania

WWII Bonus Records: YES

Pennsylvania Historical & Museum Commission
Pennsylvania State Archives
350 North Street
Harrisburg, PA 17120-0090
(717) 783-3281
www.phmc.state.pa.us

WWII Applications for Veterans' Compensation.

Records pertaining to the bonus for Pennsylvania WWII veterans. Records include the veteran's name, signature, residence, date of birth, place of birth, sex and serial number. Dates of service, branch of the service, the dates and places where the veteran entered and left active duty, residence at the time of enlistment, the names and locations of the applicants' draft boards, amount of money paid, names and address of the veteran's beneficiaries. Application also lists dependents and military status. Records are restricted. Records are released to next of kin, if veteran is deceased. Arranged alphabetically by last name.

Records of Pennsylvania National Guardsmen Mustered into World War II. 1940–1941.
Lists name and race, date and place of enlistment, grade at enlistment, name of enlisting officer, and the date and grade/rank from his prior service. Also included in these records are Declarations of the Applicants and Physical Examination Reports. Arranged alphabetically by last name.

National Guard Enlistment Records, Including 201 Files. 1867–1945.

Records for National Guard enlistments from the end of the Civil War to WWII. Records contain the name, signature, date of birth, place of birth, race, occupation, marital status, dependents, education, residence, date of enlistment, physical description and name and address of next of kin. Also includes brief medical information. Alphabetical by last name.

Master Card File of Officers in the Pennsylvania National Guard. 1934–1985.
    Index card listings of officers of the Pennsylvania National Guard. Contains information pertaining to the officer's status of service. Alphabetical by last name.

Office of Commonwealth Libraries
Bureau of State Library, 333 Market Street
Harrisburg, PA 17126-1745
(717) 783-5950
www.statelibrary.state.pa.us/libraries

Lykens & Wiconisco Homecoming Celebration: Aug. 31, Sept. 1-2, 1946, Clayton L. Peters and Harry A. Stutzman.
Contains Roll of honor and List of dead of World War II.

Off to War: Franklin Countians in World War II, Roscoe Barnes III, Burd Street Press, 1996.

War and Peace: Fulton County, 1945, Marty McCullen, Fulton County Historical Society, 1995.

Gold Star Honor Roll World War II Erie County, Pennsylvania, Erie County Historical Society, 1947.

Combat Connected Naval Casualties, World War II, by States, Navy Department, 1946.

The Historical Society of Pennsylvania
1300 Locust Street
Philadelphia, PA 19107
(215) 732-6200
www.hsp.org

World War II Commemorative Booklet: Honoring Local Servicemen on the 50th Anniversary of D-Day, June 6 1944–1994, William Tennent High School, Madrigal Singers, Minuteman Press, 1994.

Young American Patriots: The Youth of Pennsylvania in World War II, National Pub. Co, 1947?

Military Service Records of Members in the Armed Forces in World War II, Society of Colonial Wars in the Commonwealth of Pennsylvania, 1947.

Genealogical Society of Pennsylvania
215 S. Broad St, 7th Floor
Philadelphia, PA 19107-5325
(215) 545-0391
www.libertynet.org/gspa

The Adjutant General of Pennsylvania
Building S-O-47 Fisher Avenue
Annville, PA 17003-5002
(717) 861-8500

Record turned over to archives.

Veterans Affairs Regional Office
1000 Liberty Avenue
Pittsburgh, PA 15222
(800) 827-1000

Rhode Island

WWII Bonus Records: YES

State Archives and Public Records Administration
337 Westminster Street
Providence, RI 02903
(401) 222-2353, (401) 222-3199 Fax
www.state.ri.us/archives

Scrapbooks, World War II, 1941–1945.
Clippings from newspapers during WWII years. Indexed by township.

Roster of Rhode Island Women in the Armed Services of the United States.
Origin of this resource is not known. Lists the name, address and branch of service.

Discharge Records. Town of Little Compton.
Other discharge certificates filed by veterans are maintained by city or town.

Temporary Commissions Granted to Rhode Island National Guard Personnel while in Federal Service, 1941–1945.

Appointments (various); Air Corps, Engineers, Field Artillery, Dental & Medical Corps, etc 1930–1940's.

Casualty Records.
Card file of information sent by the War Department to the State Adjutant General. Includes wounded, killed, prisoner of war, missing in action, personnel returned to duty, repatriates and promotions.

Roster of Naval Non-Combat Dead, Navy Department, 1946.

State Summary of War Casualties from World War II for Navy, Marine Corps, and Coast Guard Personnel from Rhode Island, Navy Department, 1946.

The Rhode Island Historical Society
110 Benevolent Street
Providence, RI 02906
(401) 331-8575
www.rihs.org

Newspapers for WWII years.

University of Rhode Island Library
15 Lippitt Road
Kingston, RI 02881-2011
www.uri.edu/library

History and Roster of Rhode Island Masonry in World War Two, Winfield Scott Solomon, 1946.

A Musical Tribute to Rhode Island WW II Women Veterans "Honoring Those Who Served" a World War II Women's Revue, Secretary of State, 2002.
   Material includes rosters for the Women's Army Corps, Women in the Marine Corps, WAVES, SPARs, Nurse Corps, Red Cross and Women's Honor Roll.

Rhode Island Genealogical Society
PO Box 433
Greenville, RI 02828
http://users.ids.net/~ricon/rigs.html

The Adjutant General of Rhode Island
Headquarters RI National Guard
645 New London Ave
Cranston, RI   02920-3097
(401) 275-4100

National Guard records and WWII bonus records.
   The WWII bonus records contain the amount paid and service history that came from the discharge certificate. Request records giving the veteran's name, branch of service, time period of service, date of birth and serial number. Privacy Act applies to records.

Veterans Affairs Regional Office
380 Westminister Mall
Providence, RI 02903
(800) 827-1000

South Carolina

WWII Bonus Records: NO

South Carolina Department of Archives and History
8301 Parklane Road
Columbia, SC 29223
(803) 896-6100, (803) 896-6198 Fax
www.state.sc.us/scdah

The Adjutant General's office published five volumes of biographical information obtained from the discharges (and other available information) of men and women who served from the state of South Carolina. It includes last name, first name, middle initial, (Jr./Sr.), military serial number, city and state of birth, date of birth, date entered active duty, date of discharge and information concerning the veterans service, awards and units. Also lists those who were killed. Alphabetically by veteran's last name.

National Guard Records.

Company Files after induction of Selected South Carolina. National Guard Units.

National Guard Enlistment Records. 1919–1941.

Discharges and Releases 1941–1943.

Combat Connected Naval Casualties World War II, by state, Navy Department, 1946.

South Carolina Historical Society
100 Meeting Street
Charleston, SC 29401
(803) 723-3225
www.schistory.org

South Carolina Genealogical Society
PO Box 492
Columbia, SC 29202
www.scgen.org

The Adjutant General of South Carolina
#1 National Guard Road
Columbia, SC 29201-4766
(803) 806-4217

Records are in custody of the State Archives.

South Carolina Office of Veterans Affairs
1205 Pendleton Street, Suite 226
Columbia, SC 29201
(803) 734-0200, (803) 734-0197 Fax

No WWII records.

South Caroliniana Library
910 Sumter St
University of South Carolina
Columbia, SC 29208
(803) 777-3132, (803) 777-5747 Fax
www.sc.edu/library/socar/index.html

Newspapers for WWII years.

*World War II Honor List of Dead and Missing Army and
Army Air Forces Personnel. State of South Carolina,* War
Department, 1946.

*State Summary of War Casualties from World War II for
Navy, Marine Corps, and Coast Guard Personnel from South
Carolina,* Navy Department, 1946.

Veterans Affairs Regional Office
1801 Assembly Street
Columbia, SC 29201
(800) 827-1000

BLUMER, JULIUS M 44095113. B BARNWELL SC 30 OCT
19. HA HAMBERG BAMBERG CO SC. EAD ARMY 20 AUG 45.
AWD WWIIVM. HON DISCH PFC CE 5 AUG 46.

BLUNT, ANDER 34654575. B WHITEVILLE NC 25 JUL 19.
HA LORIS HORRY CO SC. EAD ARMY 7 MAY 43. OS APT
10 APR 44 TO 21 JAN 46. AWD GCMDL ACM APCM
RYUKYUS WWIIVM. HON DISCH SSGT 667 ORD AMMO CO 30
JAN 46.

BLUNT, FREDDIE 34647526. B WANDO SC 9 OCT 14. HA
JOHNS IS CHARLESTON CO SC. EAD ARMY 4 MAR 43. OS
APT 29 JAN 44 TO 6 JAN 46. AWD GCMDL CIB APCM NEW
GUINEA N SOLOMONS LUZON WWIIVM. HON DISCH PFC CO
L 369 INF 16 JAN 46.

BLUNT, ROBERT W 520219. B INDIANAPOLIS IND 2 DEC
25. HA PORT ROYAL BEAUFORT CO SC. EAD USMC 4 JAN
43. OS 16 MOS. HON DISCH PVT 17 NOV 45.

BLYTH, EDWIN K 9926556. B CHARLESTON SC 22 JUN
23. HA NAVY YARD CHARLESTON CO SC. EAD USN 14 AUG
43. AWD ACM APCM WWIIVM PLR. HON DISCH FM1C VY
CHARLESTON SC 1 FEB 46.

BLYTH, THOMAS J 9907314. B CHARLESTON SC 20 NOV
17. HA NAVY YARD CHARLESTON CO SC. EAD USN 27 JUL
45. AWD WWIIVM. HON DISCH S1C USS FARENHOLT 4 MAY
46.

BLYTHE, ALBERT A 34510872. B GREENVILLE SC 10 FEB
21. HA GREENVILLE GREENVILLE CO SC. EAD AAF 6 NOV
42. OS APT 25 JUL 44 TO 25 JAN 46. AWD ACM APCM
CHINA OFF CENT BURMA INDIA-BURMA WWIIVM. HON
DISCH PFC 1337 AAF BU 6 FEB 46.

BLYTHE, COLLINS V 9307724. B SWEETWATER TEX 16
FEB 26. HA CHARLESTON CHARLESTON CO SC. EAD USN
27 FEB 44. AWD ACM APCM 2S/S WWIIVM. HON DISCH
EM2C USS REQUISITE 5 MAY 46.

BLYTHE, EDGEWORTH M JR 0261575. B GREENVILLE SC
12 FEB 08. HA GREENVILLE GREENVILLE CO SC. EAD
ARMY 27 OCT 41. OS EAMET 10 SEP 44 TO 3 OCT 45.
AWD ADSM ACM EAMECM WWIIVM. HON SEP AD LT COL
CLAIMS TM 6813 17 JAN 46.

The Official Roster of South Carolina Servicemen and Servicewomen in World War II, 1941–46

South Dakota

WWII Bonus Records: YES

South Dakota State Archives
900 Governors Drive
Pierre, SD 57501-2217
(605) 773-3804, (605) 773-6041 Fax
www.sdhistory.org/archives.htm

The True Story of BB-57, USS South Dakota: The Queen of the Fleet, Taylor Publishing Co, 1987.

Lest We Forget: World War II Yankton County veterans.

*Other county books available for Edmunds county, Black Hills and Beadle county.

State Summary of War Casualties from World War II for Navy, Marine Corps, and Coast Guard Personnel from South Dakota, Navy Department, 1946.

Fallen Sons and Daughters of South Dakota in World War II, in World War II, Governor's Office, 2002.

Newspapers for WWII years.

South Dakota National Guard Museum
301 E Dakota Ave
Pierre, SD 57501-3225
(605) 224-9991

South Dakota in WWII. Lists some veterans that served from South Dakota. Includes name, rank, county, unit and dates of service.

May have rosters for National Guard units.

South Dakota Genealogical Society
Box 1101
Pierre, SD 57501-1101
www.rootsweb.com/~sdgenweb/gensoc/sdgensoc.html

South Dakota Army National Guard
Records Management
2823 West Main Street
Rapid City, SD 57702-8186
(605) 737-6240

National Guard records. Request records giving the
veteran's full name, date of birth and time period of service.

Department of Military and Veterans Affairs
Soldiers and Sailors Memorial Bldg
425 E Capitol Ave
Pierre, SD 57501-5070
(605) 773-3269, (605) 773-5380 Fax

WWII Bonus Records.
   Bonus records include veteran's name, serial number,
dates of service, branch, county resided in, bonus number.
Include the veterans name and serial number (if known),
with request.

Veterans Affairs Regional Office
2501 West 22nd Street
Sioux Falls, SD 57117
(800) 827-1000

Tennessee

WWII Bonus Records: NO

Tennessee State Library and Archives
403 Seventh Avenue North
Nashville, TN 37243-0312
(615) 741-2764
www.state.tn.us/sos/statelib/tslahome.htm

Tennessee World War II Veterans' Survey.
   A statewide project began 1996 to collect information
about Tennessee WWII veterans. These questionnaires were
for veterans from the state or veterans who were in the state
during the war. The record group is divided into five series.
Series I contains over 7,500 of the completed questionnaires

listed alphabetically by surname. Series II contains photographs, copies of veterans' discharges, diaries and memoirs, clippings, books, and other military service materials. Series III has donor agreements. Series IV contains the book that was published from the surveys, *Answering the Call,* which lists of 6,400 veterans. Series V is a small file of WWII questionnaires done before the Bicentennial survey.

World War Two Collection, 1941–1945.
Contains clippings on Tennesseans who served in the Navy during WWII. Includes folders for naval personnel (alphabetical), and folders about females in the WAVES.

US Naval Personnel Biographies of Tennesseans, 1943–1945.
Biographical information on Tennesseans who served in the Navy during the war. Many photographs are included.

Tennessee National Guard, Adjutant General Office Military Records, 1812–1941. (Original records)

They Served the Flag: The Second World War Veterans of Weakley County, Tennessee, Saunders; Downing, Mountain Press, 2001.

Ration Book Three, 1943: World War II Index to Registrants, Jefferson County, Tennessee, Jefferson County Genealogical Society, 1996.

Answering The Call: Tennesseans in the Second World War: A Bicentennial Project, Tennessee 200, Inc, 1996.

World War II Veterans, Wayne County, Tennessee, Turner Publishing Co, 2001.

"We Honor." World War II Memorial Booklet of Bristol area War Veterans, Patton-Crosswhite VFW Post 6975, 1951.

Maury County Remembers World War II, Maury County Historical Society, 1991.

Service Record, World War I and II Marshall County, Tennessee, VFW Bill Lowe Wheatley Post 5109, 1948.

White County's G.I. Honor Roll Book: The Army, Navy, Coast Guard, and Marine Corps. Expositor Print. Co, 1946.

World War II Honor List of Dead and Missing Army and Army Air Forces Personnel. State of Tennessee, War Department, 1946.

Combat Connected Naval Casualties, World War II, by States, Navy Department, 1946.

Microfilm Collections:

Army–Navy "E" Award Recipients, 1942–1945.

Military Absentee Ballots from 1944–1962.

National Guard Enlistment Records, 1890–1967.

United States Navy, Personnel Questionnaires Tennessee, 1942–1945.

Newspapers for WWII years. Indexed.

Tennessee Genealogical Society
PO Box 247
Brunswick, TN 38014-0247
www.rootsweb.com/~tngs

The Adjutant General of Tennessee
Houston Barracks, PO Box 41502
Nashville, TN 37204-1501
(615) 313-3001

Discharge certificates and National Guard personnel files. Must supply the county the veteran entered from and date of birth with request.

Veterans Affairs Regional Office
1190 9th Avenue, South
Nashville, TN 37203
(800) 827-1000

Texas

WWII Bonus Records: NO

Texas State Library and Archives
1201 Brazos Street, PO Box 12927
Austin, TX 78701
www.tsl.state.tx.us

Texas Adjutant General Service Records 1836–1935.
   Files from the Adjutant General's office and other agencies that contain service records information for Special Ranger Service Records, Railroad Rangers Service Records, etc. Search online *www.tsl.state.tx.us/arc/service/index.html*

Discharge Records.
   Records of discharges, if filed, are maintained at the county level. For a list of regional depositories that hold county records see *www.tsl.state.tx.us/arc/local/depositories.html*

Collection of 36th Division Materials.
   A collection of correspondence, clippings, printed material and military records pertaining to the 36th Division. Contains information from the 36th Division Association and includes personal WWII servicemen interviews.

Combat Connected Naval Casualties, World War II, by States, Navy Department, 1946.

In the Life and Lives of Brown County People, Brown County Historical Society, 1981.
   Lists brown county veterans that served in World War II. Includes surnames A–G.

USS Texas (BB35), By Egan, Lott, Sumrall, Leeward Publications, 1976.

Texas Historical Commission
PO Box 12276
Austin, TX 78711-2276
(512) 463-6100
www.thc.state.tx.us

Texas State Genealogical Society
www.rootsweb.com/~txsgs

The University of Texas at Austin
Perry-Castaneda Library
1 University Station S5466
Austin, TX 78712
(512) 495-4250
www.lib.utexas.edu

Fighting Men of Texas, Historical Publishing Co, 1948.

Heroes of World War II of the Dalhart, Texas area, Dalhart Publishing Co, 1944/45

Serving the Nation: Men and Women from Wilbarger County and adjacent territory, World War II, Vernon Daily Record, 1944/45.

In Memoriam, Texas Newspaper Publishers Assn. 1945. Lists employees of Texas newspapers who died in World War II.

World War II Honor List of Dead and Missing Army and Army Air Forces Personnel. State of Texas, War Department, 1946.

Report on project for providing memorial certificates to families of ex-students who gave their lives in World War II, Texas University, Registrar's Office, 1947.

Newspapers for WWII years. Indexed.

Texas Veterans Commission
PO Box 12277
Austin, TX 78711
(512) 463-5538, (512) 475-2395 Fax
www.tvc.state.tx.us

Casualty lists only.

The Adjutant General of Texas
PO Box 5218, Camp Mabry
Austin, TX 78763-5218
(512) 782-5031

National Guard records.
   Include the veteran's name, date of birth and time period
of service when requesting records. About 90% of records
are available for WWII.

Veterans Affairs Regional Office – Waco
1 Veterans Plaza, 701 Clay Avenue
Waco, TX 76799
(800) 827-1000

Veterans Affairs Regional Office – Houston
6900 Almeda Road
Houston, TX 77030
(800) 827-1000

Utah

WWII Bonus Records: NO

Utah State Archives and Records Service
PO Box 141021
Salt Lake City, UT 84114-1021
(801) 538-3013, (801) 538-3354
www.archives.state.ut.us

Military Service Cards, 1898–1975.
   Card file listing the military service of Utah Veterans.
Arranged alphabetically by surname.

Military Separation Forms and Benefit Records, 1917–1979.

Most contents pertain to WWII veterans and include personal information, transfer and discharged information, selective service, military service, VA insurance and pay, and authentication and signatures. Alphabetical by name.

Selective Service Cards, 1940–1957.

Cards prepared by the Utah State Historical Society's military records section. Contains the veteran's name, rank, branch of service and local draft board number. Alphabetical by veteran's last name.

Military Death Certificates, 1941–1953.

Contains death certificates of WWII and Korean War killed overseas whose final burial was in Utah. Arranged by date.

World War Military Listings, 1917–1951.

Information collected by the Utah State Historical Society of Utahans serving in the Armed Forces. Most records pertain to WWII and include casualties, wounded, missing and discharges with overseas service. Arranged alphabetical by last name.

National Guard, World War II Records, 1941–1945.

Collection consists of rosters for National Guard unit and federal unit histories for units that Utah guardsmen served in during the WWII. 40th Infantry.

Military Discharges.

Copies of discharge certificates filed with the county recorder's office. Series includes: Box Elder (1944–1952); Carbon (1944+); Duchesne (1945–1994); Emery (1923–1952); Iron (1921–1964); Juab (1944–1947); Kane (1945–1994); Millard (1944–1960); San Juan (1944–1948); Sanpete (1944–1964); Sevier (1942–1970); Uintah (1944–1992); Utah (1924–1971).

WWII Scrapbooks 1940–1948.

Contains a list of casualties.

University of Utah
201 S President's Circle Room 201
Salt Lake City, UT 84112
(801) 581-6273 (Reference)
www.utah.edu

State Summary of War Casualties from World War II for Navy, Marine Corps, and Coast Guard Personnel from Utah, Navy Department, 1946.

Utah Remembers World War II, Utah State University Press, 1991.

Utah State Historical Society
300 South Rio Grande
Salt Lake City, UT 84101-1143
(801) 533-3500
http://history.utah.gov

Newspapers for WWII years.

An Historical Index of Men and Women of Washington County Utah who served in the Military during World War II, Young, Abram Owen, Jr, 1992.

The Glory of Bingham Canyon Utah, 1941–1944, Victory Flag Society, 1944.

Utah Genealogical Association
PO Box 1144
Salt Lake City, UT 84110
(888) INFO-UGA
www.infouga.org

The Adjutant General of Utah
12953 S Minuteman Drive
Draper, UT 84020-1776
(801) 523-4400

All WWII records were turned over to the Archives.
Veterans Affairs Regional Office

Veterans Affairs Regional Office
125 S State Street
Salt Lake City, UT 84147
(800) 827-1000

Vermont

WWII Bonus Records: YES

Vermont State Archives
109 State Street
Montpelier, VT 05609-1103
(802) 828-2308
http://vermont-archives.org

Roster of Vermonters in Uniformed Service of the United States during the Second World War, 1941–1945 (2 Volumes), Adjutant General, 1972.
   Includes the veterans' name, date and place of birth, residence, dates of service, assignments and military service information.

Personal papers and scrapbook collections for WWII.

Department of Libraries
109 State Street
Montpelier, VT 05609-0601
(802) 828-3261, (802) 828-2199 Fax
http://dol.state.vt.us

Newspapers for WWII years.

Vermont Historical Society Library
60 Washington Street
Barre, VT 05641-4209
(802) 479-8500
www.vermonthistory.org

Personal paper collections for WWII.

Genealogical Society of Vermont
PO Box 1553
St. Albans, VT 05478-1006
www.rootsweb.com/~vtgsv

The Adjutant General of Vermont
State Veterans Affairs
120 State Street
Montpelier, VT 05620-4401
(802) 828-3379

Discharge certificates on file. Card files for WWII bonus records that contain military service data.

The Military Department
Green Mountain Armory, Camp Johnson
Colchester, VT 05446-3004
(802) 338-3423

No WWII records.

Veterans Affairs Regional Office
215 N Main Street
White River Junction, VT 05009
(800) 827-1000

Virginia

WWII Bonus Records: NO

The Library of Virginia
800 East Broad Street
Richmond, VA 23219-8000
(804) 692-3500
www.lva.lib.va.us

Correspondence and Data Files, 1941–1950.
   Information consisting of newspaper clippings by subject, reference notes and citations, scrapbooks and listing of Virginia WWII casualties.

Personal War Service Records of Virginia's War Dead, 1942–1945.

Collection contains letters, military service records, newspaper clippings and photographs of Virginia WWII casualties.

Separation Notices and Reports, 1942–1945.

Discharge records of Virginia servicemen and women. The majority of the collection is from 1944–1946. Arranged alphabetically by last name. At this time the collection is closed for processing.

Signal Corps Photograph Collection.

Contains over 3,500 photographs from the Hampton Roads Embarkation Series, 1942–1946.

Gold Star Honor Roll of Virginians in the Second World War, Virginia World War II History Commission, 1947.

The History of Appomattox, Virginia, also World War II–I and Spanish American War Service Record. Nathaniel Ragland Featherston, 1948

Pursuits of War; the People of Charlottesville and Albemarle County, Virginia, in the Second World War, By Gertrude Dana Parlier and others, W. Edwin Hemphill.

Roster of Catholic Men and Women who served in World War II, Diocese of Richmond, 1941–1946, Diocese of Richmond, VA, 1946.

Roster of Officers of the Hampton Roads port of Embarkation, Newport News, Virginia. Edited by Capt. J. M. Hetherington, 1946.

Serviceman's Album of Men and Women Serving the Nation in World War II. The Coalfield progress, 1945.

"We honor." World War II Memorial Booklet of Bristol area War Veterans, Patton-Crosswhite VFW Post 6975, 1951.

History of 47th Infantry Regiment, US Army, 1947.

Young American Patriots: The Youth of Virginia in World War II, National Publishing Co, 1945.

A Tribute to World War II Veterans of Russell County, Virginia, Historical Society of Russell County, 1999.

Wise County, Virginia's World War II Veterans: A Tribute, Wise County Historical Society, 1995.

State Summary of War Casualties from World War II for Navy, Marine Corps, and Coast Guard Personnel from Virginia, Navy Department, 1946.

World War II Honor List of Dead and Missing Army and Army Air Forces Personnel. State of Virginia, War Department, 1946.

Naval Non-Combat Dead, World War II [Virginia], Navy Department, 1946.

Virginia DAR Genealogical Records committee Report. Series 2, v. 45, World War I Board Registrations, General Index to Induction and Discharge Records, World War II, Scott County, Virginia, Virginia DAR, 1996.

Newspapers for WWII years.

Virginia Historical Society
PO Box 7311
Richmond, VA 23221-0311
(804) 358-4901
www.vahistorical.org

Fauquier's World War II Gold Star Heroes, John Toler, 1991.

Pursuits of War: The People of Charlottesville and Albemarle County, Virginia, in the Second World War, Hemphill, 1948.

Men from Rockingham County and Harrisonburg who lost their lives in World War II. Rockingham recorder, Harrisonburg, VA 1947.

Honor Roll of Montgomery County's sons and daughters in World War II: A chronicle of the men and women from Montgomery County who entered the service of our Armed Forces to help win the greatest war of civilization, Montgomery Co, VA War Finance Committee, 1940's.

Virginia National Guard
Building 316, Fort Pickett
Blackstone, VA 23824-6316

Records turned over the Archives.

Virginia Veterans Affairs
270 Franklin Road, SW Rm 503
Roanoke, VA 24011-2215

No WWII records.

Veterans Affairs Regional Office
210 Franklin Road, SW
Roanoke, VA 24011
(800) 827-1000

Washington

WWII Bonus Records: YES

Washington State Archives
PO Box 40236
Olympia, WA 98504-0238
(360) 753-1684, (360) 664-8814 Fax
www.secstate.wa.gov/archives

Department of Veterans' Affairs, World War II Veterans Bonus Files, 1950–1959.

Files contain the veteran's application for the WWII bonus. Includes the name, claim number, amount paid and warrant number. Also includes military service and discharge documents.

Military Department, Histories of the Washington State
Military Department, 1855–1965.
  Washington National Guard histories. Includes muster
rolls.

Military Department, Enlistment Records, 1880–1946.
  National Guard records containing enlistment papers,
name, serial number, residence, occupation, date and place
of induction, date of birth and place of birth, race, marital
status, military service history, type of discharge.
Chronological by group and then alphabetically.

Department of Veterans Affairs, Orting Soldiers Home,
  Applications for Admission, 1891–1987.

Department of Veterans Affairs, Orting Soldiers Home,
  Cemetery Records, 1891–1972.

Department of Veterans Affairs, Retsil Veterans Home,
  Member Files, 1910–1992.

Washington State Library
PO Box 42460
Olympia, WA 98504-2460
(360) 704-5200
www.statelib.wa.gov

*The War Years: A Chronicle of Washington State in World
War II,* Warren, 2000.
  Contains a list of casualties.

Battleship at War: The Epic Story of the USS Washington,
Ivan Musicant, 1986.

Newspapers for WWII years.

University Libraries
University of Washington
Box 352900
Seattle, WA 98195-2900
(206) 543-0242
www.lib.washington.edu

Combat Connected Naval Casualties, World War II, by States, Navy Department, 1946.

Try Us: The Story of the Washington Artillery in World War II, Powell A. Casey, 1971.

Washington State Historical Society
1911 Pacific Avenue
Tacoma, WA 98402
(253) 272-3500
www.wshs.org

Washington State Genealogical Society
PO Box 1422
Olympia, WA 98507-1422
www.rootsweb.com/~wasgs

The Adjutant General of Washington
Camp Murray, Bldg 1
Tacoma, WA 98430-5000
(253) 512-8000 7834

National Guard records.

Washington Department of Veterans Affairs
505 E Union, PO Box 41155
Olympia, WA 98504-1155
(360) 586-1070

WWII bonus records.
   Contains a copy of the discharge certificate and copy of application for those who applied for the bonus. Include the veteran's name and date of birth with request.

Veterans Affairs Regional Office
915 2nd Avenue
Seattle, WA 98174
(800) 827-1000

West Virginia

WWII Bonus Records: YES

West Virginia State Archives and Library
Cultural Center
1900 Kanawha Blvd East
Charleston, WV 25305-0300
(304) 558-0220, (304) 558-2044 Fax
www.wvculture.org/history

Newspapers for WWII years.

Reports of Transfer of Discharge, 1941–1945.
    Arranged alphabetically by last name. Contains military service history.

Lewis Countians in World War II: Presenting the pictures of 800 young Men and Women serving in the United States Armed Forces, Independent Publishing Co, 1943–1946.

Calhoun County in World War II, Stevens; Barrows. Calhoun Historical and Genealogical Society.

Record of Prestonians: World War II, Preston County Historical Society, 1960?

Our Patriots of America West Virginia, National Patriotic Publishers. Covers mostly the middle part of the state.

Salute to the Veteran (clippings from newspapers), Men of WWII in the News–1945, Pauline Haga, 1993.

Service Record Book of Men and Women of Madison, W.Va, and Community, VFW, Daniel Boone Post 5578.

Summers County World War Veterans.

War Veterans of Upshur County, Nathaniel Jack, 1988.

Young American Patriots: The Youth of West Virginia in World War II, National Publishing Co, 1946.

Memorial: Men and Women in Service, World War II, David Dale Johnson, 194?

West Virginia Veterans Memorial Database.
   Online database listings over 10,000 men and women from West Virginia who died in 20th-century military actions. For veterans to be included they must have either been born in West Virginia or a resident six months prior to military service.
http://wvmemory.wvculture.org/wvvetmem.html

Naval Non-Combat Dead, World War II, Navy Department, 1946.

State Summary of War Casualties from World War II for Navy, Marine Corps, and Coast Guard Personnel from West Virginia, Navy Department, 1946.

World War II Honor List of Dead and Missing Army and Army Air Forces Personnel. State of West Virginia, War Department, 1946.

Heritage History Book, McDowell County Historical Society. Included in this book is a list of 2,050 WWII   veterans from the county. (McDowell County Historical Society, HC 61, Box 37-B, Paynesville, WV 24873)

West Virginia Historical Society
PO Box 5220
Charleston, WV 25361
www.wvhistorical.com

West Virginia Genealogical Society
PO Box 249
Elkview, WV 25071
(304) 965-1179
http://rootsweb.com/~wvgs

The Adjutant General of West Virginia
1703 Coonskin Drive
Charleston, WV 25311-1085
(304) 561-6530

Separation documents for 75% of WWII veterans. Include veteran's full name, date of birth, service number (if known), and approximate dates of service with request.

West Virginia Division of Veterans Affairs
1321 Plaza E, Suite 101
Charleston, WV 25301-1400
(304) 558-3661, (304) 558-3662 Fax

WWII Bonus records. Include the veteran's name and date of birth with request.

Veterans Affairs Regional Office
640 Fourth Avenue
Huntington, WV 25701
(800) 827-1000

West Virginia Veterans Memorial

REMEMBER...

JOHN OHLEY CASDORPH, JR.
1921-1944

"Greater love hath no man than this, that a man lay down his life for his friends."
John 15:13

John Ohley Casdorph, Jr was born on September 21, 1921 in Charleston, WV. The son of John Hunt Ohley and Etta Josephine Casdorph, John was raised on the family 200 acre truck gardening farm. Naturally, Casdorph spent his youth working on the farm with the family. He had four brothers and two sisters: Caleb Henry, Charles Lamoreaux, James Firpo, Oscar Delano, Louise Elizabeth, and Rayma LaOue.

West Virginia Veterans Memorial Database, http://wvmemory.wvculture.org/ wvvetmem.html

Wisconsin

WWII Bonus Records: NO

State Historical Society of Wisconsin
816 State Street
Madison, WI 53706-1482
(608) 264-6400, (608) 264-6404 Fax
www.wisconsinhistory.org

Newspapers for WWII years.

Archives

World War II Materials, 1941–1947.

Contains mostly information pertaining to veterans from Eau Claire County. List of veterans who entered the service from Eau Claire Churches, 1942-1945 and also includes records of discharges and casualties from Eau Claire county local board #1. Also included in this collection is the War Department's and Navy Department's casualty books.

World War II Military Service Data Sheets, 1945–1946.
Oconto County.

Collection created by the Oconto County War History Commission. Consists of military service history and photographs of those who served from Oconto County during WWII. Information includes branch, dates of service, places assigned, discharge date and place, wounds or illness, casualty information or capture and awards. Other information may include marital status, schools, occupation, employer, rank, drafted or enlisted. Arranged alphabetically by last name

Military Record and Report of Separation, 1945–1946.

Collection of discharge certificates filed by the veterans of Racine County.

World War II Military Service Record Envelopes, 1934–1945.
Racine County.

Collections of military service information from those who served in the military from Racine County. Information

includes newspaper clippings, photographs of veterans in
uniform, worksheets, etc. Arranged by town then alphabetical by surname.

List of World War II dead, undated.
    Handwritten list of casualties from Racine County. In-
cludes the veteran's name, next of kin's name and address.

Repatriation of World War II dead, 1947–1950.
    Records pertaining to the return of Racine County casual-
ties from overseas temporary cemeteries for burial in Racine
County.

Library

*3600 Strong: An Honor Roll of the Men and Women of the
Procter & Gamble companies and the Buckeye Cotton Oil
Company who joined the armed forces of the United States of
America and those of the Dominion of Canada during the
years 1940–45*, Procter & Gamble, 1947.

*Honor Roll Album of Bayfield County Men and Women who
Served in World War II,* Charles M Sheridan, 1947.

Honor Roll, Lafayette County, World War Two, Martha K.
Riley, 1950.

*Service Record Book of Men and Women of Genoa City, Wis.,
and Community,* American Legion Post 183, 1947.

*Service Record Book of Men and Women of Orfordville, WI,
and Community,* American Legion Post 209, 194?.

*Service Record Book of the Men and Women of Highland,
Wisconsin, present and past,* VFW Post 9440, 1956.

The City of West Allis: Residents who served in World War II,
by Sharon L. Clow. 1992.

Wisconsin Soldiers, 14th Armored Division, World War II,
Bev Hetzel, 199-

War without Guns: This book records the contributions of Wisconsin Physicians who served in World War II during the period from Pearl Harbor, December 7, 1941 to V-J Day, August 14, 1945, The State Medical Society of Wisconsin, 1949.

World War II Honor List of Dead and Missing Army and Army Air Forces Personnel. State of Wisconsin, War Department, 1946.

Wisconsin Veterans Museum Research Center
30 W Mifflin Street
Madison, WI 53703
(608) 261-0536, (608) 264-7615 Fax
http://museum.dva.state.wi.us

Service Record Book of Men and Women of Oregon, Wisconsin & Ccommunity, VFW Post 9379, 1946.

Service Record Book of Men and Women of Galesville & Vicinity, Walsworth, 194?

Miller, G. L. Portage County Draft Registration lists for World War I and World War II, Stevens Point, WI, 2000.

Remember Pearl Harbor!: Souvenir Program, Enlistment, Earl Wallen Platoon, United States Marine Corps: Columbus Auditorium, Green Bay, December 7, 1942, Green Bay, WI: USMC Recruiting Council, 1942.
    Includes the names and hometowns of men who enlisted in the Marine Corps on December 7, 1942.

Museum has an extensive collection of oral histories.

Wisconsin State Genealogical Society
PO Box 5106
Madison, WI 53705-0106
www.rootsweb.com/~wsgs

The Adjutant General of Wisconsin
Department of Military Affairs
2400 Wright Street
Madison, WI 53704

Maintains some National Guard records.

Wisconsin Department of Veterans Affairs
PO Box 7843
Madison, WI 53707
(608) 266-1311

Discharge records. Include veteran's name, date of birth and Social Security number with request.

Veterans Affairs Regional Office
5000 West National Avenue B-6
Milwaukee, WI 53295
(800) 827-1000

Wyoming

WWII Bonus Records: NO

Wyoming State Archives
Barrett Building, 2301 Central Avenue
Cheyenne, WY 82002
(307) 777-7826, (307) 777-7044 Fax
http://wyoarchives.state.wy.us

Military Discharge Records filed with county clerks. Public record.

World War II Honor List of Dead and Missing Army and Army Air Forces Personnel. State of Wyoming, War Department, 1946.

State Summary of War Casualties from World War II for Navy, Marine Corps, and Coast Guard Personnel from Wyoming, Navy Department, 1946.

Wyoming Newspapers (not indexed).

University of Wyoming Libraries
Box 3334, University Station
Laramie, WY 82071-3334
(307) 766-2070
www-lib.uwyo.edu

The American Guidebook, VFW Post 2221, Ladies Auxillary, 1944. Albany county honor roll.

Reflections of World War II: 115th U.S. Cavalry, Wyoming National Guard, Dean Morgan Junior High School, 1993. Information about Military personnel from Casper, Wyoming during WWII.

Letters from Home: The Huntley Horn, 1944 to 1946, Margie Raben Jones, 1996.

House notes, November 1944, issued for Epsilon Delta of Sigma Nu, sponsored by Sigma Nu House Co, Sigma Nu, 1944. Contains Epsilon Delta honor roll.

Convocation honoring faculty, alumni and students of the University of Wyoming who served their country in the late world war, University of Wyoming, 1946.

Newspapers for WWII years.

Wyoming State Historical Society
PMB #184
1740H Dell Range Boulevard
Cheyenne, WY 82009-4946
http://wyshs.org

Wyoming's War Years, 1941–1945, Dr.T.A. Larson, Wyoming Historical Foundation, 1954. Contains a list of Wyoming casualties by county.

The Adjutant General of Wyoming
Tag Records Office
5500 Bishop Boulevard
Cheyenne, WY 82009-3220
(307) 772-5234/5239

National Guard records and discharge certificates. Include the veteran's name and date of birth with request.

Selective Service Cards, 1942–1946.
    Collection of draft registration cards. Their collection does not include all counties. Alphabetical by last name.

Wyoming Council of Veterans Affairs
Wyoming Army National Guard Room 101
5905 CY Ave
Casper, WY 82604
(307) 265-7372

No WWII records.

Veterans Affairs Regional Office
2360 East Pershing Boulevard
Cheyenne, WY 82001
(800) 827-1000

MILITARY SERIAL NUMBERS

Knowing the history behind a serial number can be of great importance when determining when a veteran entered the service. In some cases it can tell if the veteran was drafted or enlisted. This explanation should give some guidance on how numbers were issued for officers and enlisted personnel during WWII. Officer numbers were issued in a chronological order but enlisted numbers were issued by service commands. Service commands consisted of regions and included several states. A serial number can also be a clue as to the year a person entered the service.

Army and Army Air Forces

"Generally speaking, numbers fall into two broad categories: simple seven or eight digit numbers (in a few cases fewer digits) for male enlisted personnel, and prefixed serial numbers for other personnel. Regular Army enlisted men who entered the service before the outset of Selective Service bear seven–digit or lower serial numbers, usually beginning with "6" or "7", as 6974426, Men who enlisted in the Army of the United States have eight–digit numbers beginning with "1", the second digit indicating the Service Command of origin. For example, the serial number 14066025 would indicate that the man enlisted in the Army of the United States in the Fourth Service Command (Southeastern U.S.), Men called in federally recognized National Guard service received eight–digit numbers beginning with "2", the third digit representing the Service Command: 20107656 indicates a National Guardsman from New England (First Service Command). Men inducted or enlisted through Selective Service were given eight–digit numbers beginning with "3" or "4", the second digit representing the Service Command. The prefixed serial numbers for other than men enlisted personnel carry a designated letter: 0–(as in 0–1574257) for male commissioned officers; W–for male Warrant Officers; T– for Flight Officers of the Army Air Forces; L–for commissioned officers of the Women's Army Corps; V–for WAC Warrant Officers; A–for WAC enlisted women; R–for Hospital Dietitians, and M – for Physical Therapy Aides."

World War II Honor List of Dead and Missing Army and Army Air Forces Personnel. National Archives and Records Administration (www.archives.gov)

Army & Army Air Corps Officers

The Army and Air Force discontinued serial (service) numbers on July 1, 1969.

20,000 – 99,999	1935–1964
100,000 – 124,999	1921–1941
125,000 – 499,999	1921–1941
500,000 – 799,999	1942–1954
800,000 – 999,999	1921–1969 *
1,000,000 – 2,999,999	1942–1954

Numbers preceded by "O"

*Also given to Warrant Officers and Army Field Clerks.

Army and Army Air Corps Enlisted

6,000,000 – 7,999,999	1919–1940
10,000,000 – 10,999,999	1940–1969 *
11,000,000 – 11,142,500	1940–1945
11,142,501 – 11,188,000	1946–1948
12,000,000 – 12,242,000	1940–1945
12,242,001 – 12,321,000	1946–1948
13,000,000 – 13,197,500	1940–1945
14,000,000 – 14,204500	1940–1945
14,204,501 – 14,300,770	1946–1948
15,000,000 – 15,201,000	1940–1945
15,201,000 – 15,280,500	1946–1948
16,000,000 – 16,201,500	1940–1945
16,201,501 – 16,307,000	1946–1948
17,000,000 – 17,183,500	1940–1945
17,183,501 – 17,254,500	1946–1948
18,000,000 – 18,247,100	940–1945
18,247,101 – 18,360,800	1946
19,000,000 – 19,235,500	1940–1945
19,235,501 – 19,324,485	1946–1948
11,000,000 – 19,999,999	1940–1969 +
30,000,000 – 39,999,999	1940–1946
40,000,000 – 46,999,999	1943–1946
90,000,000 – 99,999,999	1940–1945 #

*Issued for enlistments outside the continental U.S.

+See Regular Army Numbers (enlisted) chart.

#Approximately 20,000 of these numbers were issued to the Philippine Army during WWII.

Regular Army Numbers (enlisted)

11,000,000 – 19,999,999 .... Men who enlisted in the regular Army on or after July 1, 1940.

10,100,000 – 10,199,999 .... Hawaiian Department

10,200,000 – 10,299,999 .... Panama Canal Department

10,300,000 – 10,399,999 .... Philippine Department

10,400,000 – 10,499,999 .... Puerto Rican Department

Army of the United States

31,000,000 – 39,999,999 .... Men inducted under the Selective Service Act of 1940.

30,100,000 – 30,199,999 .... Hawaiian Department

30,200,000 – 30,299,999 .... Panama Canal Department

30,300,000 – 30,399,999 .... Philippine Department

30,400,000 – 30,499,999 .... Puerto Rican Department

40,000,000 – 46,999,999 .... Men inducted under the Selective Service Act of 1940.

National Guard

Enlisted service numbers 20,000,000 – 20,999,999 were assigned between the years 1940–1946. The Army serial number description indicates that the third digit represents the service command or area of enlistment.

State Serial Number Chart

Regular army and draftee columns use the first two digits of the serial number. The National Guard column uses the first three digits.

State	Regular Army	Draftee*	National Guard
Alabama	14	34, 44	204
Alaska	19	39	209
Arizona	19	39	209
Arkansas	18	38	208
California	19	39	209
Colorado	17	37	207
Connecticut	11	31	201
Delaware	12	32, 42	202

Florida	14	34, 44	204
Georgia	14	34, 44	204
Hawaii	10	30	200
Idaho	19	39	209
Illinois	16	36, 46	206
Indiana	15	35, 45	205
Iowa	17	37	207
Kansas	17	37	207
Kentucky	15	35, 45	205
Louisiana	18	38	208
Maine	11	31	201
Maryland	13	33, 43	203
Massachusetts	11	31	201
Michigan	16	36, 46	206
Minnesota	17	37	207
Mississippi	14	34, 44	204
Missouri	17	37	207
Montana	19	39	209
Nebraska	17	37	207
Nevada	19	39	209
New Hampshire	11	31	201
New Jersey	12	32, 42	202
New Mexico	18	38	208
New York	12	32, 42	202
North Carolina	14	34, 44	204
North Dakota	17	37	207
Ohio	15	35, 45	205
Oklahoma	18	38	208
Oregon	19	39	209
Pennsylvania	13	33, 43	203
Rhode Island	11	31	201
South Carolina	14	34, 44	204
South Dakota	17	37	207
Tennessee	14	34, 44	204
Texas	18	38	208
Utah	19	39	209
Vermont	11	31	201
Virginia	13	33, 43	203
West Virginia	15	35, 45	205
Washington	19	39	209
Wisconsin	16	36, 46	206

Wyoming .... 17 .... 37 207
Panama .... 10 .... 30 200
Puerto Rico .... 10 .... 30 200
Philippines .... 10 .... 30 200
    *Entered through the Selective Service System as a
    draftee or inductee.

Examples:

19020965: Regular Army enlistee who entered the service
from Alaska, Arizona, California, Idaho, Montana,
Nevada, Oregon, Utah, or Washington. The serial
number was issued between 1940 –1945.

44006516: Enlisted personnel who entered the service
through the Selective Service System between 1943–1946.
Service command states were Alabama, Florida, Georgia,
Mississippi, North Carolina, South Carolina and
Tennessee.

20014436: National Guard enlistee number issued between
1940–1946. The service command area included Hawaii,
Panama, Puerto Rico and the Philippines.

Coast Guard

Coast Guard numbers were called signal numbers.
Discontinued on October 1, 1974.

Coast Guard Officer
1,000 – 99,999 1915–1974

Coast Guard Enlisted
200,000 – 254,999 1930–1942
255,000 – 349,999 1945–1962
500,000 – 707,999 1941–1945
3,000,000 – 3,081,999 1942–1944
4,000,000 – 4,040,999 .... 1942–1945w
5,000,000 – 5,001,499 1942
6,000,000 – 6,207,999 1941–1945
7,000,000 – 7,027,999 1943–1945
    w = Women

Marine Corps

Marine Corps also referred to as signal numbers. Discontinued July 1, 1972.

Marine Corps Officer
1 – 19,999 1920–1945
20,000 – 99,999 1941–1966
    Numbers preceded by "O"

Marine Corps Enlisted
255,000 – 349,999 .... 1933–1941m
350,000 – 499,999 .... 1941–1942m
500,000 – 599,999 .... 1942–1946m
600,000 – 670,899 .... 1943–1947m
700,000 – 799,999 .... Women
800,000 – 999,999 .... 1943–1947m
1,000,000 – 1,699,999 .... 1944–1957m
    m = Male

Navy

Navy numbers were issued by blocks of numbers allocated to entrance stations around the county. Navy numbers were discontinued July 1, 1972.

Navy Officer
501 – 124,999 1903–1941
125,000 – 199,999 1942
200,000 – 254,999 1942–1943
255,000 – 349,999 1943–1944
350,000 – 499,999 1944–1947

Navy Enlisted
2,000,000 – 9,999,999 1918–1965

8 7 0 - 0 0 - 0 1 T O 8 8 0 - 0 0 - 0 0, INCLUSIVE

BLOCK	PLACED ASSIGNED	AUTHORITY AND DATE OF ASSIGNMENT
870-00-01 to 871-64-99, inclusive	NRS, Minneapolis, Minn. (Block continued from previous page)	Recruiting C/L 131-42 dtd 15 Dec 1942
871-65-00 to 872-24-99, inclusive	NRS, Omaha, Nebr.	Recruiting C/L 131-42 dtd 15 Dec 1942
872-25-00 to 872-54-99, inclusive	NRS, Sioux Falls, S.D.	Recruiting C/L 131-42 dtd 15 Dec 1942
872-55-00 to 874-74-99, inclusive	NRS, Saint Louis, Mo.	Recruiting C/L 131-42 dtd 15 Dec 1942
874-75-00 to 875-34-99, inclusive	NRS, Toledo, Ohio	Recruiting C/L 131-42 dtd 15 Dec 1942
875-35-00 to 875-84-99, inclusive	NRS, Springfield, Ill.	Recruiting C/L 131-42 dtd 15 Dec 1942
875-85-00 to 876-14-99, inclusive	NRS, Boise, Idaho	Recruiting C/L 131-42 dtd 15 Dec 1942
876-15-00 to 876-34-99, inclusive	NRS, Cheyenne, Wyoming	Recruiting C/L 131-42 dtd 15 Dec 1942
876-35-00 to 877-54-99, inclusive	NRS, Denver, Colo.	Recruiting C/L 131-42 dtd 15 Dec 1942
877-55-00 to 877-84-99, inclusive	NRS, Helena, Montana	Recruiting C/L 131-42 dtd 15 Dec 1942
877-85-00 to 880-00-00, inclusive	NRS, Los Angeles, Calif. (Block continued on next page).	Recruiting C/L 131-42 dtd 15 Dec 1942

Master Service Number Book, US Navy Department.

Master Service Number Book is a detailed listing of navy serial numbers and what entrance station and date they were assigned. Due to the size it's impossible to include the information in this book. Contact the USS Whetstone Association for their book, *Lost Shipmates Located* $20.

USS Whetstone Assn
6200 Emerald Pine Circle
Fort Myers, FL 33912
www.usswhetstone.net

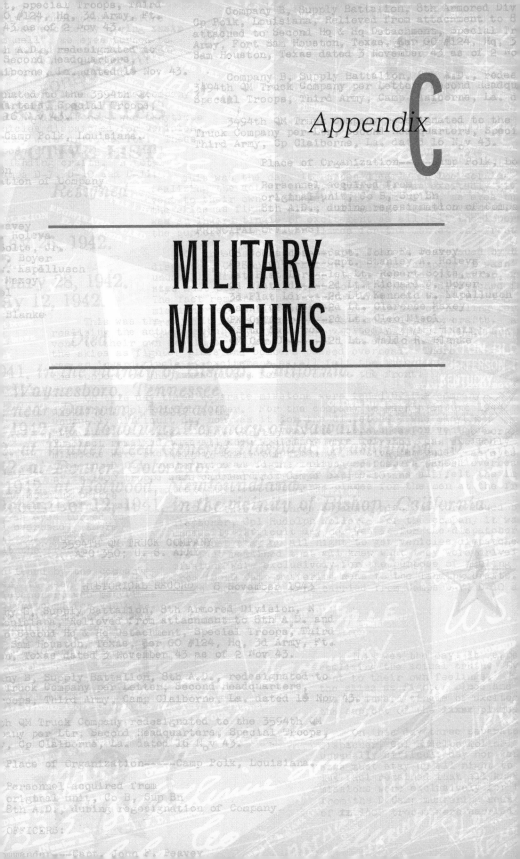

Appendix **C**

MILITARY MUSEUMS

Air Force

390TH Memorial Museum
6000 E Valencia Rd
Tucson, AZ 85706
(520) 574-0287
www.390th.org

8th Air Force Museum
PO Box 10
Barksdale AFB, LA 71110
(318) 456-3067
www.8afmuseum.net

Air Force Armament
  Museum
100 Museum Dr
Eglin AFB, FL 32542
(850) 651-1808
*www.destin-ation.com/
airforcearmamentmuseum*

Air Mobility Command
  Museum
1301 Heritage Rd
Dover AFB, DE 19902-8001
(302) 677-5938
www.amcmuseum.org

Champlin Fighter Aircraft
  Museum
4936 Fighter Aces Dr
Mesa, AZ 85205
(480) 830-4540
www.champlinfighter.com

FE Warren ICBM & Heritage
  Museum
7405 Marne Loop, Bldg 210
F E Warren, WY 82005
(307) 773-2980
*www.pawnee.com/
fewmuseum*

Hill Aerospace Museum
75th ABW/MU
7961 Wardleigh Rd
Hill AFB, UT 84056-5842
(801) 777-6868/6818
www.hill.af.mil/museum

Luna Mimbres Museum
301 S Silver St
Deming, NM 88030-3761
(505) 546-2382
*www.cityofdeming.org/
museum.html*

McChord Air Museum
PO Box 4205
McChord AFB, WA 98438-
0205
(253) 982-2485
www.mcchordairmuseum.org

Peterson Air & Space
  Museum
150 E Ent Ave
Peterson AFB, CO 80914
(719) 556–4915
*www.spacecom.af.mil/21sw/
peterson/museum/museum.htm*

South Dakota Air & Space
  Museum
PO Box 871
Elder, SD 57719
(605) 385-5189

US Air Force Museum
1100 Spaatz St
Wright Patterson, OH 45433
(937) 255-3286
www.wpafb.af.mil/museum

Army

1st Armored Division
  Museum
Baumholder, Germany
1admuseumdir@cmtymail.104asg.army.mil
www.baumholder.army.mil/
museum/museum.htm

1st Cavalry Museum
PO Box 5187
Ft Hood, TX 76545
(254) 287-3626
http://pao.hood.army.mil/
1CD_Museum

4th Infantry Division Museum
761st Tank Battalion Ave, 418
Ft Hood, TX 76544
(254) 287-8811
www.hood.army.mil/4id/
4id_museum.htm

82nd Airborne Division War
  Memorial Museum
PO Box 70119
Ft Bragg, NC 28307-0119
(910) 432-3443
www.bragg.army.mil/18abn/
museums.htm

Airborne/Special
  Operations Museum
PO Box 89
Fayetteville, NC 28302-0089
(910) 483-3003
www.asomf.org/home.htm

Camp Blanding Museum
Route 1, Box 465
Starke, FL 32091
(904) 533-3196
www.30thinfantry.org/
blanding.shtml

Don F Pratt Memorial
  Museum
Building 5702,Tennessee Ave
Ft Campbell, KY 42223-5335
(270) 798-4986
www.campbell.army.mil/pratt

Finance Corps Museum
10000 Hampton Parkway
Ft Jackson, SC 29207-7025
(803) 751-3771
www.jackson.army.mil/
Directorates/museums.htm

First Division Museum
1 S 151 Winfield Rd
Wheaton, IL 60187-6097
(630) 668-5185
www.rrmtf.org/firstdivision/
firstdivision.htm

Fort Bliss Museum
1735 Marshall Rd
Ft Bliss, TX 79916
(915) 568-3390
www.bliss.army.mil/Museum/
fort_bliss_museum.htm

Fort Huachuca Historical
  Museum
ATZS-PAM
Ft Huachuca, AZ 85613-6000
(520) 533-3898
http://huachuca-www.army.mil/
history/museum.htm

Fort Jackson Museum
2179 Sumter St
Ft Jackson, SC 29207-6102
(803) 751-7419
www.jackson.army.mil/
Directorates/museums.htm

Fort Lewis Military Museum
PO Box 331001
Ft Lewis, WA 98433-1001
(253) 967-7206
www.lewis.army.mil/DPTMS/
POMFI/museum.htm

Fort Sam Houston Museum
1207 Stanley Rd, Bldg 123
Ft Sam Houston, TX 78234
(210) 221-1886
www.cs.amedd.army.mil/
dptmsec/fshmuse.htm

Fort Sill Museum
ATZR-TM, 437 Quanah Rd
Ft Sill, OK 73503-5100
(580) 442-5123
http://sill-www.army.mil/
museum/index.htm

Fort Stewart Museum
2022 Frank Cochran Dr
Ft Stewart, GA 31314
(912) 767-7885

Frontier Army Museum
100 Reynolds Ave
Ft Leavenworth, KS 66027
(913) 648-3191
http://leav-www.army.mil/
museum

Fort Meade Museum
4674 Griffin Ave
Ft Meade, MD 20755-5094
(301) 677-6966
www.Fortmeade.army.mil/
Museum/Index.htm

Gen Patton Museum
62450 Chiriaco Rd
Chiriaco Summit, CA 92201
(760) 227-3483
www.desertusa.com/mag99/
feb/stories/paton.html

JFK Warfare Museum
Fort Bragg, NC 28310
(910) 432-4272
www.soc.mil/swcs/
swcs_home.htm

National Infantry Museum
Building 396, Baltzell Ave
Ft Benning, GA 31905-5593
(706) 545-6762
www.benningmwr.com/
museum.cfm

Patton Museum of Cavalry &
Armor
PO Box 25
Fort Knox, KY 40121
(502) 624-3812
www.generalpatton.org

Quartermaster Museum
1201 22nd St
Fort Lee, VA 23801-1601
(804) 734-4203
www.qmmuseum.lee.army.mil

Rock Island Arsenal
  Museum
ATTN SOSRI- CF
1 Rock Island Arsenal
Rock Island, IL 61299-5000
(309) 782-5021
http://riamwr.com/
museum.htm

Tropic Lightning Museum
Building 361, Waianae Ave
Schofield Barracks, HI 96857
(808) 655-0438

US Army Aviation Museum
PO Box 620610-0610
Ft Rucker, AL 36362
(334) 598-2508
www.armyavnmuseum.org

US Army Engineer Museum
427 Freedom Dr
ATTN: ATZT-PTM-PM
Ft Leonard Wood, MO 65473
(573) 596-8015
www.wood.army.mil/museum

US Army Intelligence
 Museum
ATZS-PAM
Ft Huachuca, AZ 85613-6000
(520) 533-1107
*http://138.27.35.32/history/
html/31mimuseRO.html*

US Army Medical Museum
PO Box 340244
Ft Sam Houston, TX 78234
(210) 221-6277/6358
*www.cs.amedd.army.mil/
dptmsec/amedd.htm*

US Army Military Police
 Museum
495 South Dakota Ave, 1607
Ft Leonard Wood, MO 65473
(573) 596-0131 ext 60604
*www.wood.army.mil/
usamps/history*

US Army Museum of Hawaii
 Museum Activity,
DCA, CRD, USAG-HI
Ft Shafter, HI 96858-5000
(808) 438-2821
*www.leahi.net/hams/
museum*

US Army Museum
 Noncommissioned Officers
Biggs Army Airfield
Ft Bliss, TX 79908
(915) 568-5412
*http://usasma.bliss.army.mil/
museum/index.html*

US Army Ordnance
 Museum
Building 2601
Aberdeen, MD 21005-5201
(410) 278-3602
www.ordmusfound.org

US Army Signal Corps
 Museum
Building 29807
Ft Gordon, GA 30905
(706) 791-2818
*www.gordon.army.mil/ocos/
Museum*

US Army Transportation
 Museum
300 Washington Blvd,
Besson Hall
Ft Eustis, VA 23604-5260
(757) 878-1115
*www.eustis.army.mil/
dptmsec/museum.htm*

US Army Women's Museum
2100 Adams Ave, P-5219
Ft Lee, VA 23801-2100
(804) 734-4327
www.awm.lee.army.mil

US Cavalry Museum
PO Box 2160
Fort Riley, KS 66442-0160
(785) 239-2737
http://Riley.army.mil

West Point Museum
Building 2110
West Point, NY 10996
(845) 938-2203
www.usma.edu/Museum

White Sands Museum
PO Box 224
White Sands, NM 88002
(505) 678-8824
www.wsmr-history.org

Coast Guard

US Coast Guard Museum
15 Mohegan Ave
New London, CT 06320
(860) 444-8511
www.uscg.mil/hq/g-cp/
museum/museuminfo.html

Marine Corps

Marine Corps Heritage
  Foundation
PO Box 420
Quantico, VA 22134
(703) 640-7961
www.marineheritage.org

Marine Corps Historical
  Center
1254 Charles Morris St, SE
Washington, DC 20374-5040
(202) 433-0780
http://hqinet001.hqmc.usmc.mil/
HD/MCHC.htm

MCRD Command Museum
1600 Henderson Ave, # 212
San Diego, CA 92140-5000
(619) 524-6719
www.usmchistory.com

Navy

Aircraft Carrier Hornet
  Museum
PO Box 460
Alameda, CA 94501
(510) 521-8448
www.uss-hornet.org

American Victory Mariners
  Memorial
705 Channelside Dr
Tampa, FL 33602
(813) 228-8766
www.americanvictory.org

Baltimore Maritime Museum
802 S Caroline St
Baltimore, MD 21231
(410) 396-3453
www.baltomaritimemuseum.org

Battleship North Carolina
Eagles Island, PO Box 480
Wilmington, NC 28402-0480
(910) 251-5797
www.battleshipnc.com

Boston Nat'l Historic Park
Charlestown Navy Yard
Boston, MA 02129-4543
(617) 242-5601
*www.nps.gov/bost/
Navy_Yard.htm*

Buffalo and Erie County
  Naval & Military Park
One Naval Park Cove
Buffalo, NY 14202
(716) 847-1773
www.buffalonavalpark.org

CEC/Seabee Museum
5200 2nd St, Building 59
Gulfport, MS 39501-5001
(228) 871-3164
*www.ncbc.navfac.navy.mil/
cecmuseum/gulfport.htm*

CEC/Seabee Museum NCBC
1000 23rd Ave, Bldg 99/HO
Port Hueneme, CA 93043
(805) 982-5165
*www.ncbc.navfac.navy.mil/
cecmuseum*

Destroyer Escort Historical
  Museum
PO Box 1926
Albany, NY 12201-1926
(518) 431-1943
www.ussslater.org

Freedom Park
2497 Freedom Park Rd
Omaha, NE 68110
(402) 345-1959
www.freedomparknavy.org

Great Lakes Naval
  Memorial & Museum
PO Box 1692
Muskegon, MI 49443
(231) 755-1230
www.silversides.org

H L White Marine Museum
PO Box 101
Oswego, NY 13126
(315) 342-0480
www.hleewhitemarinemuseum.com

Hampton Roads Naval
  Museum
1 Waterside Dr, Suite 248
Norfolk, VA 23510-1627
(757) 322-2987
www.hrnm.navy.mil

Independence Seaport
  Museum
211 S Columbus/Walnut St
Philadelphia, PA 19106
(215) 925-5439
www.phillyseaport.org

Intrepid Sea-Air-Space
  Museum
Pier 86 12th Ave and 46th St
New York, NY 10036
(212) 245-0072
www.intrepidmuseum.org

Louisiana War Memorial &
  USS Kidd
305 S River Rd
Baton Rouge, LA 70802
(225) 342-1942
www.usskidd.com

Muskogee War Memorial
3500 Batfish Rd
Muskogee, OK 74402
(918) 682-6294
www.ussbatfish.com

Mystic Seaport Museum
75 Greenmanville Ave
Mystic, CT 06355-0990
(860) 572-0711
www.mysticseaport.org

Nati'l Liberty Ship Memorial
Ft Mason Center, Building A
San Francisco, CA 94123
(415) 544-0100
www.ssjeremiahobrien.org

National Museum of Naval
  Aviation
1750 Radford Blvd
Pensacola, FL 32508
(850) 452-3604
www.naval-air.org

Nat'l Museum Pacific War
340 E Main St
Fredericksburg, TX 78624
(830) 997-4379
www.nimitz-museum.org

Naval Submarine Base New
  London
PO Box 571
Groton, CT 06349-5571
(800) 343-0079
www.ussnautilus.org

Naval Undersea Museum
610 Dowell St
Keyport, WA 98345
(360) 396-4148
http://num.kpt.nuwc.navy.mil

Naval War College Museum
686 Cushing Rd
Newport, RI 02841-1207
(401) 841-4052
www.nwc.navy.mil/museum

New Jersey Naval Museum
78 River St
Hackensack, NJ 07601-7110
(201) 342-3268
www.njnm.com

Patriots Point NavalMuseum
40 Patriots Point Rd
Mt Pleasant, SC 29464
(843) 884-2727
www.state.sc.us/patpt

Patuxent River Naval Air
  Museum
PO Box 407
Patuxent River, MD 20670
(301) 863-7418
www.paxmuseum.com

Project Liberty Ship
Box 25846
Baltimore, MD 21224-0846
(410) 558-0646
*www.liberty-ship.com/2001/
index.html*

SS City of Milwaukee
51 Ninth St
Manistee, MI 49660
(231) 398-0328
www.carferry.com

SS Lane Victory
Berth 94
San Pedro, CA 90733-0629
(310) 519-9545
www.lanevictoryship.com

SS Red Oak Victory
PO Box 1267
Richmond, CA 94802
(510) 237-2933
www.redoakvictory.org

The Navy Museum
805 Kidder Breese SE , 76
Washington, DC 20374-5060
(202) 433-4882
www.history.navy.mil/branches/
org8-1.htm

UDT Seal Museum
3300 N State Rd A1A
Fort Pierce, FL 34949
(561) 595-5845
www.navysealteams.com/
options.htm

US Naval Academy Museum
118 Maryland Ave
Annapolis, MD 21402-5034
(410) 293-2108
www.nadn.navy.mil/Museum

US Navy Supply Corps
  Museum
1425 Prince Ave
Athens, GA 30606-2205
(706) 354-7349
www.nscs.cnet.navy.mil/
service2.asp?ID=6

USS Alabama
2703 Battleship Parkway
PO Box 65
Mobile, AL 36601
(800) 426-4929
www.ussalabama.com

USS Arizona Memorial
  National Park
1 Arizona Memorial Place
Honolulu, HI 96818-3145
(808) 422-2771
www.arizonamemorial.org

USS Bowfin Submarine
  Museum & Park
11 Arizona Memorial Dr
Honolulu, HI 96818-3104
(866) 836-0317
www.bowfin.org

USS Cavalla
Seawolf Park
Galveston, TX 77550
(409) 744-7854
www.cavalla.org

USS Cod Submarine
1089 E 9th St
Cleveland, OH 44114
(216) 566-8770
www.usscod.org

USS Constellation
301 E Pratt St
Baltimore, MD 21202-3134
(410) 539-1797
www.constellation.org

USS Lexington Museum
2914 N Shoreline Blvd
Corpus Christi, TX 78403
(361) 888-4873
www.usslexington.com

USS LST 325
4763 E 10th Rd
Earlville, IL 60518-6203
(815) 627-9077
http://lstmemorial.org

USS Massachusetts
Battleship Cove
Fall River, MA 02721
(508) 678 -1100
www.battleshipcove.org

USS Missouri Memorial
PO Box 6339
Honolulu, HI 96818-4572
(808) 423-2263
www.ussmissouri.com

USS New Jersey
62 Battleship Place
Camden, NJ 08103-3302
(856) 966-1652
www.battleship-newjersey.com

USS Orleck Memorial
PO Box 3005
Orange, TX 77631-3005
(409) 882-9191
www.ussorleck.org

USS Pampanito
PO Box 470310
San Francisco, CA 94147
(415) 775-1943
*www.maritime.org/
pamphome.htm*

USS Potomac
PO Box 2064
Oakland, CA 94604-2064
(510) 627-1215
www.usspotomac.org

USS Requin (SS-481)
1 Allegheny Ave
Pittsburgh, PA 15212
(412) 237-1550
*www.csc.clpgh.org/exhibits/
requin.asp*

USS Texas
3523 Highway 134
La Porte, TX 77571
(281) 479-2431
*www.tpwd.state.tx.us/park/
battlesh/battlesh.htm*

Wisconsin Maritime
  Museum
75 Maritime Dr
Manitowoc, WI 54220
(920) 684-0218
http://wimaritimemuseum.org

Joint

Congressional Medal of
  Honor Museum
40 Patriots Point Rd
Mt Pleasant, SC 29464
(843) 884-8862
*www.cmohs.org/society/
museum.htm*

Military Historians
  Westbrook Museum
North Main St
Westbrook, CT 06498
(860) 399-9460

Museum of World War II
8 Mercer Rd
Natick, MA 01760
(508) 651-7695
www.museumofworldwarii.com

National Atomic Museum
PO Box 5800, MS 1490
Albuquerque, NM 87185
(505) 245-2136
www.atomicmuseum.com

National D-Day Museum
945 Magazine St
New Orleans, LA 70130
(504) 527-6012
www.ddaymuseum.org

Nat'l Purple Heart Museum
PO Box 3214
Enfield, CT 06083-3214
www.nphm.org

National Guard

45th Infantry Div Museum
2145 NE 36th
Oklahoma City, OK 73111
(405) 424-5313
www.45thdivisionmuseum.com

5th Reg Armory Museum
29th Division Street
Baltimore, MD 21201-2288
(410) 576-6160
www.mdmilitaryhistory.org/
index.htm

Alabama National Guard
Museum
6900 43rd Avenue N
Birmingham, AL 35206
(256) 847-4184
www.ngaal.org/museum.htm

Arizona Military Museum
5636 E McDowell Rd
Phoenix, AZ 85008-3495
(602) 267-2676
www.az.ngb.army.mil/
Museum/museum.htm

Arkansas National Guard
Museum
Camp Robinson
N Little Rock, AR 72199
(501) 212-5215
www.arngmuseum.com

Armed Forces Museum
Building 850
Camp Shelby, MS 39407
(601) 558-2757
www.ngms.state.ms.us/
campshelby/Museum

California Military Museum
1119 Second St
Sacramento, CA 95814
(916) 442-2883
http://militarymuseum.org

Ft Douglas Military Museum
32 Potter St
Ft Douglas, UT 84113
(801) 581-1251
www.fortdouglas.org

Historical Society/Georgia
Nat'l Guard
PO Box 17965
Atlanta, GA 30316-0965
(404) 624-6061
www.hsgng.org

Idaho Military History
Museum
4040 W Guard St
Boise, ID 83705-5004
(208) 422-4841
http://inghro.state.id.us/
museum

Illinois State Military
Museum
1301 N MacArthur Blvd
Springfield, IL 62702-2399
(217) 761-3910
www.il.ngb.army.mil

Iowa Gold Star Museum
7700 NW Beaver Dr
Johnston, IA 50131-1902
(515) 252-4531
www.iowanationalguard.com

Kentucky Military History
Museum
100 W Broadway
Frankfort, KY 40601-1931
(502) 564-3265
www.kyhistory.org/Museums/
Kentucky_Military_History_Museum.htm

Massachusetts National
Guard Museum
44 Salisbury St
Worcester, MA 01609-3126
(508) 797-0334
www.state.ma.us/guard/
museum/museum.htm

Montana Military Museum
PO Box 125
Ft Harrison, MT 59636-0125
www.montanaguard.com/
museum.htm

Museum of the Kansas
National Guard
6700 SW Topeka Blvd
Topeka, KS 66619-1401
(785) 862-1020
http://skyways.lib.ks.us/
museums/kng/index.html

National Guard Militia
Museum of NJ
PO Box 277
Sea Grit, NJ 08750
(732) 974-5966
www.nj.gov/military/
museum/index.html

New York State Military
Museum
61 Lake Ave
Saratoga Sprgs, NY 12866
(518) 583-0184
www.dmna.state.ny.us/
historic/museum.html

Oregon Military Museum
PO Box 2516
Clackamas, OR 97015-2516
(503) 557-5359
www.swiftview.com/
~ormilmuseum

Puerto Rico NG Museum
APARTADO 9023786
San Juan, PR 00902-3786
(787) 289-1675
www.pinacolada.net/
prngmuseum/index.html

South Carolina Military
Museum
1 National Guard Rd, 42
Columbia, SC 29201-4766
(803) 413-8897
www.scguard.com/museum

South Dakota NG Museum
301 E Dakota Ave
Pierre, SD 57501-3225
(605) 224-9991
www.state.sd.us/military/
Military/museum.htm

Texas Military Forces
  Museum
PO Box 5210
Austin, TX 78763-5218
(512) 782-5659
www.kwanah.com/txmilmus

Wisconsin Army and Air NG
  Museum
Volk Field ANGB
Camp Douglas, WI 54618
(608) 427-1280
*www.volkfield.ang.af.mil/
doc/museum1.htm*

DEPARTMENT OF VETERANS AFFAIRS NATIONAL CEMETERIES

Cemetery	Contact

Alabama

Ft Mitchell National Cemetery
553 Highway 165
Ft Mitchell, AL 36856-4403
Russell County
(334) 855-4731

Mobile National Cemetery	Barrancas Nat'l Cemetery
1202 Virginia Street	80 Hovey Road
Mobile, AL 36604-2366	Pensacola, FL 32508-1054
Mobile County	(850) 453-4108

Alaska

Ft Richardson Nat'l Cemetery	Ft Richardson Nat'l Cemetery
997 Davis Highway	PO Box 5498
Ft Richardson, AK 99505-7000	Ft Richardson, AK 99505-0498
Anchorage County	(907) 384-7075

Sitka National Cemetery	Ft Richardson Nat'l Cemetery
803 Sawmill Creek Road	PO Box 5498
Sitka, AK 99835-7455	Ft Richardson, AK 99505-0498
Sitka County	(907) 384-7075

Arizona

Nat'l Memorial Cemetery of Arizona
23029 N Cave Creek Road
Phoenix, AZ 85024-7500
Maricopa County
(480) 513-3600

Prescott National Cemetery	Nat'l Memorial Cemetery AZ
500 N US Highway 89	23029 N Cave Creek Road
Prescott, AZ 86301-5001	Phoenix, AZ 85024-7500
Yavapai County	(480) 513-3600

Arkansas

Fayetteville National Cemetery
700 S Government Avenue
Fayetteville, AR 72701-6456
Washington County
(479) 444-5051

Cemetery	Contact

Ft Smith National Cemetery
522 Garland Street
Ft Smith, AR 72901-2400
Sebastian County
(479) 783-5345

Little Rock National Cemetery
2523 Confederate Boulevard
Little Rock, AR 72206-2404
Pulaski County
(501) 324-6401

California

Cemetery	Contact
Ft Rosecrans National Cemetery 1700 Cabrillo Monument Dr San Diego, CA 92106 San Diego County	Ft Rosecrans Na'l Cemetery PO Box 6237 San Diego, CA 92166-0237 (619) 553-2084
Golden Gate National Cemetery 1300 Sneath Lane San Bruno, CA 94066-2099 San Mateo County (650) 761-1646	
Los Angeles National Cemetery 950 S Sepulveda Boulevard Los Angeles, CA 90049-3456 Los Angeles County (310) 268-4494	
Riverside National Cemetery 22495 Van Buren Boulevard Riverside, CA 92518-2798 Riverside County (909) 653-8417	
San Francisco National Cemetery Presidio of San Francisco San Francisco, CA 94129 San Francisco County	Golden Gate Nat'l Cemetery 1300 Sneath Lane San Bruno, CA 94066-2099 (650) 761-1646

Cemetery   **Contact**

San Joaquin Valley National Cemetery
32053 McCabe Road
Gustine, CA 95322-9749
Merced County
(209) 854-1040

Colorado

Ft Logan National Cemetery
3698 S Sheridan Boulevard
Denver, CO 80235-2952
Denver County
(303) 761-0117

Ft Lyon National Cemetery   Ft Logan National Cemetery
VA Medical Center   3698 S Sheridan Boulevard
Ft Lyon, CO 81038   Denver, CO 80235-2952
Las Animas County   (303) 761-0117

Florida

Barrancas National Cemetery
80 Hovey Road
Pensacola, FL 32508-1054
Escambia County
(850) 453-4108

Bay Pines National Cemetery   Bay Pines National Cemetery
10000 Bay Pines Boulevard N   PO Box 477
St Petersburg, FL 33708   Bay Pines, FL 33744-0477
Pinellas County   (727) 398-9426

Florida National Cemetery
6502 SW 102nd Avenue
Bushnell, FL 33513-8914
Sumter County
(352) 793-7740

St Augustine National Cemetery   Florida National Cemetery
104 Marine Street   6502 SW 102nd Avenue
St Augustine, FL 32084-5004   Bushnell, FL 33513-8914
St Johns County   (352) 793-7740

Cemetery	Contact

Georgia

Marietta National Cemetery 500 Washington Avenue NE Marietta, GA 30060-2102 Cobb County	Ft Mitchell National Cemetery 553 Highway 165 Ft Mitchell, AL 36856-4403 (334) 855-4731

Hawaii

National Memorial Cemetery of the Pacific
2177 Puowaina Drive
Honolulu, HI 96813-1729
Honolulu County
(808) 532-3720

Illinois

Abraham Lincoln National Cemetery
27034 S Diagonal Road
Elwood, IL 60421-9304
Will County
(815) 423-9958

Alton National Cemetery 600 Pearl Street Alton, IL 62003 Madison County	Jefferson Barracks Cemetery 2900 Sheridan Road St Louis, MO 63125-4166 (314) 260-8720
Camp Butler National Cemetery 5063 Camp Butler Road Springfield, IL 62707-9722 Sangamon County (217) 492-4070	
Danville National Cemetery 1900 E Main Street Danville, IL 61832-5100 Vermilion County (217) 554-4550	
Mound City National Cemetery Junction Highway 37 & 51 Mound City, IL 62963 Pulaski County	Jefferson Barracks Cemetery 2900 Sheridan Road St Louis, MO 63125-4166 (314) 260-8720

Cemetery	**Contact**
Quincy National Cemetery 36th and Maine Street Quincy, IL 62301 Adams County	Rock Island National Cemetery PO Box 737 Moline, IL 61266-0737 (309) 782-2094
Rock Island National Cemetery Building 118 Rock Island, IL 61299-7090 Rock Island County	Rock Island National Cemetery PO Box 737 Moline, IL 61266-0737 (309) 782-2094

Indiana

Crown Hill National Cemetery 700 W 38th Street Indianapolis, IN 46208-4240 Marion County	Marion National Cemetery 1700 E 38th Street Marion, IN 46953-4568 (765) 674-0284
Marion National Cemetery 1700 E 38th Street Marion, IN 46953-4568 Grant County (765) 674-0284	
New Albany National Cemetery 1943 Ekin Avenue New Albany, IN 47150-1749 Floyd County	Zachary Taylor Nat'l Cemetery 4701 Brownsboro Road Louisville, KY 40207-1746 (502) 893-3852

Iowa

Keokuk National Cemetery 1701 J Street Keokuk, IA 52632-3142 Lee County	Rock Island National Cemetery PO Box 737 Moline, IL 61266-0737 (309) 782-2094

Kansas

Ft Leavenworth Nat'l Cemetery Biddle Boulevard Ft Leavenworth, KS 66027 Leavenworth County	Leavenworth Nat'l Cemetery PO Box 1694 Leavenworth, KS 66048-9594 (913) 758-4105

Cemetery	Contact
Ft Scott National Cemetery 900 N National Ft Scott, KS 66701-8375 Bourbon County	Ft Scott National Cemetery PO Box 917 Ft Scott, KS 66701-0917 (620) 223-2840
Leavenworth National Cemetery 4101 S 4th Street Leavenworth, KS 66048-5014 Leavenworth County	Leavenworth Nat'l Cemetery PO Box 1694 Leavenworth, KS 66048-5014 (913) 758-4105

Kentucky

Camp Nelson National Cemetery 6980 Danville Road Nicholasville, KY 40356-9594 Jessamine County (859) 885-5727	
Cave Hill National Cemetery 701 Baxter Avenue Louisville, KY 40204-1775 Jefferson County	Zachary Taylor Nat'l Cemetery 4701 Brownsboro Road Louisville, KY 40207-1746 (502) 893-3852
Danville National Cemetery 277 N 1st Street Danville, KY 40422-1601 Boyle County	Camp Nelson Nat'l Cemetery 6980 Danville Road Nicholasville, KY 40356-9594 (859) 885-5727
Lebanon National Cemetery 20 Highway 208 Lebanon, KY 40033-9418 Marion County	Zachary Taylor Nat'l Cemetery 4701 Brownsboro Road Louisville, KY 40207-1746 (502) 893-3852
Lexington National Cemetery 833 W Main Street Lexington, KY 40508-2021 Fayette County	Camp Nelson Nat'l Cemetery 6980 Danville Road Nicholasville, KY 40356-9594 (859) 885-5727
Mill Springs National Cemetery 9044 W Highway 80 Nancy, KY 42544-8756 Pulaski County	Camp Nelson Nat'l Cemetery 6980 Danville Road Nicholasville, KY 40356-9594 (859) 885-5727

Cemetery	**Contact**

Zachary Taylor National Cemetery
4701 Brownsboro Road
Louisville, KY 40207-1746
Jefferson County
(502) 893-3852

Louisiana

Alexandria National Cemetery 209 E Shamrock Street Pineville, LA 71360-6553 Rapides County	Natchez National Cemetery 41 Cemetery Road Natchez, MS 39120-2036 (601) 445-4981
Baton Rouge National Cemetery 220 N 19th Street Baton Rouge, LA 70806-3634 East Baton Rouge County	Port Hudson Nat'l Cemetery 20978 Port Hickey Road Zachary, LA 70791-6722 (225) 654-3767

Port Hudson National Cemetery
20978 Port Hickey Road
Zachary, LA 70791-6722
East Baton Rouge County
(225) 654-3767

Maine

Togus National Cemetery 1 VA Medical/Regional Office Cntr Togus, ME 04330 Kennevac County	Massachusetts Nat'l Cemetery Connery Avenue Bourne, MA 02532 (508) 563-7113

Maryland

Annapolis National Cemetery 800 W Street Annapolis, MD 21401-3602 Anne Arundel County	Baltimore National Cemetery 5501 Frederick Avenue Catonsville, MD 21228-2199 (410) 644-9696

Baltimore National Cemetery
5501 Frederick Avenue
Catonsville, MD 21228-2199
Baltimore City County
(410) 644-9696

Cemetery	**Contact**
Loudon Park National Cemetery 3445 Frederick Avenue Baltimore, MD 21229-3812 Baltimore City County	Baltimore National Cemetery 5501 Frederick Avenue Catonsville, MD 21228-2199 (410) 644-9696

Massachusetts

Massachusetts National Cemetery
Connery Avenue
Bourne, MA 02532
Barnstable County
(508) 563-7113

Michigan

Ft Custer National Cemetery
15501 Dickman Road
Augusta, MI 49012
Kalamazoo County
(616) 731-4164

Minnesota

Ft Snelling National Cemetery
7601 34th Avenue S
Minneapolis, MN 55450-1105
Hennepin County
(612) 726-1127

Mississippi

Biloxi National Cemetery
400 Veterans Avenue
Biloxi, MS 39531-2410
Harrison County
(228) 388-6668

Corinth National Cemetery 1551 Horton Street Corinth, MS 38834-5842 Alcorn County	Memphis National Cemetery 3568 Townes Avenue Memphis, TN 38122-1299 (901) 386-8311

Natchez National Cemetery
41 Cemetery Road
Natchez, MS 39120-2027
Adams County, (601) 445-4981

Cemetery	Contact

Missouri

Jefferson Barracks National Cemetery
2900 Sheridan Road
St Louis, MO 63125-4166
St Louis County
(314) 260-8720

Jefferson City National Cemetery
1024 E McCarty Street
Jefferson City, MO 65101-4808
Cole County

Jefferson Barracks Cemetery
2900 Sheridan Road
St Louis, MO 63125-4166
(314) 260-8720

Springfield National Cemetery
1702 E Seminole Street
Springfield, MO 65804-2438
Greene County
(417) 881-9499

Nebraska

Ft McPherson National Cemetery
12004 S Spur 56A
Maxwell, NE 69151-1031
Lincoln County
(308) 582-4433

New Jersey

Beverly National Cemetery
916 Bridgeboro Road
Beverly, NJ 08010-1736
Burlington County
(609) 877-5460

Finn's Point National Cemetery
Ft Mott Road
Salem, NJ 08079-0542
Salem County

Beverly National Cemetery
916 Bridgeboro Road
Beverly, NJ 08010-1736
(609) 877-5460

New Mexico

Ft Bayard National Cemetery
300 Camino De Paz
Ft Bayard, NM 88036
Grant County

Ft Bliss National Cemetery
PO Box 6342
Ft Bliss, TX 79906
(915) 564-0201

Cemetery   **Contact**

Santa Fe National Cemetery
501 N Guadalupe Street
Santa Fe, NM 87501-1455
Santa Fe County
(505) 988-6400, (877) 353-6295

New York

Bath National Cemetery
Department of VA
San Juan Avenue
Bath, NY 14810
Grant County
(607) 664-4853

Calverton National Cemetery
210 Princeton Boulevard
Calverton, NY 11933-1030
Suffolk County
(631) 727-5410/5770

Cypress Hills National Cemetery   Long Island National Cemetery
625 Jamaica Avenue   2040 Wellwood Avenue
Brooklyn, NY 11208-1203   Farmingdale, NY 11735-1211
Kings County   (631) 454-4949

Long Island National Cemetery
2040 Wellwood Avenue
Farmingdale, NY 11735-1211
Suffolk County
(631) 454-4949

Saratoga National Cemetery
200 Duell Road
Schuylerville, NY 12871-1721
Saratoga County
(518) 581-9128

Woodlawn National Cemetery
1825 Davis Street
Elmira, NY 14901-1061
Chemung County
(607) 732-5411

Cemetery	Contact

North Carolina

New Bern National Cemetery
1711 National Avenue
New Bern, NC 28560-3023
Craven County
(252) 637-2912

Raleigh National Cemetery
501 Rock Quarry Road
Raleigh, NC 27610-3353
Wake County

Salisbury National Cemetery
202 Government Road
Salisbury, NC 28144-5655
(704) 636-2661/4621

Salisbury National Cemetery
202 Government Road
Salisbury, NC 28144-5655
Rowan County
(704) 636-2661/4621

Wilmington National Cemetery
2011 Market Street
Wilmington, NC 28403-1017
New Hanover County

New Bern National Cemetery
1711 National Avenue
New Bern, NC 28560-3023
(252) 637-2912

Ohio

Dayton National Cemetery
VAMC, 41 Third Street

Dayton, OH 45428-1008
Montgomery County
(937) 262-2115

Ohio Western Reserve Cemetery
10175 Rawiga Road
Rittman, OH 44270-0008
Medina County

Ohio Western Reserve Cemetery
PO Box 8
Rittman, OH 44270-0008
(330) 335-3069

Oklahoma

Ft Gibson National Cemetery
1423 Cemetery Road
Ft Gibson, OK 74434-8106
Muskogee County
(918) 478-2334

Cemetery	Contact
Ft Sill National Cemetery 24665 N S Road 260 Elgin, OK 73538 Commanche County	Ft Sill National Cemetery RR 1 Box 5224 Elgin, OK 73538-9762 (580) 492-3200

Oregon

Eagle Point National Cemetery
2763 Riley Road
Eagle Point, OR 97524-6543
Jackson County
(541) 826-2511

Roseburg National Cemetery 913 NW Garden Valley Blvd Roseburg, OR 97470-6523 Douglas County	Eagle Point National Cemetery 2763 Riley Road Eagle Point, OR 97524-6543 (541) 826-2511

Willamette National Cemetery
11800 SE Mount Scott Boulevard
Portland, OR 97266-6937
Clackamas County
(503) 273-5250

Pennsylvania

Indiantown Gap National Cemetery
RR 2, Box 484, Indiantown Gap Road
Annville, PA 17003-9618
Lebanon County
(717) 865-5254

Philadelphia National Cemetery Haines Street and Limekiln Pike Philadelphia, PA 19138 Philadelphia County	Beverly National Cemetery 916 Bridgeboro Road Beverly, NJ 08010-1736 (609) 877-5460

Puerto Rico

Puerto Rico National Cemetery
Avenue Cementario Nacional #50
BO Hato Tejas
Bayamon, PR 00960
Bayamon County
(787) 798-6720

Cemetery	Contact

South Carolina

Beaufort National Cemetery
1601 Boundary Street
Beaufort, SC 29902-3947
Beaufort County
(843) 524-3925

Florence National Cemetery
803 E National Cemetery Road
Florence, SC 29506-3232
Florence County
(843) 669-8783

South Dakota

Black Hills National Cemetery 20901 Pleasant Valley Dr Sturgis, SD 57785-8947 Meade County	Black Hills National Cemetery PO Box 640 Sturgis, SD 57785-0640 (605) 347-3830/7299
Ft Meade National Cemetery Old Stone Road Sturgis, SD 57785 Meade County	Black Hills National Cemetery PO Box 640 Sturgis, SD 57785-0640 (605) 347-3830/7299
Hot Springs National Cemetery VA Medical Center 500 N 5th Street Hot Springs, SD 57747-1480 Fall River County	Black Hills National Cemetery PO Box 640 Sturgis, SD 57785-0640 (605) 347-3830/7299

Tennessee

Chattanooga National Cemetery
1200 Bailey Avenue
Chattanooga, TN 37404-2899
Hamilton County
(423) 855-6590

Knoxville National Cemetery 939 Tyson Street NW Knoxville, TN 37917-7143 Knox County	Chattanooga Nat'l Cemetery 1200 Bailey Avenue Chattanooga, TN 37404-2899 (423) 855-6590

Cemetery	Contact

Memphis National Cemetery
3568 Townes Avenue
Memphis, TN 38122-1299
Shelby County
(901) 386-8311

Mountain Home Nat'l Cemetery
VA Medical Center Building 117
Memorial Avenue
Mountain Home, TN 37684-5001
Washington County

Mountain Home Cemetery
PO Box 8
Mntn Home, TN 37684-0008
(423) 979-3535

Nashville National Cemetery
1420 Gallatin Road S
Madison, TN 37115-4619
Davidson County
(615) 736-2839

Texas

Dallas Ft-Worth National Cemetery
2000 Mountain Creek Parkway
Dallas, TX 75211-6702
Dallas County
(214) 467-3374

Ft Bliss National Cemetery
5200 Fred Wilson Boulevard
Ft Bliss, TX 79906
El Paso County

Ft Bliss National Cemetery
PO Box 6342
Ft Bliss, TX 79906-0342
(915) 564-0201

Ft Sam Houston Nat'l Cemetery
1520 Harry Wurzbach Road
San Antonio, TX 78209
Bexar County
(210) 820-3891/3894

Houston National Cemetery
10410 Veterans Memorial Drive
Houston, TX 77038-1502
Harris County
(281) 447-8686/0580

Cemetery

Contact

Kerrville National Cemetery
3600 Memorial Boulevard
Kerrville, TX 78028-5799
Kerr County

Ft Sam Houston Cemetery
1520 Harry Wurzbach Road
San Antonio, TX 78209
(210) 820-3891/3894

San Antonio National Cemetery
517 Paso Hondo Street
San Antonio, TX 78202
San Antonio County

Ft Sam Houston Cemetery
1520 Harry Wurzbach Road
San Antonio, TX 78209
(210) 820-3891/3894

Virginia

Alexandria National Cemetery
1450 Wilkes Street
Alexandria, VA 22314-3424
Alexandria City County

Quantico National Cemetery
PO Box 10
Triangle, VA 22172-0010
(703) 221-2183

Balls Bluff National Cemetery
Route 7
Leesburg, VA 22075
Loudon County

Culpeper National Cemetery
305 US Avenue
Culpeper, VA 22701-3141
(540) 825-0027

City Point National Cemetery
10th Avenue and Davis Street
Hopewell, VA 23860
Hopewell City County

Ft Harrison National Cemetery
8620 Varina Road
Richmond, VA 23231-8246
(804) 795-2031

Cold Harbor National Cemetery
Route 156 N
Mechanicsville, VA 23111
Hanover County

Ft Harrison National Cemetery
8620 Varina Road
Richmond, VA 23231-8246
(804) 795-2031

Culpeper National Cemetery
305 US Avenue
Culpeper, VA 22701-3141
Culpeper County
(540) 825-0027

Danville National Cemetery
721 Lee Street
Danville, VA 24541-2119
Danville City County

Salisbury National Cemetery
202 Government Road
Salisbury, NC 28144-5655
(704) 636-2661/4621

Cemetery	**Contact**

Ft Harrison National Cemetery
8620 Varina Road
Richmond, VA 23231-8246
Henrico County
(804) 795-2031

Glendale National Cemetery 8301 Willis Church Road Richmond, VA 23231-7908 Henrico County	Ft Harrison National Cemetery 8620 Varina Road Richmond, VA 23231-8246 (804) 795-2031

Hampton National Cemetery
Cemetery Road at Marshall Avenue
Hampton, VA 23667
Hampton City County
(757) 723-7104

Quantico National Cemetery 18424 Joplin Road Triangle, VA 22172 Prince William County	Quantico National Cemetery PO Box 10 Triangle, VA 22172-0010 (703) 221-2183
Richmond National Cemetery 1701 Williamsburg Road Richmond, VA 23231-3427 Richmond City County	Ft Harrison National Cemetery 8620 Varina Road Richmond, VA 23231-8246 (804) 795-2031
Seven Pines National Cemetery 400 E Williamsburg Road Sandston, VA 23150-1641 Henrico County	Ft Harrison National Cemetery 8620 Varina Road Richmond, VA 23231-8246 (804) 795-2031
Staunton National Cemetery 901 Richmond Avenue Staunton, VA 24401-4902 Staunton City County	Culpeper National Cemetery 305 US Avenue Culpeper, VA 22701-3141 (540) 825-0027
Winchester National Cemetery 401 National Avenue Winchester, VA 22601-5210 Winchester City County	Culpeper National Cemetery 305 US Avenue Culpeper, VA 22701-3141 (540) 825-0027

Cemetery	Contact

Washington

Tahoma National Cemetery
18600 SE 240th Street
Covington, WA 98042-4868
King County
(425) 413-9614

West Virginia

Grafton National Cemetery 431 Walnut Street Grafton, WV 26354-1748 Taylor County	West Virginia Nat'l Cemetery RR 3, Box 127 Grafton, WV 26354-9523 (304) 265-2044

West Virginia National Cemetery
RR 3 Box 127
Grafton, WV 26354-9523
Taylor County
(304) 265-2044

Wisconsin

Wood National Cemetery
5000 W National Ave, Bld 1301
Milwaukee, WI 53295-0002
Milwaukee County
(414) 382-5300

MILITARY REUNION
ASSOCIATIONS

Listed are just some of the WWII–era military reunion associations. Check their website for contact information. For more military reunion listings check *www.militaryusa.com/reunions.html*

AIR FORCE

15TH AF 461ST BOMB GRP
1943–45
www.461st.org

191ST CSS MSS
All Years
http://miairguard.freeyellow.com

1ST AACS MOBILE MOB
All Years
http://1stmob.users1.50megs.com

317TH TRP CAR WING
1941+
www.usaf317thvet.org

8TH AF 446TH BOMB GRP H
1943–45
www.446bg.com

98TH BOMB GRP VETS ASSN
All Years
*http://members.aol.com/
bombgrp98/index.html*

9TH AF 315TH TCG
1942–45
http://315group.20megsfree.com

AEROMEDICAL EVAC ASSN
1942+
www.jps.net/everwa

B 47 STRATOJET ASSN
All Years
www.b-47.com

BAD 2 ASSN
All Years
www.military.com/bad2warton

P 47 THUNDERBOLT PILOTS
1941–45
www.p47pilots.com

PERRIN FIELD AFB
1941–71
www.perrinairforcebase.net

USAF AIRCREW LIFE
SUPPORT
All Years
www.usafals.net

WEBB AFB
All Years
www.webbafbreunion.com

ARMY

100TH INF DIV ASSN
1942–47
www.100thww2.org

101ST ABN ASSN
All Years
www.screamingeagle.org

101ST ABN DIV 101 AV
All Years
www.a101avn.org

104TH INF DIV NATL
TIMBERWOLF
1941–45
www.104infdiv.org

13TH ENG COMBAT BN
All Years
http://13thengineerbn.homestead.com

14TH CAV ASSN
All Years
www.14cav.org

17TH ART REG
All Years
www.17thartilleryregiment.org

1ST INF DIV SOCIETY OF
All Years
www.bigredone.org

22ND INF REG SOCIETY
All Years
www.22ndinfantry.org

24TH INF DIV ASSN NATL
1940+
*http://home.att.net/~victory24/
index.htm*

25TH INF DIV ASSN
All Years
http://www.25thida.com

2ND ARM DIV ASSN
1941–45
www.2ndarmoredhellonwheels.com

2ND INDIANHEAD DIV ASSN
All Years
www.swiftsite.com/2ida

30TH FIELD ART BN
1941+
www.hardchargers.com

34TH BMB GP H
1943–45
www.excel–tech.com/34ᵗʰ

36TH INF DIV
1940+
*www.ghg.net/burtond/36th/
36infdivassoc*

3RD ARM DIV SPEARHEAD
1941–91
www.3ad.org

3RD INF REG "THE OLD GUARD"
All Years
www.oldguard.org

4TH INF DIV (IVY) NATL
All Years
www.4thinfantry.org

506TH INF 3RD BN (ABN)
All Years
www.currahee.org

50ST PARACHUTE INF REG
1942–45
www.geocities.com/vamburgey

5TH ARM DIV ASSN
1940–45
www.5ad.org

5TH SPECIAL FORCES CPT 38
All Years
www.sfa38.org

70TH INF DIV ASSN
1943–46
www.trailblazersww2.org

720TH MP BN
All Years
www.720mp.org

7TH INF REG
All Years
www.cottonbalers.com

807TH TANK DEST BN
1941–45
http://www.807thtdbn.org

82ND ABN DIV ASSN
All Years
*www.fayettevillenc.com/
airborne82dassn*

82ND COMBAT ENG
1941–46
www.82ndengineers.org

8603RD 3RD ASA
1945–70
www.cianathq.org

88TH INF DIV ASSN
All Years
www.88infdiv.org

931ST SIGNAL BN AVN
1943–45
*http://freepages.military.rootsweb.com/
~army931sb*

94TH INF DIV ASSN
1941–45
http://www.94thinfdiv.com

97TH SIGNAL BN
1942–93
www.triedandtrue.org

99TH INF DIV ASSN
1941+
www.99div.com

9TH INF DIV 60TH IR 5TH BN
All Years
www.5thbattalion.org

AMERICAL DIV ASSN
All Years
www.americal.org

ARMY AIR TRAFFIC
CONTROLLERS
All Years
www.armyatc.org

ARMY SECURITY AGENCY
ALPINERS
1945–57
*http://members.aol.com/
asavets/alpine/alpine.htm*

CAMP BRECKINRIDGE
1942–62
www.breckinridge–arts.org

CAMP GORDON JOHNSTON
1942+
www.campgordonjohnston.com

COMBAT INFANTRYMEN
All Years
www.cianathq.org

ENGINNER OCS ASSN
(TEOCSA)
All Years
www.teocsa.org

GLIDER PILOTS
1941–45
www.ww2gp.org

OV–1 MOHAWK ASSN
All Years
www.ov–1mohawk.org

RAINBOW DIV OF WWII
1941–45
www.rainbowvets.org

SIGNAL CORPS OCS
1941+
www.isgroup.net/sigcocs

COAST GUARD

BERING SEA PATROL AK
1941–45
www.mardigrasfun.com/bsp

LIGHTSHIP SAILORS
All Years
www.uscglightshipsailors.org

USCGC INGHAM WHEC 35
1941–45
www.fredsplace.org

MARINE CORPS

1ST MAR DIV
1941+
www.1stmarinedivisionassociation.org

22ND MAR ASSN
1942–46
www.22dmarines.org

4TH MAR DIV 3RD BN
All Years
www.thundering–third.org

DELTA BATT 2/11
All Years
www.delta211usmc.org

HMR HMR L HMM 262
All Years
www.hmm–262.com

MARINE CORPS MUSTANG
All Years
www.dell.homestead.com/
mustang

MARINE EMBASSY GUARD
All Years
www.embassymarine.org

MCB 53 ASSN
1942–69
www.angelfire.com/pa/
mcb53aa/index.html

USMC TANKERS ASSN
All Years
www.usmcvta.org

USS HORNET MAR DET
CV8/CV12
All Years
www.usmcvta.org

WOMEN MARINES ASSN
All Years
www.womenmarines.org

NAVY

4TH SPECIAL SEABEES
1941–45
http://members.aol.com/
elliott233/mel.html

AROU 1/2/3/4/5/140
1943–45
www.intella.net/aroun

DESTROYER ESCORT
  SAILORS
All Years
www.desausa.org

INTL CHIEF PETTY OFFICER
All Years
http://goatlocker.exis.net/icpoa/
index.html

LCT FLOTILLAS
1941–45
http://ww2lct.org

MCB 11
All Years
www.mcb11.com

NAVY HELICOPTER ALUMNI
1945+
www.navhelo.org

NAVY MUSICIANS
All Years
www.geocities.com/Pentagon/
Bun

NCS LONDONDERRY
All Years
www.navcommsta–
londonderry.freeservers.com

PATROL CRAFT SAILORS
1940–50
www.ww2pcsa.org

S CHINA PATROL ASIATIC
1941–45
www.geocities.com/vienna/5047

SITE ONE HOLY LOCH SCTL
All Years
www.hollyloch.com

SUBIC BAY MARINE
1945–92
http://subicbaymarines.com

ULITHI NAVAL REUNION
1944–45
www.shsu.edu/~stdbma11/
ulithi/2002reunion.html

USN ARMED GUARD
1941–45
http://armed–guard.com

USN CRYPTOLOGIC VETS
All Years
www.usncva.org

USS ALBANY CA 123/CG 10
1944+
www.ussalbany.org

USS ALGOL AKA 54
All Years
www.ussalgolaka54.org

USS AMERICA CV 66
All Years
www.ussamerica.org

USS ANDERSON GEN A E
AP/TAP 111
1943–58
www.ussgeneralanderson.org

USS ARCHERFISH AGSS 311
All Years
www.archerfish.com

USS ASHLAND LSD 1/48
1943+
www.ussashland.org

USS BANG SS 385
1943–72
www.ussbang.com

USS BECUNA SS 319
1941–45
www.ssbn508.org

USS BEXAR APA/LPA 237
1945–70
http://www.ussbexar.com

USS BLENNY SS 324
1941–45
www.webenet.net/~ftoon/
memory/f_memory.html

USS BOGUE CVE 9
1941–45
www.geocities.com/Athens/
Cyprus/1207/bogue.html

USS BOXER
CV/CVA/CVS21/LPH4
1945–69
www.ussboxer.com

USS BRINKLEY BASS DD 887
1945+
www.ussbrinkleybass.com

USS BRYANT DD 665
1943–45
www.winslowsupply.com/
bryant

USS BUSH DD 529
1943–45
www.ussbush.com

USS CABILDO LSD–16
1945–70
http://members.aol.com/
cabildousn

USS CHARA AKA 58/AE 31
1944–72
www.usschara.com

USS COLONIAL LSD 18
1945–70
www.geocities.com/
uss_colonial/lsd

USS COOLBAUGH DE 217
1943–73
www.usscoolbaugh.org

USS CRONIN DE/DEC 704
All Years
www.usscronin.org

USS DEHAVEN DD 727 469
All Years
www.ussdehaven.org

USS DES MOINES CA 134
All Years
http://ussdesmoines.com

USS DOYLE DD 494/DMS 34
1941–54
*www.geocities.com/
bensonclass/macomb.html*

USS DUNCAN DD 485
1942–45
www.ussduncan.org

USS EDWARDS RS DD 950
All Years
www.dd950.com

USS FESSENDEN DE/DER142
1942–60
*www.crosswinds.net/
~fessenden*

USS FRANKLIN SSBN 640
All Years
www.ssbn640.com

USS GEARING DD 710
1945–73
www.ussgearingdd710.com

USS GRANT U S SSBN 631
All Years
www.delphi.com/ssbn631

USS GRAY FF 1054
All Years
*http://
ussgrayff1054.hypermart.net*

USS GREAT SITKIN AE 17
1945–73
www.greatsitkin.org

USS GREENE EUGENE
A DD/DDR 711
All Years
www.destroyers.org

USS GUARDFISH SSN 612
All Years
http://guardfish.org

USS HAYNSWORTH DD 700
All Years
www.uss–haynsworth.com

USS HENRICO APA 45
1943–68
www.interpoint.net/~henrico

USS HISSEM DE/DER 400
All Years
www.usshissem.org

USS INDIANA BB 58
1942–46
*www.geocities.com/pentagon/
quarters/785*

USS KENNEBEC A0 36
1942–70
www.usskennebec.org

USS KEPHART DE 207/APD61
1942–46
www.ormocbattle.com

USS LCI NATL
1944–46
www.mightymidgets.org

USS LEE ROBERT E SSBN 601
All Years
www.ssbn601.com

USS LINDENWALD LSD 6
1943–68
www.usslindenwald.com

USS LST 883 LST 883
1945–59
www.drg–ent.com/883

USS LST ASSN CARL CHPT
1941+
www.uslst.org

USS MACOMB DD458/DMS 23
1941–54
*www.geocities.com/
bensonclass/macomb.html*

USS MACON CA 132
1945–61
www.britesites.com/macon.htm

USS MARCUS ISLAND CVE 77
1943–46
www.marcusisland.org

USS MENARD APA 201
1944–55
www.ussmenard.com

USS MEREDITH
DD165/434/729/890
1941–45
*www.sierratel.com/daycare/
meredith*

USS METIVIER DE 582
All Years
www.de582.com

USS MILWAUKEE AOR 2
All Years
www.ussmilwaukee.com

USS MISSOURI BB 63
1941+
http://ussmissouri.org

USS MT MCKINLEY
AGC 7/LCC 7
1944–70
www.ussmtmckinley.com

USS NECHES AO 47/AO 5
1942–70
*www.geckotech.com/
ussnechesao47*

USS NOBLE APA 218
1944–66
www.ussnoble.com

USS ORLECK DD 886
1945+
www.ussorleck.com

USS OWENS JC DD 776
1944–73
www.jcowensdd776.org

USS PERRY DD 844
1940–73
www.ussperry.com

USS PICKAWAY APA 222
1944–70
*www.angelfire.com/co2/
pickawayapa222/apa222.html*

USS POCONO AGC/LCC 16
All Years
www.usspocono.org

USS POLK COUNTY LST 1084
1945–69
http://usspolkcounty.weblogger.com

USS POWER DD 839
1945–77
www.usspower.com

USS PURSUIT AM 108/AGS 17
1943–60
www.usspursuitreunion.org

USS QUAPAW ATF 110
1945–85
www.ussquapaw.com

USS RADFORD DD/DDE 446
1942–69
www.ussradford446.org

USS RASHER SS 269
1943–71
www.ussrasher.org

USS RENSHAW DD/DDE 499
All Years
*www.destroyers.org/uss–
renshaw*

USS ROBINSON DD 562
1944–64
www.ussronbinson.org

USS ROBINSON FM DE 220
1944–60
www.de220.com

USS RONQUIL SS 396
1944–71
http://ussronquil.com

USS SAN FRANCISCO CA 38
1941–45
*www.geocities.com/
mariwether.geo/sfa.html*

USS SEADRAGON SSN 584
All Years
*www.ssn584.homestead.com/
index.html*

USS SEVERN AO 61
1944–74
www.usssevern.com

USS SHELTON DD 790/DE 407
1943–73
www.icss.net/~rbpetro

USS SHUBRICK DD 639
1942–45
www.ussduncan.org

USS SIMPSON DD 221
1941–46
*http://home.gci.net/
~fourpiperdestroyer*

USS SMAll YearsEY DD 565
All Years
http://pages.prodigy.net/dd565

USS ST LO & VC 65
All Years
www.stlomidway6365.org

USS STRONG DD 758/DD 467
1944–88
http://uss–corry.com

USS SUMTER APA 52
1943–46
www.geocities.com/uss_sumter

USS SURFBIRD
AM/MSF/ADG 383
All Years
*http://home.attbi.com/
~surfbird_383*

USS TANG SS 563
All Years
*www.geocities.com/rrowe50/
tang.html*

USS THOMAS LLOYD
DD/DDE 764
All Years
www.angelfire.com/hi2/DD764

USS TOPEKA CL 67
1944–49
*http://hometown.aol.com/
jwtopeka67*

USS TRUXTUN DE 282/APD 98
1940–46
*http://home.gci.net/
~fourpiperdestroyer*

USS TUCSON CL 98/SSN 770
1945–49
www.css7.navy.mil/tucson.htm

USS TURNER
DD/DDR 834/DD 648
1944–69
www.ussturner.org

USS UVALDE AKA 88
1944–68
http://ussuvalde.com

USS VESOLE DD/DDR 878
1945–83
www.ussvesole.org

USS WALDRON DD 699
1941–73
www.inetport.com/~rwells/
usswaldron.htm

USS WASHINGTON BB 56
1945+
www.usswashington.com

USS WEEKS JOHN W DD 701
1944–70
www.ussjwweeks701.org

USS WESTCHESTER COUNTY
LST 1167
All Years
www.lst1167.com

USS WHETSTONE LSD 27
1945–70
www.usswhetstone.net

USS WHITMAN DE 24
1943–45
www.desausa.org

USS WILTSIE DD 716
All Years
http://home.fuse.net/usswiltsie

USS WISCONSIN BB 64
All Years
www.usswisconsin.org

USS WORCESTER CL 144
All Years
www.ussworcester.com

USS YMS 425 YMS 305
1944–46
www.ussyms425.com

VA 176 "THUNDERBOLTS"
All Years
http://geocities.com/pentagon/
2908

VP 8 ALUMNI ASSN
All Years
www.vpnavy.com/
vp8news.html

JOINT
AIR INTELLIGENCE TRAIN
All Years
http://afaitc.server101.com/
index.htm

BERLIN AIRLIFT VETS
1945–94
www.berlinveterans.com

FLEET TUG SAILORS NATL
All Years
www.nafts.com

MT ECKSTEIN RIMBACH W
   GERMANY
All Years
www.geocities.com/
rimbach_2001

USS ANTIETAM
CV/CVA//CVS 36/CG 54
1945–62
www.ussantietam.com
USS BAYFIELD APA 33
1943–69
http://geocities.com/
ussbayfieldapa33

USS BOSTON + MAR DET
CA69 CAG1 SSN703
All Years
www.ussboston.org

USS DANIELS J CG 27
All Years
www.ussjosephusdaniels.com

USS KIRKPATRICK DE/DER 318
All Years
www.nafts.com

USS LANSING
DE/DER 388/WDE 488
1943–65
www.usslansing.org

USS ROCKAWAY (NAVY&CG)
AVP 29
1942–72
www.cccnews.net/rockaway

USS SARATOGA
CV3/CVA/CV60
All Years
www.usssaratoga.com

FEDERAL RECORDS CENTERS

The 4ᵗʰ WWII draft registrations cards are now open to the public and available from the appropriate federal records center.

National Archives and Records Administration
Pacific Region - Laguna Niguel
24000 Avila Road
Laguna Niguel, CA 92677-3497
(949) 360-2641, (949) 360-2624 Fax
www.archives.gov/facilities/ca/laguna_niguel.html

Clark County, Nevada

National Archives and Records Administration
Pacific Region – San Francisco
1000 Commodore Drive
San Bruno, CA 94066-2350
(650) 876-9009, (650) 876-9233 Fax
www.archives.gov/facilities/ca/san_francisco.html

California, Hawaii, and Nevada except Clark County

National Archives and Records Administration
Rocky Mountain Region - Denver
Bldg. 48, Denver Federal Center
PO Box 25307
Denver, CO 80225-0307
(303) 236-0817, (303) 236-9297 Fax
www.archives.gov/facilities/co/denver.html

Arizona, Colorado, Montana, New Mexico, Utah, and Wyoming

National Archives and Records Administration
Southeast Region
1557 St Joseph Avenue
East Point, GA 30344-2593
(404) 763-7474, (404) 763-7059 Fax
www.archives.gov/facilities/ga/atlanta.html

Alabama, Florida, Georgia, Kentucky, Mississippi, North Carolina, South Carolina, Tennessee

National Archives and Records Administration
Great Lakes Region
7358 South Pulaski Road
Chicago, IL 60629-5898
(773) 581-7816, (312) 353-1294 Fax
www.archives.gov/facilities/il/chicago.html

Illinois, Indiana, Michigan, Ohio, and Wisconsin

National Archives and Records Administration
Northeast Region – Boston
Frederick C. Murphy Federal Center
380 Trapelo Road
Waltham, MA 02452-6399
(781) 663-0130, (781) 647-8088 Fax
www.archives.gov/facilities/ma/boston.html

Connecticut, Maine, Massachusetts, New Hampshire,
Rhode Island, and Vermont

National Archives and Records Administration
Northeast Region – New York
201 Varick Street
New York, NY 10014-4811
(212) 401-1628, (212) 401-1638
www.archives.gov/facilities/ny/new_york_city.html

New York (Manhattan, Queens, Brooklyn, Staten Island,
and Bronx), New Jersey, Puerto Rico, and Virgin Islands

National Archives and Records Administration
Central Plains Region – Kansas City
2312 East Bannister Road
Kansas City, MO 64131-3011
(816) 926-6920, (816) 926-6982 Fax
www.archives.gov/facilities/mo/kansas_city.html

Iowa, Kansas, Minnesota, Missouri, Nebraska,
North Dakota, and South Dakota

National Archives and Records Administration
Central Plains Region – Lee's Summit
200 Space Center Drive
Lee's Summit, MO 64064-1182
(816) 823-6272, (816) 823-5249 Fax
www.archives.gov/facilities/mo/lees_summit.html

New York (some counties)

National Archives and Records Administration
Mid-Atlantic Region
900 Market Street
Philadelphia, PA 19107-4292
(215) 597-3000, (215) 597-2303 Fax
*www.archives.gov/facilities/pa/philadelphia_center_
city.html*

Delaware, Maryland, Pennsylvania, Virginia,
and West Virginia

National Archives and Records Administration
Southwest Region – Fort Worth
501 West Felix St, Building 1
PO Box 6216
Fort Worth, TX 76115-3405
(817) 334-5525, (817) 334-5511 Fax
www.archives.gov/facilities/tx/fort_worth.html

Arkansas, Louisiana, Oklahoma, and Texas

National Archives and Records Administration
Pacific Alaska Region – Seattle
6125 Sand Point Way NE
Seattle, WA 98115-7999
(206) 526-6501, (206) 526-6575 Fax
www.archives.gov/facilities/wa/seattle.html

Idaho, Montana, Oregon, and Washington

National Archives and Records Administration
Pacific Alaska Region – Anchorage
654 West Third Avenue
Anchorage, AK 99501-2145
(907) 271-2441, (907) 271-2442 Fax
www.archives.gov/facilities/ak/anchorage.html
Alaska

Washington National Records Center
4205 Suitland Road
Suitland, MD 20746-8001
(301) 778-1600, (301) 778-1521
www.archives.gov/facilities/md/suitland.html
Washington, DC, Philippines, and American Samoa

Presidential Libraries for WWII Research
Franklin D Roosevelt Library
4079 Albany Post Road
Hyde Park, NY 12538-1999
(845) 229-8114, (845) 229-0872 Fax
www.fdrlibrary.marist.edu

Harry S Truman Library
500 West US Highway 24
Independence, MO 64050-1798
(816) 833-1400, (816) 833-4368 Fax
www.trumanlibrary.org

PAY CHARTS

ANNUAL PAY AND ALLOWANCES OF COMMISSIONED AND WARRANT OFFICERS, NAVY AND NAVAL RESERVE

Flag officers

Rank	Pay	Personal cash allowance	With dependents — Rental[12]	With dependents — Subsistence[4]	Without dependents — Rental[13]	Without dependents — Subsistence[4]
Admirals	8,000	2,200	1,440	511.00	1,260	255.50
Vice admirals	8,000	500	1,440	511.00	1,260	255.50
Rear admirals (upper half)	8,000		1,440	511.00	1,260	255.50
Rear admirals (lower half)	6,000		1,440	511.00	1,260	255.50

PAY (Dollars) — SERVICE FOR LONGEVITY[1]

RANK AND SERVICE FOR PAY PERIOD PURPOSES[2]	Pay period	Base pay[3]	Over 3 years	Over 5 years	Over 6 years	Over 9 years	Over 10 years	Over 12 years	Over 15 years	Over 17 years	Over 18 years	Over 20 years	Over 21 years	Over 23 years	Over 24 years	Over 27 years	Over 30 years	With dep. Rental[12]	With dep. Subsistence[4]	Without dep. Rental[13]	Without dep. Subsistence[4]
Commodores and captains	6	4,000	4,200		4,400	4,600		4,800	5,000		5,200		5,400		5,600	5,800	6,000	1,440	511.00	1,260	255.50
Commanders: Over 30 years[3]	6	4,000															6,000	1,440	511.00	1,260	255.50
Commanders: Under 30 years	5	3,500	3,675		3,850	4,025		4,200	4,375		4,550		4,725		4,900	5,075		1,440	766.50	1,260	255.50
Lieutenant commanders: Over 23 years[3]	5	3,500												4,725	4,900	5,075	5,250	1,440	766.50	1,260	255.50
Lieutenant commanders: Under 23 years	4	3,000	3,150		3,300	3,450		3,600	3,750		3,900		4,050					1,260	766.50	1,080	255.50
Lieutenants: Over 17 years[3]	4	3,000								3,750	3,900		4,050		4,200	4,350	4,500	1,260	766.50	1,080	255.50
Lieutenants: Under 17 years	3	2,400	2,520		2,640	2,760		2,880	3,000									1,080	511.00	900	255.50
Lieutenants (junior grade): Over 10 years[3]	3	2,400					2,760	2,880	3,000		3,120		3,240		3,360	3,480	3,600	1,080	766.50	900	255.50
Lieutenants (junior grade): Under 10 years	2	2,000	2,100		2,200	2,300												900	511.00	720	255.50
Ensigns: Over 5 years[3]	2	2,000		2,100	2,200	2,300		2,400	2,500		2,600		2,700		2,800	2,900	3,000	900	511.00	720	255.50
Ensigns: Under 5 years	1	1,800	1,890															720	511.00	540	255.50
Commissioned warrant officers:[4] Over 20 years, creditable record	4	3,000										3,900	4,050		4,200	4,350	4,500	1,260	766.50	1,080	255.50
Over 10 years, creditable record	3	2,400					2,760	2,880	3,000		3,120		3,240		3,360	3,480	3,600	1,080	511.00	900	255.50
Under 10 years	(*)	2,100	2,205		2,310	2,415		2,520	2,625		2,730		2,835		2,940	3,045	3,150	900	511.00	720	255.50
Warrant officers	1	1,800	1,890		1,980	2,070		2,160	2,250		2,340		2,430		2,520	2,610	2,700	720	511.00	540	255.50

MONTHLY PAY OF ENLISTED MEN, NAVY AND NAVAL RESERVE

Pay grade	Classification	Base pay[2]	Years of service[1]									
			Over 3 years	Over 6 years	Over 9 years	Over 12 years	Over 15 years	Over 18 years	Over 21 years	Over 24 years	Over 27 years	Over 30 years
1st	Chief petty officers with permanent appointments	$138.00	$144.90	$151.80	$158.70	$165.60	$172.50	$179.40	$186.30	$193.20	$200.10	$207.00
	Chief petty officers with acting appointments	126.00	132.30	138.60	144.90	151.20	157.50	163.80	170.10	176.40	182.70	189.00
2d	Petty officers, first class	114.00	119.70	125.40	131.10	136.80	142.50	148.20	153.90	159.60	165.30	171.00
	Stewards, first class											
	Cooks, first class											
3d	Petty officers, second class	96.00	100.80	105.60	110.40	115.20	120.00	124.80	129.60	134.40	139.20	144.00
	Stewards, second class											
	Cooks, second class											
4th	Petty officers, third class	78.00	81.90	85.80	89.70	93.60	97.50	101.40	105.30	109.20	113.10	117.00
	Stewards, third class											
	Cooks, third class											
5th	Seaman, first class	66.00	69.30	72.60	75.90	79.20	82.50	85.80	89.10	92.40	95.70	99.00
	Fireman, first class											
	Hospital apprentice, first class											
	Bugler, first class											
	Steward's mate, first class											
6th	Seaman, second class	54.00	56.70	59.40	62.10	64.80	67.50	70.20	72.90	75.60	78.30	81.00
	Fireman, second class											
	Hospital apprentice, second class											
	Bugler, second class											
	Steward's mate, second class											
7th	Apprentice seaman	50.00	52.50	55.00	57.50	60.00	62.50	65.00	67.50	70.00	72.50	75.00
	Steward's mate, third class											

[1]For purposes of computing longevity pay of enlisted men, active Federal service in the Army, Navy, Marine Corps, Coast Guard, Coast and Geodetic Survey, and Public Health Service, and the Reserve components thereof, shall be counted; and in addition, service (active and inactive) in the active National Guard of the several States, Territories, and District of Columbia, enlisted Reserve Corps of the Army, Naval Reserve (including Fleet Reserve), Naval Reserve Force, Marine Corps Reserve, Marine Corps Reserve Force, and Coast Guard Reserve. Service in the National Guard Reserve and inactive National Guard, and inactive service on the retired list, shall not be counted. All other enlisted men are entitled to the pay shown in the appropriate columns, i.e., base pay plus an

[2]Base pay is payable only to enlisted men with less than 3 years of service. Increase of 5 percent for each 3 years of service up to 30 years.

ARMY PAY TABLES 1625

Monthly rates of pay of enlisted men of the army, effective 1 June 1942, under act 16 June 1942, including 20 percent increase for foreign service or sea duty, and enlisted personnel of the Women's Army Corps, as provided by the act of 1 July 1943, effective 30 September 1943.

Grade	Base pay	Over 3 years' service	Over 6 years' service	Over 9 years' service	Over 12 years' service	Over 15 years' service	Over 18 years' service	Over 21 years' service	Over 24 years' service	Over 27 years' service	Over 30 years' service
First grade—Master sergeant, first sergeant	$165.60	$172.50	$179.40	$186.30	$193.20	$200.10	$207.00	$213.90	$220.80	$227.70	$234.60
Second grade—Technical sergeant	135.80	143.50	148.40	153.30	159.60	165.30	171.00	176.70	182.40	188.10	193.80
Third grade—Staff sergeant, technician third grade	115.20	120.00	124.80	129.60	134.40	139.20	144.00	148.80	153.60	158.40	163.20
Fourth grade—Sergeant, technician fourth grade	93.60	97.50	101.40	105.30	109.20	113.10	117.00	120.90	124.80	128.70	132.60
Fifth grade—Corporal, technician fifth grade	79.20	82.50	85.80	89.10	92.40	95.70	99.00	102.30	105.60	108.90	112.20
Sixth grade—Private first class	64.80	67.50	70.20	72.90	75.60	78.30	81.00	83.70	86.40	89.10	91.80
Seventh grade—Private	60.00	62.50	65.00	67.50	70.00	72.50	75.00	77.50	80.00	82.50	85.00

Monthly rates of pay of enlisted men of the army, effective 1 June 1942, under act 16 June 1942, including flying pay and 20 percent increase for foreign service or sea duty, and enlisted personnel of the Women's Army Corps, as provided by the act of 1 July 1943, effective 30 September 1943.

Grade	Service	Base pay	Over 3 years' service	Over 6 years' service	Over 9 years' service	Over 12 years' service	Over 15 years' service	Over 18 years' service	Over 21 years' service	Over 24 years' service	Over 27 years' service	Over 30 years' service
First grade—Master sergeant, first sergeant	Regular	$165.60	$172.50	$179.40	$186.30	$193.20	$200.10	$207.00	$213.90	$220.80	$227.70	$234.60
	Flying	82.80	86.25	89.70	93.15	96.60	100.05	103.50	106.95	110.40	113.85	117.30
	Total	248.40	258.75	269.10	279.45	289.80	300.15	310.50	320.85	331.20	341.55	351.90
Second grade—Technical sergeant	Regular	136.80	143.50	148.20	153.30	159.60	165.30	171.00	176.70	182.40	188.10	193.80
	Flying	68.40	71.25	74.10	76.95	79.80	82.65	85.50	88.35	91.20	94.05	96.90
	Total	205.20	213.75	222.30	230.85	239.40	247.95	256.50	265.05	273.60	282.15	290.70
Third grade—Staff sergeant, technician third grade	Regular	115.20	120.00	124.80	129.60	134.40	139.20	144.00	148.80	153.60	158.40	163.20
	Flying	57.60	60.00	62.40	64.80	67.20	69.60	72.00	74.40	76.80	79.20	81.60
	Total	172.80	180.00	187.20	194.40	201.60	208.80	216.00	223.20	230.40	237.60	244.80
Fourth grade—Sergeant, technician fourth grade	Regular	93.60	97.50	101.40	105.30	109.20	113.10	117.00	120.90	124.80	128.70	132.60
	Flying	46.80	48.75	50.70	52.65	54.60	56.55	58.50	60.45	62.40	64.35	66.30
	Total	140.40	146.25	152.10	157.95	163.80	169.65	175.50	181.35	187.20	193.05	198.90
Fifth grade—Corporal, technician fifth grade	Regular	79.20	82.50	85.80	89.10	92.40	95.70	99.00	102.30	105.60	108.90	112.20
	Flying	39.60	41.25	42.90	44.55	46.20	47.85	49.50	51.15	52.80	54.45	56.10
	Total	118.80	123.75	128.70	133.65	138.60	143.55	148.50	153.45	158.40	163.35	168.30
Sixth grade—Private first class	Regular	64.80	67.50	70.20	72.90	75.60	78.30	81.00	83.70	86.40	89.10	91.80
	Flying	32.40	33.75	35.10	36.45	37.80	39.15	40.50	41.85	43.20	44.55	45.90
	Total	97.20	101.25	105.30	109.35	113.40	117.45	121.50	125.55	129.60	133.65	137.70
Seventh grade—Private	Regular	60.00	62.50	65.00	67.50	70.00	72.50	75.00	77.50	80.00	82.50	85.00
	Flying	30.00	31.25	32.50	33.75	35.00	36.25	37.50	38.75	40.00	41.25	42.50
	Total	90.00	93.75	97.50	101.25	105.00	108.75	112.50	116.25	120.00	123.75	127.50

DISTINGUISHED SERVICE AWARDS

Medal of Honor—M. H.		$2.00
Distinguished Flying Cross—D. F. C.		2.00
Distinguished Service Cross—D. S. C.		2.00
Distinguished Service Medal—D. S. M.		2.00

Soldiers' Medal—S. M ... $2.00

For each bar in lieu of medal of honor, distinguished flying cross, distinguished service cross, distinguished service medal, or soldiers' medal. ... 2.00

1616   ARMY REGISTER, 1944

RATES OF PAY ALLOWED BY LAW TO OFFICERS OF THE ARMY, ANNEXED TO THE ARMY
30 AUG.

Pay of officers

(Act 16 June 1942 (56 Stat. 359), effective 1 June 1942,

NOTE.—The following rates of pay also apply to Reserve and National Guard officers, as provided by the act of 30 September 1943 (with certain exceptions as to allowances for dependents); and female physicians

Grade	Pay period	Annual base pay	Service						
			Less than 3 years	Over 3 years	Over 5 years	Over 6 years	Over 9 years	Over 10 years	Over 12 years
General of the Armies of the United States		$13,500	$1,125.00	$1,125.00	$1,125.00	$1,125.00	$1,125.00	$1,125.00	$1,125.00
General or Chief of Staff [1]		8,000	666.67	666.67	666.67	666.67	666.67	666.67	666.67
Lieutenant general		8,000	666.67	666.67	666.67	666.67	666.67	666.67	666.67
Major general		8,000	666.67	666.67	666.67	666.67	666.67	666.67	666.67
Brigadier general		6,000	500.00	500.00	500.00	500.00	500.00	500.00	500.00
Colonel	6	4,000	333.33	350.00	350.00	366.67	383.33	383.33	400.00
Lieutenant colonel:									
Over 30 years' service	6	4,000							
Less than 30 years' service	5	3,500	291.67	306.25	306.25	320.83	335.42	335.42	350.00
Major:									
Over 23 years' service	5	3,500							
Less than 23 years' service	4	3,000	250.00	262.50	262.50	275.00	287.50	287.50	300.00
Captain:									
Over 17 years' service	4	3,000							
Less than 17 years' service	3	2,400	200.00	210.00	210.00	220.00	230.00	230.00	240.00
First lieutenant:									
Over 10 years' service	3	2,400						230.00	240.00
Less than 10 years' service	2	2,000	166.67	175.00	175.00	183.33	191.67		
Second lieutenant:									
Over 5 years' service	2	2,000			175.00	183.33	191.67	191.67	200.00
Less than 5 years' service	1	1,800	150.00	157.50					

ARMY PAY TABLES · 1617

REGISTER CONFORMABLY TO THE RESOLUTION OF THE HOUSE OF REPRESENTATIVES
1842

in active service

as amended by act 2 Dec. 1942, effective 1 June 1942)

2 Dec. 1942, effective 1 June 1942; officers of the Women's Army Corps, as provided by the act of 1 July 1943, effective
and surgeons, as provided by the act of 16 April 1943 (except allowances for dependents).

Service								Rental		Subsistence [1] (30-day month)	
Over 15 years	Over 17 years	Over 18 years	Over 21 years	Over 23 years	Over 24 years	Over 27 years	Over 30 years	With dependents	No dependents	With dependents	No dependents
$1,125.00	$1,125.00	$1,125.00	$1,125.00	$1,125.00	$1,125.00	$1,125.00	$1,125.00	(2)	(2)		
666.67	666.67	666.67	666.67	666.67	666.67	666.67	666.67	$120	$105	$42	$21
666.67	666.67	666.67	666.67	666.67	666.67	666.67	666.67	120	105	42	21
666.67	666.67	666.67	666.67	666.67	666.67	666.67	666.67	120	105	42	21
500.00	500.00	500.00	500.00	500.00	500.00	500.00	500.00	120	105	42	21
416.67	416.67	433.33	450.00	450.00	466.67	483.33	500.00	120	105	42	21
							500.00	120	105	42	21
364.58	364.58	379.17	393.75	393.75	408.33	422.92		120	105	63	21
				393.75	408.33	422.92	437.50	120	105	63	21
312.50	312.50	325.00	337.50					105	90	63	21
	312.50	325.00	337.50	337.50	350.00	362.50	375.00	105	90	63	21
250.00								90	75	42	21
250.00	250.00	260.00	270.00	270.00	280.00	290.00	300.00	90	75	42	21
								75	60	42	21
208.33	208.33	216.67	225.00	225.00	233.33	241.67	250.00	75	60	42	21
								60	45	42	21

3. PAY FOR FOREIGN SERVICE OR SEA DUTY.—The base pay of any commissioned officer shall be increased by 10 per
centum for any period of service while on sea duty or duty in any place beyond the continental limits of the United States
or in Alaska. The per centum increases herein authorized shall be included in computing increases in pay for aviation
and submarine duty. This section shall be effective from December 7, 1941, and shall cease to be in effect twelve months
after the termination of the present war is proclaimed by the President. (See sec. 2, act 16 June 1942 (56 Stat. 360; 37
U. S. C. 102; M. L., 1939, Sup. II. sec. 1371c–2).)

4. AIDES.—Additional pay is authorized for aides to a major general, not more than three in number, who shall be in
the grade of captain or lieutenant. (R. S. 1098; 10 U. S. C. 498; M. L., 1939, sec. 157.)

Additional pay is authorized for aides to a brigadier general, not more than two in number, who shall be in the grade
of lieutenant. (R. S. 1098; 10 U. S. C. 498; M. L., 1939, sec. 157.)

An aide to a major general is allowed $200 and an aide to a brigadier general $150 per year in addition to the pay of his
rank. (R. S. 1261; 10 U. S. C. 692; M. L., 1939, sec. 1421.)

Pay for aides to officers holding a permanent rank of brigadier general or major general, but who are temporarily holding higher rank (such as lieutenant general) is authorized as shown in preceding paragraphs. See 22 Comp. Gen. 335.

The aides to a lieutenant general of a higher rank than those authorized by R. S. 1098 may not be paid.

5. SAVING CLAUSE.—No person, active or retired, shall suffer any reduction in any pay, allowances, or compensation
to which he was entitled upon the effective date of this act. (See sec. 19, act 16 June 1942 (56 Stat. 369; 37 U. S. C. 119,
M. L., 1939, Sup. II, sec. 1371c–19).)

Pay of warrant officers and flight officers of the Army, effective 1 June 1942, under act 16 June 1942

Grade	Annual base pay	Monthly rates											Rental		Subsistence[1] (30-day month)	
		Less than 3 years' service	Over 3 years' service	Over 6 years' service	Over 9 years' service	Over 12 years' service	Over 15 years' service	Over 18 years' service	Over 21 years' service	Over 24 years' service	Over 27 years' service	Over 30 years' service	With dependents	No dependents	With dependents	No dependents
Chief warrant officers (especially designated by Secretary of War)	$3,000.00	$250.00	$262.50	$275.00	$287.50	$300.00	$312.50	$325.00	$337.50	$350.00	$362.50	$375.00	$105	$90	$63	$21
Chief warrant officers (especially designated by Secretary of War). Masters, Army Mine Planter Service.	2,400.00	200.00	210.00	220.00	230.00	240.00	250.00	260.00	270.00	280.00	290.00	300.00	90	75	42	21
Chief warrant officers (except masters, Army Mine Planter Service) and chief engineers.	2,400.00	200.00	210.00	220.00	230.00	240.00	250.00	260.00	270.00	280.00	290.00	300.00	90	75	42	21
First mates and first assistant engineers, Army Mine Planter Service.	2,100.00	175.00	183.75	192.50	201.25	210.00	218.75	227.50	236.25	245.00	253.75	262.50	75	60	42	21
Warrant officers (junior grade); second mates and second assistant engineers, Army Mine Planter Service.	1,950.00	162.50	170.62	178.75	186.88	195.00	203.13	211.25	219.38	227.50	235.63	243.75	60	45	42	21
Army Mine Planter Service and flight officers.	1,800.00	150.00	157.50	165.00	172.50	180.00	187.50	195.00	202.50	210.00	217.50	225.00	60	45	42	21

[1] For a greater or less number of days than 30 the amount of subsistence allowance should be correspondingly increased or decreased.

NOTES

1. LONGEVITY PAY.—Every person paid under the provisions of this section shall receive an increase of 5 per centum of the base pay of his period for each three years of service, not exceeding thirty years. (See sec. 8, act 16 June 1942 (56 Stat. 362; 37 U. S. C. 108; M. L., 1939, Sup. II, sec. 1371c-8).)

2. FLYING PAY.—Warrant officers shall receive an increase of 50 per centum of their pay when by orders of competent authority they are required to participate regularly and frequently in aerial flights, and when in consequence of such orders they do participate in regular and frequent flights. (See sec. 18, act 16 June 1942 (56 Stat. 368; 37 U. S. C. 118; M. L., 1939, Sup. II, sec. 1371c-18).)

3. PARACHUTE DUTY.—Any warrant officer, not in flying-pay status, who is assigned or attached as a member of a parachute unit, including parachute-jumping schools, and for whom parachute jumping is an essential part of his military duty and who has received a rating as a parachutist or is undergoing training for such a rating shall receive while engaged upon parachute duty, additional pay at the rate of $100 per month. (See sec. 18, act 16 June 1942 (56 Stat. 368; 37 U. S. C. 118; M. L., 1939, Sup. II, 1371c-18).)

4. SOLDIERS' HOME DEDUCTIONS.—Deductions for the maintenance of the United States Soldiers' Home will be made from the pay of warrant officers of the Regular Army and Regular Army Reserve, but not from the pay of other warrant officers. (See A.R. 35-2220.)

5. LIMITATION ON PAY AND ALLOWANCES.—When the total pay and allowances of a warrant officer shall exceed the rate of $458.33 per month, the amount of the allowances shall be reduced by the amount above $458.33. (See sec. 8, act 16 June 1942 (56 Stat. 362; 37 U. S. C. 108; M. L., 1939, Sup. II, sec. 1371c-8).)

Pay and allowances of members of the Army Nurse Corps and other female personnel of the Medical Department, having relative Commissioned Rank, under act 22 December 1942

Grade	Relative Rank	Pay period	Annual base pay	Less than 3 years	Over 3 years	Over 6 years	Over 9 years	Over 12 years	Over 15 years	Over 18 years	Over 21 years	Over 24 years	Over 27 years	Over 30 years	Rental	Subsistence [2] (30-day month)
The superintendent, A. N. C.	Colonel	6	4,000	333.33	350.00	366.67	383.33	400.00	416.67	433.33	450.00	466.67	483.33	500.00	105.00	21.00
Assistant superintendents and directors, A. N. C. (designated by Secretary of War)	Lieutenant colonel	5	3,500	291.67	306.25	320.83	335.42	350.00	364.58	379.17	393.75	408.33	422.92	437.50	105.00	21.00
Director of dietitians [3] Director of physical therapy aides [3]	Major or	4	3,000	250.00	262.50	275.00	287.50	300.00	312.50	325.00	337.50	350.00	362.50	375.00	90.00	21.00
Assistant superintendents Assistant directors	Major	3	2,400	200.00	210.00	220.00	230.00	240.00	250.00	260.00	270.00	280.00	290.00	300.00	75.00	21.00
Chief dietitians Chief physical therapy aides Head nurses	Captain	3	2,400	200.00	210.00	220.00	230.00	240.00	250.00	260.00	270.00	280.00	290.00	300.00	75.00	21.00
Head dietitians Head physical therapy aides Head nurses	First lieutenant	2	2,000	166.67	175.00	183.33	191.67	200.00	208.33	216.67	225.00	233.33	241.67	250.00	60.00	21.00
Nurses Dietitians Physical therapy aides	Second lieutenant	1	1,800	150.00	157.50	165.00	172.50	180.00	187.50	195.00	202.50	210.00	217.50	225.00	45.00	21.00

NOTES

During the present war and for 6 months thereafter, the members of the Army Nurse Corps shall have relative rank and receive pay and money allowances for subsistence and rental of quarters as now or hereafter provided by law, for commissioned officers, without dependents, of the Regular Army in the 6th to the 1st pay periods, respectively. (See sec. 1, act 22 December 1942 (56 Stat. 1072; M. L., 1939, Sup. II, sec. 2165i-1).)

[2] For a greater or less number of days than 30, the amount of subsistence allowance should be correspondingly increased or decreased. (See secs. 5 and 13, act 16 June 1942 (56 Stat. 361, 366; 37 U. S. C. 105, 113; M. L., 1939, Sup. II, secs. 137ic-5 and 137ic-13).)

[3] One chief dietitian may be designated by the Secretary of War as Director of Dietitians and one chief physical therapy aide may be designated by the Secretary of War as Director of Physical Therapy Aides, each to have the relative rank of major and receive the pay and allowances of the third pay period. (See sec. 3, act 22 December 1942 (56 Stat. 1073; 10 U. S. C. 164; M. L., 1939, Sup. II, sec. 2165i-3).)

1. LONGEVITY PAY.—Every person paid under the provisions of the act of 22 Dec. 1942, shall receive an increase of 5 per centum of the base pay of her period for each 3 years of service up to 30 years. (See sec. 3, act 22 December 1942 (56 Stat. 1073; 10 U. S. C., 164; M. L., 1939, Sup. II, sec. 2165i-3).)

FLYING PAY.—Nurses shall be entitled to receive an increase of 50 per centum of their pay when by orders of competent authority they are required to participate regularly and frequently in aerial flights, and when in consequence of such orders they do participate in regular and frequent flights. (See sec. 18, act 16 June 1942 (56 Stat. 366; 37 U. S. C 118; M. L., 1939, Sup. II, sec. 137ic-18).)

3. PAY FOR FOREIGN SERVICE OR SEA DUTY.—Every person paid under the provisions of the act of 22 Dec. 1942, shall receive during any period of service while on sea duty as such duty may be defined by the Secretary of War, or duty in any place beyond the continental limits of the United States or in Alaska, an increase in base pay of 10 per centum. (See sec. 3, act 22 December 1942 (56 Stat. 1073; 10 U. S. C. 164; M. L., 1939, Sup. II, sec. 2165i-3).)

4. MEMBERS OF ARMY NURSE CORPS—ACTIVE SERVICE AS CONTRACT NURSE.—Active service as contract nurse prior to 2 Feb. 1901, and service as a reserve nurse on active duty since 2 Feb. 1901, shall be included in computing service of members of the Army Nurse Corps. (See sec. 3, act 22 December 1942 (56 Stat. 1073; 10 U. S. C. 164; M. L., 1939, Sup. II, sec. 2165i-3).)

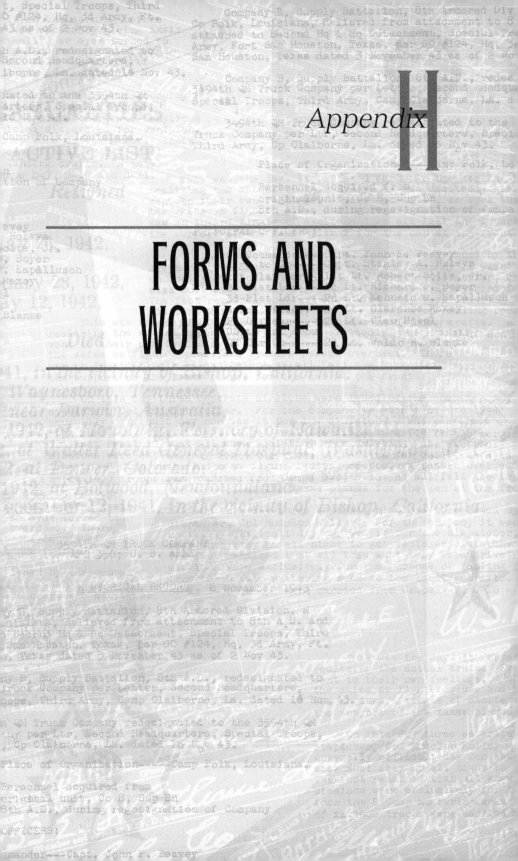

Appendix

H

FORMS AND WORKSHEETS

Freedom of Information Act Request

This is a sample letter for contacting federal agencies concerning a Freedom of Information Act (FOIA) request:

[Date]
[Agency Head or FOIA Officer]
[Name of Agency]
[Address]

To Whom It May Concern:

Under the Freedom of Information Act, 5 USC, subsection 532, I am requesting access to, or copies of [identify the records as clearly and specifically as possible].

If there are any fees for copying or researching the records please let me know in advance before fulfilling my request [or, please supply the records without informing me of the cost if the fees do not exceed $_____, which I agree to pay].

[Optional] I am requesting this information because [state the reason(s) if you think it will help obtain the information].

If you deny all or any part of this request, please cite each specific exemption that justifies your refusal to release the information and notify me of appeal procedures available under the law.

If you have any questions about this request, you may contact me by [telephone, e-mail, address].

Sincerely,
[Your name]
Sample Letter

Individual Data Worksheet

Full Legal Name: _____
                  First   middle   last

Date of birth: ___/___/___

Address before entering the military:

_____
City   County   State

WWII Draft Card ❑ Yes ❑ No
Military serial number: _____

Social Security number: _____ - _____ - _____

Branch of Service: ❑ Army ❑ Army Air Corps
❑ Coast Guard ❑ Marine Corps ❑ Navy

National Guard: ❑ Yes ❑ No
If yes, National Guard Service:
Dates of Service: From _____ To _____

Rank: _____

Retired Military? ❑ Yes ❑ No

Awards Received: _____
_____

Citations: _____
_____

Units/Ships Assignments: _____
_____

(Continued on next page)

MOS (military Occupation Specialty) and description:
_____
_____

Military Histories: _____

Newspaper Articles: _____

Reunion Association: ❑ Yes ❑ No
If yes, Contact information:
_____
_____

WWII Casualty
Date of death: ____/____/____

Cause of Death: _____
_____
_____

Place of burial: ❑ Overseas ❑ United States
Cemetery (name and address):
_____
_____

Location of grave: ❑ Plot ❑ Row ❑ Grave
Impression of headstone: ❑ Yes ❑ No
Obituary: ❑ Yes ❑ No
Next of kin: _____
If deceased, Date of death: ____/____/____
Cause of death, if known.
Place of death: _____
Cemetery (name and address): _____
_____
Location of grave: _____
_____

Obtaining Military Records

The US Locator Service (a private firm) specializes in locating and obtaining copies of service and medical records of discharged, deceased or military retired veterans who served in the US military during the following periods:

- Air Force, 1947 to present

- Army enlisted, 1 November 1912 to present

- Army officer, 1 July 1917 to present

- Coast Guard, 1 January 1898 to present

- Marine Corps, 1 January 1905 to present

- Navy enlisted, 1 January 1886 to present

- Navy officer, 1 January 1903 to present

Specifically, they can provide the following:

- DD Form 214 or other active duty separation documents

- Complete military service records
  (also known as 201 files, service jackets, etc.)

- Complete military medical records

- Military dependent medical records

- Record search only with no copies

Costs for services range from $50 for a search only with no copies, to $110 for copies of complete records.

Normal turnaround time for most records is two to four weeks, but there are some exceptions:

- A record or document is located outside the St. Louis metropolitan area

- A record was destroyed in the 1973 fire at the NPRC in St. Louis, Missouri and alternate sources will be checked

- A dependent medical record is requested

- The client or someone else had made a recent previous request to the NPRC.

In most cases the firm will require a signed authorization form from the veteran, dependent or next of kin. A copy is available on the next page.

For more information on any of these services and prices, please contact:

US Locator Service
PO Box 140194
St. Louis, MO 63114-0194
(314) 423-0860 Phone/fax
uslocator@earthlink.net

Military Records Authorization

    I request and authorize that representatives of US Locator Service be allowed to review my military and/or civilian service personnel and medical records, and/or auxiliary records in the same manner as if I presented myself for this purpose. I specifically authorize the National Personnel Records Center, St. Louis, Missouri, or other custodians of my military records, to release to US Locator Service a complete copy of my military personnel and related medical records.

    I am willing that a photocopy and/or fax of this authorization be considered as effective and as valid as the original.

Signature _____ Date _____/_____/_____

Name of Veteran _____
(Last name, First name, Middle)

Social Security #_____Service #_____

Branch of Service _____Rank _____

Present military status ❑ None, completely separated.

❑ Active Duty ❑ Reserve ❑ Retired

Dates of service _____

Date of birth _____/_____/_____ Place of birth _____

Type of Record Requested: ❑ DD 214, Report of Separation

❑ Service ❑ Medical ❑ Other _____

If veteran is deceased, Date of death_____/_____/_____

Relationship_____ (*Please include proof of death*)

Name_____ Address_____

City_____State_____Zip_____Phone_____

Payment (payable to US Locator Service)

Enclosed is ❑ Check ❑ Money order $_____

Please charge ❑ Visa ❑ MasterCard ❑ AMEX ❑ Discover
$_____

Card # _____ Expiration date ___/___

Name/Signature_____

US Locator Service * Box 140194 * St Louis, MO 63114-0194 * (314) 423-0860

Glossary

Armed Forces

Army, Coast Guard, Marine Corps and Navy. The Air Force became a separate branch after WWII.

Casualty

"Any person who is lost to the organization by having been declared dead, duty status - whereabouts unknown, missing, ill, or injured."
DOD Dictionary of Military and Associated Terms

Department of Veteran Affairs

Formerly called Veterans Administration. This government agency provides services and benefits for veterans. Millions of WWII veterans used the GI Bill to go to college after the war.

Freedom of Information Act

A federal law requiring U.S. government agencies and the Armed Forces to release records to the public on request, unless the information is exempted by the Privacy Act or for national security reasons. Common abbreviation is FOIA.

Identifying Information

Information used to identify and locate someone, such as: name, Social Security number, military service number, date of birth, ship or unit assigned, physical description, and state originally from.

Military Service Number

Also known as serial number. It wasn't until after WWII they used the term service number.

Muster roll

A list of names of officers and enlisted personnel in a military unit or ship's company.

National Archives

The federal repository of historical documents. The National Personnel Records Center is part of the National Archives and Records Administration.

Next of Kin

If a veteran is deceased then the next of kin is allowed to obtain military records. Next of kin is considered to be unremarried widow or widower, mother, father, son, daughter, bother or sister. At this time grandchildren, nieces or nephews are not considered next of kin.

Officer Registers

Books published by each branch of the service containing name, rank, serial number or Social Security number (depending on the year), date of birth, and other biographical information. WWII registers only contain the serial number.

Privacy Act

A federal law designed to protect an individual's constitutional right to privacy. The law also allows for the disclosure to an individual of information that the federal government maintains on that person.

Rank

A grade, rating, or position in a military organization's hierarchy.

Reserve Components

During WWII reserve components consisted of Army Reserve, Coast Guard Reserve, Marine Corps Reserve, Navy Reserve and Army National Guard.

Retired Military Member

A person who has completed 20 or more years of duty in any of the military components and is receiving retired pay (there are some exceptions to the 20–year service period). He may be retired from active duty or from a reserve component. A member of a reserve component is not eligible for retired pay until he reaches age 60. A military member may also retire from active duty for disability due to injury or illness, with less than 20 years of active service.

Signal Number

The Coast Guard, Navy and Marine Corps' term for the identifying number. Same as the military serial number.

Serial Number

A number formerly used by the armed forces to identify members. A military serial number is releasable information and is not protected under the Privacy Act. The serial number was discontinued in the late 1960's and early 1970's. Also known as Service number.

Ship Roster

A list of personnel assigned to a U.S. Navy ship at a particular point in time. The roster will include name (first, middle initial and last), rank and serial number for WWII era rosters.

Social Security Number

The nine–digit number issued by the Social Security Administration. A military serial/service number and a Social Security number are two different numbers.

Unit Roster

A military document that contains a list of individuals who were assigned to a particular military unit. Roster includes name (first, middle initial, and last), rank, and serial number.

Veteran

A person who has served on active duty in one or more of the armed forces.

Veterans Affairs Claim Number

The number assigned by the Department of Veterans Affairs when a veteran makes a claim for benefits. This number should be obtained when requesting the veteran's records from the Veterans Affairs office.

About The Author

Debra Johnson Knox is a South Carolina licensed private investigator. She and her father Lt. Col. Richard S. Johnson started Military Information Ent, Inc. in 1988, specializing in locating former military personnel and military research. Since her father's death in 1999 she has continued her work as an investigator and researcher, co-authoring two books, *How To Locate Anyone Who Is or Has Been in the Military* and *Find Anyone Fast*. She lives in South Carolina with her family.

Bookstore

How To Locate Anyone Who Is or Has Been in the Military: Armed Forces Locator Guide by Richard S. Johnson and Debra Johnson Knox.

Learn all conceivable means of locating current or former military members of the Air Force, Army, Coast Guard, Marine Corps, Navy, Reserve and National Guard. New chapters in this updated and expanded edition include: Verifying Military Service, Locating Women Veterans and Case Studies. 299 pages. $22.95

They Also Served: Military Biographies of Uncommon Americans by Scott Baron.

A fascinating collection of over 500 condensed military biographies of extraordinary Americans. The people profiled are known for their achievements outside the military. Prominent in their fields, whether it be law, medicine or the arts, their one commonality is that when our country called, they answered. Many interesting stories, facts, and trivia fill this wonderful, patriotic book. 333 pages, $15.95.

Find Anyone Fast (3rd edition) by Richard S. Johnson and Debra Johnson Knox.

Father/daughter private investigators explain how easy it is to find relatives, old romances, military buddies, deadbeat parents, or just about anyone. Includes how to use the Internet and state-of-the-art computer searches. 262 pages, $16.95.

Please add $6.05 shipping/handling to all orders.
Send to:

MIE Publishing
PO Box 17118
Spartanburg, SC 29301
(800) 937-2133, (864) 595-0813 Fax
www.militaryusa.com

Index

G

G–3 journal
Good Conduct Medal, 91
    Army, 101
    Coast Guard, 102
    Marine Corps, 91, 102
    Navy, 91, 102
Guadalcanal American Memorial, 76
Guadalcanal campaign, 76

H

H J Saunders, 136
Hardy, George, 83, 84
Hardy, John E., 83
Henri-Chapelle American Cemetery, 77
Honolulu Memorial, 77
Hospital admission cards, 21
    sample, 21
*How to Locate Anyone Who is or Has
    Been in the Military,* 129
Human resources information ctr, 124,

I

Identifying information, 22
    definition, 349
Interlibrary loan, 15, 17, 71, 74
Iowa Gold Star Museum, 31

K

Knox, Debra Johnson, 137, 352

L

Legion of Merit, 97
*List of Regular and Reserve Commis-
    sioned and Warrant Officers on
    Active Duty in Order of Precedence,*
    12, 70, 71,
    sample, 12-13
Lorraine American Cemetery, 77
Luxembourg American Cemetery, 77
Lyon Research, 45

M

Manila American Cemetery, 77
Marine Corps Expeditionary Medal, 103
Marine Corps Historical Center, 44, 73

Marine Corps Records,
    battle honors, 39
    histories, 45
    individual, 3-4, 5
    Internet sources, 39
    statistics, 40
Medal of Honor, 91, 94, 95
Medals of America, 26, 107, 136
Medals of American Press, 93
Medals of World War II, 93
Medals, Chapter five,
    cases, 108, 136
    displays, 108, 136
    examples of, Chapter five
    obtaining, 26-27, 135
Memorabilia, 135
Memorial Day, 107
Memorials, 133
Military & patriotic organizations, 126-
    128
Military academies, 24, 61, 67
Military colleges, 24, 61, 67
Military historical offices, 44
Military Information Ent, 129,
Military insignia, 135, 136,
Military museums, 31, 32, 42-43, 133,
    Appendix C
Military occupation specialty, 25-26
    sources, 26
Military records,
    complete, 111
    fire, 5, 7
    individual, Chapter 1, 31
    medical, 3,
    obtaining professionally, 6-7
    organizational, Chapter 2
    What if Records were burned? 5, 7
Military reunions, 85
    Internet sources, 87
Military reunion associations, Appendix
    E, 62, 85, 126,
Military serial numbers, Appendix B,
    (*see* serial number)
Military service number,
    definition, 349
Missing air crew reports, 37
Mission and Combat Reports of the
    Fifth Fighter Command, 1942–45, 38
Morning reports, 31, 32, 34
    samples, 33

NOTES

NOTES

NOTES

NOTES

NOTES

NOTES